# COLONELS IN BLUE

# COLONELS IN BLUE
## UNION ARMY COLONELS OF THE CIVIL WAR

*The New England States:*
*Connecticut, Maine, Massachusetts, New Hampshire, Rhode Island, Vermont*

ROGER D. HUNT

**Schiffer Military History**
Atglen, PA

*In memory*
*of*
*my parents*

Book design by Robert Biondi.
Union officer shoulder board on front dust jacket from the collection of Robert G. Borrell, Sr.


Library of Congress Catalog Number: 00-111941.



Printed in China.
ISBN: 0-7643-1290-1



Published by Schiffer Publishing Ltd.
4880 Lower Valley Road
Atglen, PA 19310
Phone: (610) 593-1777
FAX: (610) 593-2002
E-mail: Schifferbk@aol.com.
Visit our web site at: www.schifferbooks.com
Please write for a free catalog.
This book may be purchased from the publisher.
Please include $3.95 postage.
Try your bookstore first.

In Europe, Schiffer books are distributed by:
Bushwood Books
6 Marksbury Ave.
Kew Gardens
Surrey TW9 4JF
England
Phone: 44 (0)208 392-8585
FAX: 44 (0)208 392-9876
E-mail: Bushwd@aol.com.
Free postage in the UK. Europe: air mail at cost.
Try your bookstore first.

# Introduction

At the beginning of the Civil War the Regular Army of the United States numbered only 1,098 officers and 15,304 enlisted men. Faced with this shortage of manpower in suppressing the escalating rebellion, President Abraham Lincoln issued a call for 75,000 militia for three months service on April 15, 1861 and then a call for 500,000 volunteers for three years service on July 22, 1861. These calls for troops and others issued later in the war specified that the various state governors would appoint the commanding officers of the regiments raised in their states.

Patriotic fervor throughout the Northern states resulted in spirited competition to complete the organization of regiments to meet the state quotas. In most cases the prospective commanders of these regiments were prominent citizens whose military background (if any) consisted of service in a local militia organization. In general the early war Union army colonels were known more for their patriotic enthusiasm than for their military competence. Many of them were more successful in convincing their fellow townsmen to enlist than they were in actually leading them into battle. Fortunately for the Union cause, the colonels who stayed in the service soon acquired the necessary military skills or were replaced by subordinates who proved their capabilities on the field of battle.

This book is the first in a series of books containing photographs and biographical sketches of that diverse group of motivated citizens who attained the rank of colonel in the Union army, but failed to win promotion to brigadier general or brevet brigadier general. This volume presents the colonels who commanded regiments from the six New England states: Connecticut, Maine, Massachusetts, New Hampshire, Rhode Island and Vermont. Preceding the chapter for each state is a breakdown by regiment of all the colonels who commanded regiments from that state, with the name of each colonel being followed by the dates of his service. Included in this breakdown are the colonels who were promoted beyond the rank of colonel, with their final rank indicated in bold letters. Those indicated as attaining the rank of brigadier general are covered in the book *Generals in Blue,* by Ezra J. Warner, while those attaining the rank of brevet brigadier general are covered in the book *Brevet Brigadier Generals in Blue,* by Roger D. Hunt and Jack R. Brown.

Some explanatory notes are necessary concerning the content of the biographical sketches:

1.) The date associated with each rank is generally the date when the colonel was commissioned or appointed rather than the date when he was mustered at that rank. However, the date of muster was used whenever the date of commission or appointment was not available. The reader should be aware that these dates were constantly being revised by the War Department, so that any hope of providing totally accurate dates is virtually impossible.
2.) The word "Colonel" is italicized to indicate that the colonel was commissioned or appointed as colonel but never mustered as such.
3.) The following abbreviations are used in the text:

| | |
|---|---|
| AAG | Assistant Adjutant General |
| ACP | Appointment, Commission, and Personal |
| ADC | Aide-de-Camp |
| AIG | Assistant Inspector General |
| AQM | Assistant Quartermaster |
| Brig. | Brigadier |

| | |
|---|---|
| Bvt. | Brevet |
| CB | Commission Branch |
| Co. | County or Company |
| CSA | Confederate States Army |
| DOW | Died of Wounds |
| GAR | Grand Army of the Republic |
| Gen. | General |
| GSW | Gun Shot Wound |
| KIA | Killed in Action |
| MOLLUS | Military Order of the Loyal Legion of the United States |
| NGSNY | National Guard State of New York |
| NHDVS | National Home for Disabled Volunteer Soldiers |
| RQM | Regimental Quartermaster |
| Twp. | Township |
| US | United States |
| USA | United States Army |
| USAMHI | United States Army Military History Institute |
| USCT | United States Colored Troops |
| USMA | United States Military Academy |
| USV | United States Volunteers |
| VRC | Veteran Reserve Corps |
| Vol. | Volume |

# Acknowledgments

The following individuals provided valuable assistance in the preparation of this volume:

Alan C. Aimone, US Military Academy Library, West Point, NY
Stephen Allen, Laconia, NH
Robert B. Angelovich, Torrington, CT
Gil Barrett, Laurel, MD
Richard Baumgartner, Huntington, WV
Anna Blodgett, Augusta, ME
Everitt Bowles, Woodstock, GA
Mike Brackin, Manchester, CT
Erwin R. Brigham, Reston, VA
Samuel G. Butler, Jr., Winterport, ME
Tom Canterbury, Huntington Library, San Marino, CA
Marilynn Catanzaro, Bucksport, ME
Richard F. Carlile, Dayton, OH
Paul A. Carnahan, Vermont Historical Society, Montpelier, VT
David W. Charles, Jr., Lancaster, PA
Raymond L. Collins, Alexandria, VA
Allison Cywin, Rhode Island Historical Society, Providence, RI
Henry Deeks, Acton, MA
Bill Dekker, Caldwell, NJ
James Enos, Carlisle, PA
Jerry Everts, Lambertville, MI
William Gladstone, West Palm Beach, FL
Randy Hackenburg, US Army Military History Institute, Carlisle, PA
Thomas Harris, New York, NY
Michael A. Hogle, Okemos, MI
Ed Italo, Chicago, IL
Craig T. Johnson, Towson, MD
Gordon O. F. Johnson, Alexandria, VA
Alan Jutzi, Huntington Library, San Marino, CA
Dennis Keesee, Westerville, OH
Jeff Kowalis, Orland Park, IL
John W. Kuhl, Pittstown, NJ
Theresa La Bianca, Green-Wood Cemetery, Brooklyn, NY
Michael J. McAfee, Newburgh, NY
Robert F. MacAvoy, Clark, NJ
John F. McCormack, Jr., West Chester, PA
Thomas L. MacDonald, Eustis, ME
Edward McGuire, New York State Library, Albany, NY
Benedict R. Maryniak, Lancaster, NY
Steve Meadow, Danbury, CT
Ruth Mitchell, Maryland Historical Society, Baltimore, MD
Tom Molocea, North Lima, OH
Philip Murphy, Mechanicsburg, PA
Olaf, Oakland, CA
Seward R. Osborne, Olivebridge, NY
Ronn Palm, Kittanning, PA
Nicholas P. Picerno, Springfield, VT
Brian Pohanka, Alexandria, VA
Patrick E. Purcell, Wayne, PA
Edmund J. Raus, Jr., Manassas, VA
Stephen B. Rogers, Ithaca, NY
Alan J. Sessarego, Gettysburg, PA
Alice D. Sheriff, New London County Historical Society, New London, CT
Dr. Richard J. Sommers, US Army Military History Institute, Carlisle, PA
Christopher Steele, Massachusetts Historical Society, Boston, MA

Edward Steers, Jr., Berkeley Springs, WV
Larry Strayer, Dayton, OH
Karl Sundstrom, North Riverside, IL
Richard Tibbals, Oak Park, IL
Robert C. Trownsell, Bensenville, IL
Ken C. Turner, Ellwood City, PA
Michael W. Waskul, Ypsilanti, MI
Roy Wells, Maine State Archives, Augusta, ME
Michael J. Winey, US Army Military History Institute, Carlisle, PA
Robert J. Younger, Morningside Bookshop, Dayton, OH
Buck Zaidel, Cromwell, CT
Dave Zullo, Olde Soldier Books, Gaithersburg, MD

I am also indebted to the staffs of the following libraries for their capable assistance:

Beardsley Memorial Library, Winsted, CT
Concord Free Public Library, Concord, MA
Connecticut Historical Society, Hartford, CT
Connecticut State Library, Hartford, CT
Dover Public Library, Dover, NH
Family History Library, Salt Lake City, UT
Hornell Public Library, Hornell, NY
Huntington Library, San Marino, CA
Library of Congress, Washington, DC
Maine State Archives, Augusta, ME
Maine State Library, Augusta, ME
Maryland Historical Society, Baltimore, MD
Minnesota Historical Society, St. Paul, MN
National Archives, Washington, DC
National Society Daughters of the American Revolution, Washington, DC
New Albany Floyd County Public Library, New Albany, IN
New England Historic Genealogical Society, Boston, MA
New London County Historical Society, New London, CT
Newport Public Library, Newport, RI
New York Genealogical and Biographical Society, New York City, NY
New York State Library, Albany, NY
Pennsylvania State Library, Harrisburg, PA
Pollard Memorial Library, Lowell, MA
Rhode Island Historical Society, Providence, RI
Taunton Public Library, Taunton, MA
US Army Military History Institute, Carlisle, PA
US Military Academy Library, West Point, NY
Vermont Historical Society, Montpelier, VT
Worcester Public Library, Worcester, MA

# COLONELS IN BLUE

*Chapter I*

# CONNECTICUT

**1st Cavalry**

| | | |
|---|---|---|
| William S. Fish | Jan. 21, 1864 | Dismissed April 25, 1864 |
| Erastus Blakeslee | June 6, 1864 | Discharged Oct. 26, 1864 **Bvt. Brig. Gen.** |
| Brayton Ives | Jan. 17, 1865 | Mustered out Aug. 2, 1865 **Bvt. Brig. Gen.** |

**1st Heavy Artillery**

| | | |
|---|---|---|
| Levi Woodhouse | May 23, 1861 | Resigned Aug. 31, 1861 |
| Robert O. Tyler | Aug. 31, 1861 | Promoted **Brig. Gen., USV** Nov. 29, 1862 |
| Henry L. Abbot | Jan. 19, 1863 | Mustered out Sept. 25, 1865 **Bvt. Brig. Gen.** |

**2nd Heavy Artillery**

| | | |
|---|---|---|
| Leverette W. Wessells | July 28, 1862 | Resigned Sept. 15, 1863 |
| Elisha S. Kellogg | Jan. 23, 1864 | KIA June 1, 1864 |
| Ranald S. Mackenzie | July 10, 1864 | Promoted **Brig. Gen., USV** Oct. 19, 1864 |
| James Hubbard | Jan. 25, 1865 | Mustered out Aug. 18, 1865 **Bvt. Brig. Gen.** |

**1st Infantry**

| | | |
|---|---|---|
| Daniel Tyler | April 23, 1861 | Promoted **Brig. Gen., USV** May 10, 1861 |
| George S. Burnham | May 10, 1861 | Mustered out July 31, 1861 |

**2nd Infantry**

| | | |
|---|---|---|
| Alfred H. Terry | May 7, 1861 | Mustered out Aug. 7, 1861 Later **Major Gen., USV** |

**3rd Infantry**

| | | |
|---|---|---|
| John Arnold | May 14, 1861 | Resigned May 29, 1861 |
| John L. Chatfield | May 31, 1861 | Mustered out Aug. 12, 1861 |

**4th Infantry** (see 1st Heavy Artillery)

**5th Infantry**

| | | |
|---|---|---|
| Orris S. Ferry | July 23, 1861 | Promoted **Brig. Gen., USV** March 17, 1862 |
| George D. Chapman | April 7, 1862 | Resigned Jan. 28, 1863 |
| Warren W. Packer | March 1, 1863 | Discharged Oct. 20, 1864 |
| Henry W. Daboll | Jan. 28, 1865 | Mustered out July 19, 1865 |

**6th Infantry**

| | | |
|---|---|---|
| John L. Chatfield | Sept. 13, 1861 | DOW Aug. 9, 1863 |
| Redfield Duryee | Dec. 10, 1863 | Resigned May 29, 1864 |
| Alfred P. Rockwell | June 18, 1864 | Discharged Feb. 9, 1865 **Bvt. Brig. Gen.** |

**7th Infantry**

| | | |
|---|---|---|
| Alfred H. Terry | Sept. 17, 1861 | Promoted **Brig. Gen., USV** April 25, 1862 |
| Joseph R. Hawley | June 20, 1862 | Promoted **Brig. Gen., USV** Sept. 13, 1864 |
| Seager S. Atwell | July 1, 1865 | Mustered out July 20, 1865 |

**8th Infantry**

| | | |
|---|---|---|
| Edward Harland | Oct. 5, 1861 | Promoted **Brig. Gen., USV** Nov. 29, 1862 |
| John E. Ward | March 9, 1863 | Discharged March 14, 1865 |

**9th Infantry**

| | | |
|---|---|---|
| Thomas W. Cahill | Nov. 1, 1861 | Discharged Oct. 26, 1864 |

**10th Infantry**

| | | |
|---|---|---|
| Charles L. Russell | Oct. 26, 1861 | KIA Feb. 8, 1862 |
| Albert W. Drake | Feb. 8, 1862 | Died June 5, 1862 |
| Ira W. Pettibone | June 5, 1862 | Resigned Nov. 15, 1862 |
| John L. Otis | March 14, 1863 | Discharged Oct. 18, 1864 **Bvt. Brig. Gen.** |
| Edwin S. Greeley | Feb. 16, 1865 | Mustered out Aug. 25, 1865 **Bvt. Brig. Gen.** |

**11th Infantry**

| | | |
|---|---|---|
| Thomas H. C. Kingsbury | Nov. 27, 1861 | Resigned March 26, 1862 |
| Henry W. Kingsbury | April 25, 1862 | KIA Sept. 17, 1862 |
| Griffin A. Stedman, Jr. | Sept. 25, 1862 | DOW Aug. 6, 1864 **Bvt. Brig. Gen.** |
| Randall H. Rice | May 14, 1865 | Discharged Sept. 18, 1865 |

**12th Infantry**

| | | |
|---|---|---|
| Henry C. Deming | Dec. 31, 1861 | Discharged Jan. 31, 1863 |
| Ledyard Colburn | Jan. 31, 1863 | Resigned June 29, 1864 |

**13th Infantry**

| | | |
|---|---|---|
| Henry W. Birge | Nov. 5, 1861 | Promoted **Brig. Gen., USV** Oct. 6, 1863 |
| Charles D. Blinn | Nov. 24, 1863 | Discharged Jan. 6, 1865 |

**14th Infantry**

| | | |
|---|---|---|
| Dwight Morris | Aug. 23, 1862 | Discharged Aug. 14, 1863 |
| Theodore G. Ellis | Oct. 11, 1863 | Mustered out May 31, 1865 **Bvt. Brig. Gen.** |

**15th Infantry**

| | | |
|---|---|---|
| Dexter R. Wright | Aug. 26, 1862 | Resigned Feb. 13, 1863 |
| Charles L. Upham | April 18, 1863 | Mustered out June 27, 1865 |

**16th Infantry**

| | | |
|---|---|---|
| Francis Beach | Aug. 24, 1862 | Discharged June 24, 1865 |

**17th Infantry**

| | | |
|---|---|---|
| William H. Noble | Aug. 29, 1862 | Mustered out July 19, 1865 **Bvt. Brig. Gen.** |

**18th Infantry**

| | | |
|---|---|---|
| William G. Ely | Aug. 22, 1862 | Discharged June 27, 1865 **Bvt. Brig. Gen.** |

**19th Infantry** (see 2nd Heavy Artillery)

**20th Infantry**

| | | |
|---|---|---|
| Samuel Ross | Sept. 8, 1862 | Discharged June 26, 1865 **Bvt. Brig. Gen.** |

**21st Infantry**

| | | |
|---|---|---|
| Arthur H. Dutton | Sept. 5, 1862 | DOW June 5, 1864 **Bvt. Brig. Gen.** |
| Thomas F. Burpee | June 9, 1864 | DOW June 11, 1864 |
| Hiram B. Crosby | June 27, 1864 | Discharged Sept. 14, 1864 |

**22nd Infantry**

| | | |
|---|---|---|
| George S. Burnham | Sept. 20, 1862 | Mustered out July 7, 1863 |

**23rd Infantry**

| | | |
|---|---|---|
| Charles E. L. Holmes | Nov. 14, 1862 | Discharged June 18, 1863 |

**24th Infantry**

| | | |
|---|---|---|
| Samuel M. Mansfield | Nov. 18, 1862 | Mustered out Sept. 30, 1863 |

**25th Infantry**

| | | |
|---|---|---|
| George P. Bissell | Nov. 11, 1862 | Mustered out Aug. 26, 1863 |

**26th Infantry**

| | | |
|---|---|---|
| Thomas G. Kingsley | Nov. 10, 1862 | Mustered out Aug. 17, 1863 |

**27th Infantry**

| | | |
|---|---|---|
| Richard S. Bostwick | Oct. 22, 1862 | Mustered out July 27, 1863 |

**28th Infantry**

| | | |
|---|---|---|
| Samuel P. Ferris | Nov. 15, 1862 | Mustered out Aug. 28, 1863 |

**29th Infantry (Colored)**

| | | |
|---|---|---|
| William B. Wooster | March 8, 1864 | Resigned Aug. 21, 1865 |

## John Arnold

Colonel, 3 CT Infantry, May 14, 1861. Resigned May 29, 1861, due to "physical disability produced by overtaxing an already weakened system."

**Born:** Feb. 6, 1819 Chatham, CT
**Died:** Jan. 10, 1875 New Haven, CT
**Occupation:** Carriage manufacturer, hotelkeeper and in later life, patrolman on the police force
**Offices/Honors:** Captain of the New Haven Grays, 1850-51. Brigadier General, 2 Brigade, Connecticut State Militia, 1858-60.
**Miscellaneous:** Resided New Haven, CT. Described as "tall, erect, well-formed, and a fine soldier."
**Buried:** Evergreen Cemetery, New Haven, CT (Heart Avenue, Lot 38, unmarked)
**References:** Obituary, *New Haven Morning Journal and Courier*, Jan. 13, 1875. Military Service File, National Archives. Jerome B. Lucke. *History of the New Haven Grays.* New Haven, CT, 1876.

*Seager Schuyler Atwell*
*Roger D. Hunt Collection, USAMHI. Beers & Mansfield, National Gallery, 242 Chapel Street, New Haven, CT.*

## Seager Schuyler Atwell

Corporal, Co. F, 1 CT Infantry, April 17, 1861. Honorably mustered out, July 31, 1861. 2 Lieutenant, Co. C, 7 CT Infantry, Sept. 6, 1861. 1 Lieutenant, Co. F, 7 CT Infantry, Sept. 1, 1862. Captain, Co. C, 7 CT Infantry, July 7, 1863. Lieutenant Colonel, 7 CT Infantry, Nov. 22, 1864. Colonel, 7 CT Infantry, July 1, 1865. Honorably mustered out, July 20, 1865.

**Born:** Jan. 24, 1836 Durham, CT
**Died:** June 2, 1911 Providence, RI
**Occupation:** Mechanic before war. Farmer and shore dinner caterer after war. Described as the most prominent clambake man in the country, serving 1,250,000 people in 23 years.
**Miscellaneous:** Resided Durham, CT; Portage, WI; and Meriden, CT, before war; near New Bern, NC, 1867-71; Cranston, RI; and Providence, RI
**Buried:** North Burial Ground, Providence, RI (Section 21, Lot 4134)
**References:** Pension File, National Archives. Obituary, *Providence Journal*, June 3, 1911. Stephen Walkley. *History of the 7th Connecticut Volunteer Infantry.* Southington, CT, 1905.

*Seager Schuyler Atwell*
*Massachusetts MOLLUS Collection, USAMHI.*

## Francis Beach

1 Lieutenant, 4 US Artillery, April 29, 1861. 1 Lieutenant, Acting ADC, Staff of Brig. Gen. Philip St. George Cooke, Dec. 1861-Aug. 1862. Captain, 4 US Artillery, Aug. 14, 1862. Colonel, 16 CT Infantry, Aug. 24, 1862. Called "Little Moustache" and "Black Eye" by the men of the 16th Connecticut. Commanded 2 Brigade, Getty's Division, 18 Army Corps, Dec. 1863-Jan. 1864. Captured Plymouth, NC, April 20, 1864. Confined Libby Prison, Richmond, VA. Paroled May 2, 1864. Honorably mustered out of volunteer service, June 24, 1865.

**Born:** May 2, 1835 Hartford, CT
**Died:** Feb. 5, 1873 New York City, NY
**Education:** Graduated US Military Academy, West Point, NY, 1857
**Occupation:** Regular Army (Captain, 4 US Artillery, retired Aug. 22, 1871)
**Miscellaneous:** Resided Hartford, CT; and New York City, NY
**Buried:** Arlington National Cemetery, Arlington, VA (Section 3, Lot 1401). Cenotaph in Cedar Hill Cemetery, Hartford, CT (Section 2, Lot 1).
**References:** *Annual Reunion,* Association of the Graduates of the US Military Academy, 1873. Pension File and ACP File, National Archives. Obituary, *Hartford Daily Courant,* Feb. 7, 1873. Bernard F. Blakeslee. *History of the 16th Connecticut Volunteers.* Hartford, CT, 1875. William R. Cutter, editor. *Genealogical and Family History of the State of Connecticut.* New York City, NY, 1911.

*Seager Schuyler Atwell (1897)*
*Massachusetts MOLLUS Collection, USAMHI.*

## George Perkins Bissell

Colonel, 25 CT Infantry, Sept. 15, 1862. Honorably mustered out, Aug. 26, 1863.

**Born:** July 22, 1827 Rochester, NY
**Died:** April 11, 1891 New York City, NY
**Occupation:** Banker. Long active in the Hartford City Guard, he was a prime mover in securing the Memorial Arch to the memory of Hartford soldiers and sailors.
**Offices/Honors:** Paymaster General, Staff of Governor Jewell, 1869-70.
**Miscellaneous:** Resided Hartford, CT. Brother of Colonel Josiah W. Bissell. He and Bvt. Brig. Gen. Joseph C. Jackson married sisters.

*Francis Beach*
*State Archives, Connecticut State Library.*

**Buried:** Cedar Hill Cemetery, Hartford, CT (Section 1, Lot 21)

**References:** Obituary Circular, Whole No. 350, New York MOLLUS. Obituary, *Hartford Courant*, April 13, 1891. *The 25th Connecticut Volunteers in the War of the Rebellion.* Rockville, CT, 1913.

*George Perkins Bissell*
*State Archives, Connecticut State Library. Prescott & Gage, Photographers, 368 Main Street, Hartford, CT.*

*George Perkins Bissell*
*Roger D. Hunt Collection, USAMHI. Wilson Brothers, 258 Main Street, Hartford, CT.*

## Charles D. Blinn

Captain, Co. C, 13 CT Infantry, Feb. 18, 1862. Volunteered for the "Forlorn Hope" storming party at Port Hudson, LA, June 15, 1863. Lieutenant Colonel, 13 CT Infantry, Oct. 29, 1863. Colonel, 13 CT Infantry, Nov. 24, 1863. Honorably mustered out, Jan. 6, 1865.

**Born:** Aug. 26, 1840 Sharon, CT
**Died:** Nov. 4, 1883 Asheville, NC
**Occupation:** Dry goods merchant
**Offices/Honors:** Deputy Sheriff, Litchfield Co., CT, 1882-83
**Miscellaneous:** Resided Cornwall, Litchfield Co., CT, before war; and New Milford, Litchfield Co., CT, after war.
**Buried:** Center Cemetery, New Milford, CT
**References:** Pension File, National Archives. Theodore S. Gold. *Historical Records of the Town of Cornwall, CT.* Hartford, CT, 1904. Obituary, *Danbury News*, Nov. 14, 1883. Homer B. Sprague. *History of the 13th Infantry Regiment of Connecticut Volunteers.* Hartford, CT, 1867.

*George Perkins Bissell*
*Massachusetts MOLLUS Collection, USAMHI.*

*Charles D. Blinn*
*Courtesy of Henry Deeks. Anderson's Photographic Gallery, 61 Camp Street, New Orleans, LA.*

*Right:*
*Charles D. Blinn*
*Massachusetts MOLLUS Collection, USAMHI.*

## Richard Stone Bostwick

Private, Co. G, 2 CT Infantry, May 7, 1861. Honorably mustered out, Aug. 7, 1861. Colonel, 27 CT Infantry, Oct. 22, 1862. Captured Chancellorsville, VA, May 3, 1863. Confined in Libby Prison, Richmond, VA. Paroled May 23, 1863. Honorably mustered out, July 27, 1863.

**Born:** Dec. 22, 1831 New Haven, CT
**Died:** Jan. 5, 1906 Brooklyn, NY
**Occupation:** Clerk in early life. Later became an oyster dealer.
**Miscellaneous:** Resided New Haven, CT, to 1864; Norfolk, VA, 1864-68; New York City, NY, 1869-80; and Brooklyn, NY, 1880-1906.
**Buried:** Grove Street Cemetery, New Haven, CT (Sylvan Avenue, Tier 1, Lot 20)
**References:** Henry A. Bostwick. *Genealogy of the Bostwick Family in America.* New York City, NY, 1901. Jerome B. Lucke. *History of the New Haven Grays.* New Haven, CT, 1876. Winthrop D. Sheldon. *The "Twenty Seventh," A Regimental History.* New Haven, CT, 1866. Pension File, National Archives.

*Richard Stone Bostwick (1876)*
*History of the New Haven Grays.*

*Richard Stone Bostwick*
*Courtesy of Buck Zaidel. Filley & Gilbert, 337 Chapel Street, New Haven, CT.*

## George Sumner Burnham

Lieutenant Colonel, 1 CT Infantry, April 23, 1861. Colonel, 1 CT Infantry, May 10, 1861. Honorably mustered out, July 31, 1861. Colonel, 22 CT Infantry, Sept. 20, 1862. Honorably mustered out, July 7, 1863. Captain, AQM, USV, May 18, 1864. Honorably mustered out, Aug. 10, 1865.

**Born:** March 31, 1828 Hartford, CT

**Died:** Aug. 27, 1893 Hartford, CT

**Occupation:** Bookkeeper and clerk before war. Merchant dealing in paints and oils after war.

**Miscellaneous:** Resided Hartford, CT.

**Buried:** Cedar Hill Cemetery, Hartford, CT (Section 4, Lot 15)

**References:** Pension File, National Archives. Obituary, *Hartford Courant*, Aug. 28, 1893.

*George Sumner Burnham*
*Massachusetts MOLLUS Collection, USAMHI.*

*George Sumner Burnham*
*Massachusetts MOLLUS Collection, USAMHI.*

*Right:*
*George Sumner Burnham*
*Roger D. Hunt Collection, USAMHI. Brady's National Photographic Portrait Gallery.*

## Thomas Francis Burpee

Captain, Co. D, 14 CT Infantry, July 12, 1862. Major, 21 CT Infantry, Aug. 25, 1862. Lieutenant Colonel, 21 CT Infantry, Sept. 5, 1862. *Colonel,* 21 CT Infantry, June 8, 1864. GSW breast, Cold Harbor, VA, June 9, 1864, while going the rounds as brigade officer of the day.

**Born:** Feb. 17, 1830 Stafford, CT
**Died:** June 11, 1864 DOW White House, VA
**Occupation:** Woolen mill superintendent.
**Miscellaneous:** Resided Rockville, Tolland Co., CT. Active in Connecticut State Militia since the age of nineteen, he was Major, 5 CT State Militia, at the beginning of the war.
**Buried:** Grove Hill Cemetery, Rockville, CT
**References:** *The Story of the 21st Regiment Connecticut Volunteer Infantry.* Middletown, CT, 1900. *The Connecticut War Record.* Vol. 2, No. 3 (Oct. 1864). William R. Cutter, editor. *Genealogical and Family History of the State of Connecticut.* New York City, NY, 1911.

*George Sumner Burnham*
*Massachusetts MOLLUS Collection, USAMHI.*

*Thomas Francis Burpee*
*Roger D. Hunt Collection, USAMHI.*

*Right:*
*Thomas Francis Burpee*
*Massachusetts MOLLUS Collection, USAMHI.*

## Thomas William Cahill

Colonel, 9 CT Infantry, Sept. 3, 1861. Commanded 2 Brigade, Department of the Gulf, upon death of Brig. Gen. Thomas Williams, Baton Rouge, LA, Aug. 5, 1862. Commanded Defenses of New Orleans, Dec. 16, 1862-Jan. 9, 1863. Commanded 2 Brigade, 2 Division, 19 Army Corps, May 12, 1863-Aug. 15, 1863. Commanded 2 Brigade, 4 Division, 19 Army Corps, Aug. 15, 1863-Feb. 15, 1864. Honorably mustered out, Oct. 26, 1864.

**Born:** Aug. 12, 1826 Charlestown, MA
**Died:** Aug. 31, 1869 New Haven, CT
**Occupation:** Learned the trade of ornamental plasterer and later became a partner in a firm engaged in the masonry business
**Offices/Honors:** New Haven Common Council, 1857-58. New Haven Alderman, 1859-61. New Haven Street Commissioner, 1861 and 1869.
**Miscellaneous:** Resided New Haven, CT, where he was captain of the Washington-Erina Guards (and subsequently the Emmet Guard).
**Buried:** St. Bernard's Cemetery, New Haven, CT
**References:** Thomas H. Murray. *History of the 9th Regiment Connecticut Volunteer Infantry.* New Haven, CT, 1903. Obituary, *New Haven Morning Journal and Courier*, Sept. 1, 1869. Pension File, National Archives. William A. Croffut and John M. Morris. *Military and Civil History of Connecticut During the War of 1861-65.* New York City, NY, 1869.

*Thomas William Cahill*
*Military and Civil History of Connecticut During the War of 1861-65.*

## George Dunham Chapman

Major, 5 CT Infantry, June 21, 1861. Lieutenant Colonel, 5 CT Infantry, Oct. 23, 1861. Colonel, 5 CT Infantry, April 8, 1862. Captured Cedar Mountain, VA, Aug. 9, 1862. Confined at Libby Prison, Richmond, VA. Paroled Sept. 24, 1862. Discharged for disability, Jan. 28, 1863, due to tuberculosis.

**Born:** May 14, 1829 Middletown, CT
**Died:** Jan. 10, 1907 Middletown, CT
**Occupation:** Hardware manufacturer, specializing in harnesses and saddlery
**Offices/Honors:** Connecticut Senate, 1893
**Miscellaneous:** Resided Middletown, Middlesex Co., CT

*Right:*
*Thomas William Cahill*
*History of the 9th Regiment Connecticut Volunteer Infantry.*

**Buried:** Indian Hill Cemetery, Middletown, CT
**References:** *Proceedings for 1907: Reports of Reunion Organizations of Connecticut Volunteers for 1906 With Necrological Record.* Obituary, *Middletown Penny Press*, Jan. 10, 1907. Military Service File, National Archives. Edwin E. Marvin. *The 5th Regiment Connecticut Volunteers.* Hartford, CT, 1889.

*George Dunham Chapman (postwar)*
*Massachusetts MOLLUS Collection, USAMHI.*

## John Lyman Chatfield

Major, 1 CT Infantry, April 23, 1861. Lieutenant Colonel, 1 CT Infantry, May 10, 1861. Colonel, 3 CT Infantry, May 31, 1861. Honorably mustered out, Aug. 12, 1861. Colonel, 6 CT Infantry, Sept. 13, 1861. Commanded 1 Brigade, 1 Division, Department of the South, April 1862-July 1862. Commanded District of Beaufort, SC, 10 Army Corps, Oct. 1862. Shell wound right thigh, Pocotaligo, SC, Oct. 22, 1862. GSW left leg and right hand, Fort Wagner, SC, July 18, 1863.

**Born:** Sept. 13, 1826 Oxford, CT
**Died:** Aug. 9, 1863 DOW Waterbury, CT

*John Lyman Chatfield*
*Massachusetts MOLLUS Collection, USAMHI. S.A. Cooley, Premium Cartes de Visite, Beaufort, SC.*

*John Lyman Chatfield*
*Massachusetts MOLLUS Collection, USAMHI. G.N. Granniss, Photographer, Waterbury, CT.*

**Education:** Apprenticed to a builder at the age of 17, he developed unusual mechanical skills while working as a journeyman builder.

**Occupation:** After about three years as head mechanic for the Waterbury Lumber and Coal Co., he associated with his brother in the building business.

**Offices/Honors:** Captain of the Waterbury City Guard.

**Miscellaneous:** Resided Derby, CT; New Haven, CT; and Waterbury, CT, 1852-63.

**Buried:** Riverside Cemetery, Waterbury, CT (Section G, Lot 13)

**References:** *The Connecticut War Record,* Vol. 1, No. 12 (July 1864). Joseph Anderson, editor. *The Town and City of Waterbury, CT.* New Haven, CT, 1896. Charles K. Cadwell. *The Old 6th Regiment, Its War Record.* New Haven, CT, 1875.

## Ledyard Colburn

Major, 2 CT Infantry, May 7, 1861. Honorably mustered out, Aug. 7, 1861. Lieutenant Colonel, 12 CT Infantry, Dec. 31, 1861. Superintendent of Military Railroads, Department of the Gulf, Nov. 24, 1862. Colonel, 12 CT Infantry, Jan. 31, 1863. Supervised construction of the steamer "Colonel Colburn" in the Quartermaster service. Resigned June 29, 1864, due to "pressing private business," urgent domestic affairs, and also to allow the promotion of Lieutenant Colonel Frank H. Peck, who had commanded the regiment for the past 18 months while he was on detached service.

**Born:** Aug. 1825 Stafford, CT

**Died:** Aug. 14, 1888 Polo, Ogle Co., IL

**Occupation:** Mechanical engineer before war. Railroad superintendent and machinist after war.

**Miscellaneous:** Resided Birmingham (now Derby), New Haven Co., CT; New Orleans, LA; Chicago, IL; and Polo, Ogle Co., IL

**Buried:** Oakcliff Cemetery, Derby, CT

**References:** Pension File and Military Service File, National Archives.

## Hiram Benjamin Crosby

Private, Co. C, 18 CT Infantry, July 26, 1862. Major, 21 CT Infantry, Sept. 5, 1862. Provost Marshal, 9 Army Corps, Staff of Brig. Gen. Orlando B. Willcox, Oct.-Dec. 1862. Lieutenant Colonel, 21 CT Infantry, June 12, 1864. *Colonel,* 21 CT Infantry, June 27, 1864. Discharged for disability, Sept. 14, 1864, on account of typhoid fever and chronic diarrhea.

*Hiram Benjamin Crosby*
*Roger D. Hunt Collection, USAMHI. W.H. Jennings, Photographer, Corner Main and Shetucket Streets, Norwich, CT.*

**Born:** Dec. 25, 1830 Norwich, CT
**Died:** Oct. 7, 1900 New York City, NY
**Education:** Graduated Dartmouth College, Hanover, NH, 1854.
**Occupation:** Lawyer
**Miscellaneous:** Resided Norwich, CT; Pelham, Westchester Co., NY; and New York City, NY.
**Buried:** Kensico Cemetery, Valhalla, NY (Section 33, Katonah Plot, Lot 3728)
**References:** Henry A. Hazen and S. Lewis B. Speare, editors. *A History of the Class of 1854 in Dartmouth College.* Boston, MA, 1898. *The Story of the 21st Regiment Connecticut Volunteer Infantry During the Civil War.* Middletown, CT, 1900. Pension File, National Archives. William H. Hodgkins, editor. *Military Record of the Sons of Dartmouth.* Boston, MA, 1907.

*Hiram Benjamin Crosby*
*The Story of the 21st Regiment Connecticut Volunteer Infantry.*

## Henry W. Daboll

1 Lieutenant, Co. G, 5 CT Infantry, June 21, 1861. Captain, Co. H, 5 CT Infantry, Nov. 2, 1861. Major, 5 CT Infantry, Aug. 3, 1863. Lieutenant Colonel, 5 CT Infantry, Aug. 31, 1863. *Colonel,* 5 CT Infantry, Jan. 28, 1865. Bvt. Colonel, USV, March 13, 1865, for good conduct during the war. Honorably mustered out, July 19, 1865.

**Born:** June 18, 1834 Astoria, Long Island, NY
**Died:** Dec. 9, 1879 Vallejo, CA
**Occupation:** Machinist in a New London (CT) foundry and a Mystic (CT) machine shop before war. Moving to California in 1868, he became Engineer of the Mare Island Navy Yard, 1874-79.
**Miscellaneous:** Resided New London, New London Co., CT; Mystic, New London Co., CT; and Vallejo, Solano Co., CA.
**Buried:** Cedar Grove Cemetery, New London, CT (Section 17, Lot 60)
**References:** Obituary, *New London Evening Telegram*, Dec. 11, 1879. Obituary, *Norwich Bulletin*, Dec. 13, 1879. Edwin E. Marvin. *The 5th Regiment Connecticut Volunteers.* Hartford, CT, 1889.

*Right:*
*Henry W. Daboll*
*Courtesy of Henry Deeks. Bundy & Williams, 314 & 326 Chapel Street, New Haven, CT.*

*Henry W. Daboll*
*Massachusetts MOLLUS Collection, USAMHI.*

*Henry W. Daboll (postwar)*
*Courtesy of the author. James G. Smith, Virginia Street, Vallejo, CA.*

## Henry Champion Deming

Colonel, 12 CT Infantry, Oct. 15, 1861. Mayor of New Orleans, LA, Oct. 1862-Jan. 1863. Resigned and honorably discharged, Jan. 31, 1863, due to the severe illness of his wife.

**Born:** May 23, 1815 Colchester, CT
**Died:** Oct. 9, 1872 Hartford, CT
**Education:** Graduated Yale University, New Haven, CT, 1836. Graduated Harvard University Law School, Cambridge, MA, 1839.
**Occupation:** Lawyer and author
**Offices/Honors:** Connecticut House of Representatives, 1849-50, 1859-61 (Speaker 1861). Connecticut Senate, 1851. Mayor of Hartford, CT, 1854-58, 1860-61. US House of Representatives, 1863-67. US Collector of Internal Revenue, 1869-72.
**Miscellaneous:** Resided Hartford, CT. Author of a biography of Ulysses S. Grant and a eulogy of Abraham Lincoln.
**Buried:** Spring Grove Cemetery, Hartford, CT (Section H, Lot 92)
**References:** Charles F. Ritter and Jon L. Wakelyn. *American Legislative Leaders, 1850-1910.* Westport, CT, 1989. Richard Burton, editor. *Men of Progress: Connecticut.* Boston, MA, 1898. Military Service File, National Archives.

*Henry Champion Deming*
*State Archives, Connecticut State Library.*

*Henry Champion Deming*
*Massachusetts MOLLUS Collection, USAMHI.*

*Henry Champion Deming*
*Roger D. Hunt Collection, USAMHI.*

## Albert Waldo Drake

1 Lieutenant, Rifle Co. A, 1 CT Infantry, April 18, 1861. Honorably mustered out, July 31, 1861. Lieutenant Colonel, 10 CT Infantry, Oct. 26, 1861. *Colonel,* 10 CT Infantry, Feb. 9, 1862.

**Born:** Feb. 21, 1835 South Windsor, CT
**Died:** June 5, 1862 South Windsor, CT, of consumption
**Education:** Attended Williams College, Williamstown, MA. Graduated Yale University, New Haven, CT, 1857.
**Occupation:** Lawyer
**Offices/Honors:** Connecticut House of Representatives, 1858
**Miscellaneous:** Resided South Windsor, Hartford Co., CT
**Buried:** Center Cemetery, South Windsor, CT
**References:** Henry R. Stiles. *History of Ancient Windsor.* Hartford, CT, 1891. William A. Croffut and John M. Morris. *Military and Civil History of Connecticut During the War of 1861-65.* New York City, NY, 1869. Military Service File, National Archives.

*Albert Waldo Drake*
*History of Ancient Windsor.*

## Redfield Duryee

Private, Co. D, 1 CT Infantry, April 22, 1861. Private, Co. D, 3 CT Infantry, May 1, 1861. 1 Lieutenant, Adjutant, 3 CT Infantry, June 4, 1861. Honorably mustered out, Aug. 12, 1861. 1 Lieutenant, Adjutant, 6 CT Infantry, Sept. 13, 1861. Lieutenant Colonel, 6 CT Infantry, Sept. 21, 1863. Colonel, 6 CT Infantry, Nov. 27, 1863. Commanded Howell's Brigade, District of Hilton Head, SC, Feb. 6, 1864-April 25, 1864. Discharged for disability, May 29, 1864, due to chronic diarrhea.

**Born:** May 19, 1841 NY
**Died:** April 20, 1904 Washington, DC
**Occupation:** Clerk, US War Department, eventually becoming Assistant Chief of the Record and Pension Division.
**Miscellaneous:** Resided Waterbury, CT; Rutland, VT; and Washington, DC, after 1867
**Buried:** Arlington National Cemetery, Arlington, VA (Section 1, Lot 474)
**References:** Pension File, National Archives. Obituary, *Washington Post*, April 22, 1904. Obituary, *Hartford Daily Courant*, April 23, 1904. Charles K. Cadwell. *The Old 6th Regiment, Its War Record.* New Haven, CT, 1875.

*Right:*
*Albert Waldo Drake*
*Military and Civil History of Connecticut During the War of 1861-65.*

*Redfield Duryee*
*Massachusetts MOLLUS Collection, USAMHI. G.N. Granniss, Photographer, Waterbury, CT.*

*Redfield Duryee*
*Massachusetts MOLLUS Collection, USAMHI.*

## Samuel Peters Ferris

2 Lieutenant, 8 US Infantry, June 24, 1861. 1 Lieutenant, 8 US Infantry, Feb. 19, 1862. Colonel, 28 CT Infantry, Oct. 18, 1862. Commanded 1 Brigade, 3 Division, 19 Army Corps, June 14, 1863-July 10, 1863. Honorably mustered out of volunteer service, Aug. 28, 1863. Provost Marshal, 9 Army Corps, Sept. 17, 1864-Oct. 9, 1864.

**Born:** Jan. 6, 1840 Stamford, CT
**Died:** Feb. 4, 1882 Fort Russell, WY Territory
**Education:** Graduated US Military Academy, West Point, NY, June 1861
**Occupation:** Regular Army (Captain, 4 US Infantry, March 23, 1869).
**Miscellaneous:** Resided Stamford, Fairfield Co., CT.
**Buried:** St. Andrews Episcopal Churchyard, Stamford, CT
**References:** Pension File and ACP File, National Archives. Obituary, *Stamford Advocate*, Feb. 10, 1882. Mary Elizabeth Sergent. *An Unremaining Glory.* Middletown, NY, 1997. George W. Cullum. *Biographical Register of the Officers and Graduates of the US Military Academy.* Boston and New York, 1891.

## William Stebbins Fish

Captain, Co. C, 1 CT Cavalry, Oct. 5, 1861. Acting ADC, Staff of Major Gen. Robert C. Schenck, July-Aug. 1862. Major, 1 CT Cavalry, Aug. 15, 1862. Lieutenant Colonel, 1 CT Cavalry, March 21, 1863. Provost Marshal, Middle Department, 8 Army Corps, Jan. 23, 1863-Jan. 16, 1864. Colonel, 1 CT Cavalry, Jan. 21, 1864. His vigorous prosecution of the duties of Provost Marshal had created many enemies, who succeeded in having him arrested on Jan. 24, 1864 and imprisoned in Old Capitol Prison, Washington, DC. After a lengthy court-martial, he was cashiered April 21, 1864, for "conduct prejudicial to good order and military discipline" and for "using false accounts and vouchers . . . for the purpose of obtaining false claims against the Government." Sentenced to the Albany (NY) Penitentiary, he appealed his case through friends to President Lincoln, who on Aug. 19, 1864 asked the Judge Advocate General to re-examine the case. Finally, on Dec. 19, 1864 President Lincoln ordered that he be pardoned for the "unexecuted part of his sentence" and released from custody. He was later restored to full rank with back pay by order of President Johnson, who had thoroughly examined the case and was satisfied of his innocence.

Samuel Peters Ferris
Meade Album, Civil War Library & Museum, Philadelphia, PA.

William Stebbins Fish
Courtesy of Erwin R. Brigham. From oil painting by Eastman Johnson.

William Stebbins Fish (postwar)
Courtesy of Gordon O. F. Johnson. Scholfield & Tingley, Mystic, CT.

*Members of Co. C, 1st Connecticut Cavalry, including William S. Fish (seated, coat open). Courtesy of Gordon O. F. Johnson.*

**Born:** Aug. 25, 1833 Groton, CT
**Died:** April 10, 1879 Glasgow, Scotland
**Occupation:** Engaged in the export/import business. Described as "a prominent business man and usually successful in his ventures."
**Miscellaneous:** Resided Mystic, New London Co., CT, to 1872; and Glasgow, Scotland, 1872-79.
**Buried:** Fish Cemetery, near West Mystic, CT
**References:** Research Files of Gordon O. F. Johnson, Alexandria, VA. Lester W. Fish. *The Fish Family in England and America.* Rutland, VT, 1948. Pension File and Military Service File, National Archives. Obituary, *New London Evening Telegram*, April 26, 1879.

*William Stebbins Fish and wife, Hortense (postwar)*
*Courtesy of Gordon O. F. Johnson.*

## Charles Edward Latimer Holmes

Colonel, 23 CT Infantry, Nov. 14, 1862. Commanded District of La Fourche, Department of the Gulf, April-May 1863. Discharged for disability, June 18, 1863, due to the effects of chronic diarrhea, kidney affection and intermittent fever.

**Born:** May 15, 1832 Waterbury, CT
**Died:** April 28, 1884 Ansonia, CT
**Occupation:** Brass and silver manufacturer.

**Miscellaneous:** Resided Waterbury, CT; Plymouth, CT; Middletown, CT; and New York City, NY. Widely known as a writer of patriotic verse.
**Buried:** Riverside Cemetery, Waterbury, CT (Section B, Lots 83-87)
**References:** Joseph Anderson, editor. *The Town and City of Waterbury, CT.* New Haven, CT, 1896. Obituary, *Waterbury Daily Republican*, April 29, 1884. Obituary, *Hartford Daily Courant*, April 30, 1884.

## Elisha Strong Kellogg

Captain, Co. B, 1 CT Heavy Artillery, May 22, 1861. Major, 1 CT Heavy Artillery, March 1, 1862. Lieutenant Colonel, 2 CT Heavy Artillery, Sept. 11, 1862. Colonel, 2 CT Heavy Artillery, Jan. 23, 1864. GSW head, Cold Harbor, VA, June 1, 1864.

**Born:** Nov. 27, 1824 Glastonbury, CT
**Died:** June 1, 1864 KIA Cold Harbor, VA
**Occupation:** Engaged in mechanical pursuits after an early career as a sailor and California pioneer.
**Miscellaneous:** Resided Winsted, CT; and Derby, CT.

*Elisha Strong Kellogg*
*USAMHI.*

*William Stebbins Fish*
*Maryland Historical Society, Baltimore, MD. Bendann Brothers, Baltimore, MD*

**Buried:** Forest View Cemetery, Winsted, CT
**References:** Timothy Hopkins. *The Kelloggs in the Old World and the New.* San Francisco, CA, 1903. *The Connecticut War Record.* Vol. 2, No. 2 (Sept. 1864). Obituary, *Winsted Herald*, June 10, 1864. Theodore F. Vaill. *History of the 2nd Connecticut Volunteer Heavy Artillery.* Winsted, CT, 1868.

## Henry Walter Kingsbury

1 Lieutenant, 5 US Artillery, May 14, 1861. Acting ADC, Staff of Major Gen. Irvin McDowell, June 8, 1861-Dec. 13, 1861. Colonel, 11 CT Infantry, April 25, 1862. GSW leg, foot, shoulder and abdomen, Antietam, MD, Sept. 17, 1862.

**Born:** Dec. 25, 1836 Chicago, IL
**Died:** Sept. 18, 1862 DOW Antietam, MD
**Education:** Graduated US Military Academy, West Point, NY, May 1861
**Occupation:** Regular Army (1 Lieutenant, 5 US Artillery).
**Miscellaneous:** Resided Washington, DC. Son-in-law of Brig. Gen. Joseph P. Taylor. Brother-in-law of CSA Lieutenant General Simon B. Buckner. Brother-in-law of Bvt. Brig. Gen. John McLean Taylor. His widow married Bvt. Brig. Gen. Albert G. Lawrence.
**Buried:** Oak Hill Cemetery, Washington, DC (Lot 640). Cenotaph in Congregational Church Cemetery, Hamburg, CT.
**References:** Frederick J. Kingsbury. *The Genealogy of the Descendants of Henry Kingsbury.* Hartford, CT, 1905. Mary Elizabeth Sergent. *They Lie Forgotten: The United States Military Academy, 1856-1861.* Middletown, NY, 1986.

## Thomas Humphrey Cushing Kingsbury

Lieutenant Colonel, 5 CT Infantry, July 23, 1861. Colonel, 11 CT Infantry, Nov. 27, 1861. Discharged for disability, March 26, 1862, due to failing health caused by typhoid pneumonia.

**Born:** Dec. 23, 1806 New Orleans, LA
**Died:** Aug. 8, 1880 Franklin, CT
**Education:** Attended US Military Academy, West Point, NY (Class of 1832)
**Occupation:** Farmer

*Right:*
*Elisha Strong Kellogg*
*Roger D. Hunt Collection, USAMHI.*

**Offices/Honors:** Connecticut House of Representatives, 1869 and 1872-73.

**Miscellaneous:** Resided Jefferson, Ashtabula Co., OH; Franklin, New London Co., CT; and Yantic, New London Co., CT

**Buried:** Plains Cemetery, Franklin, CT

**References:** Frederick J. Kingsbury. *The Genealogy of the Descendants of Henry Kingsbury.* Hartford, CT, 1905. Pension File, National Archives. Obituary, *Norwich Bulletin*, Aug. 10, 1880.

*Henry Walter Kingsbury (1861)*
*USAMHI.*

*Henry Walter Kingsbury*
*Courtesy of Gil Barrett.*

*Right:*
*Henry Walter Kingsbury*
*Massachusetts MOLLUS Collection, USAMHI.*

## Thomas Gibbs Kingsley

Colonel, 26 CT Infantry, Nov. 10, 1862. GSW face, right shoulder, and right thigh, Port Hudson, LA, May 27, 1863. Honorably mustered out, Aug. 17, 1863.

**Born:** Aug. 29, 1820 Franklin, CT
**Died:** Sept. 21, 1884 Middletown, CT
**Occupation:** Farmer, school teacher, and bookkeeper. Secretary and Treasurer of Shetucket Foundry Co., Norwich, CT, in 1868.
**Offices/Honors:** Connecticut House of Representatives, 1859.
**Miscellaneous:** Resided Franklin, New London Co., CT; and Yantic, New London Co., CT.
**Buried:** Yantic Cemetery, Norwich, CT (Section 5, Lot 22)
**References:** Pension File, National Archives. Obituary, *Norwich Bulletin*, Sept. 23, 1884. William A. Kingsley, editor. *Kingsley Family of America.* Baltimore, MD, 1980.

*Thomas Gibbs Kingsley*
*Courtesy of Buck Zaidel. N.D. Morgan, Photographic Artist, Rockwell Building, 166 Main Street, Norwich, CT.*

*Right:*
*Thomas Gibbs Kingsley*
*Courtesy of Henry Deeks.*

## Samuel Mather Mansfield

2 Lieutenant, Corps of Engineers, June 17, 1862. Acting ADC, Staff of Major Gen. Joseph K. F. Mansfield, July-Sept. 1862. Colonel, 24 CT Infantry, Nov. 18, 1862. 1 Lieutenant, Corps of Engineers, March 3, 1863. Honorably mustered out of volunteer service, Sept. 30, 1863. Captain, Corps of Engineers, Aug. 15, 1864.

**Born:** Sept. 23, 1839 Middletown, CT
**Died:** Feb. 18, 1928 Boston, MA
**Education:** Graduated US Military Academy, West Point, NY, 1862
**Occupation:** Regular Army (Brigadier General, retired Feb. 21, 1903)
**Offices/Honors:** Chairman of the Massachusetts Harbor and Land Commission, 1906-12
**Miscellaneous:** Resided Middletown, CT; and Boston, MA. Son of Major General Joseph K. F. Mansfield.
**Buried:** Indian Hill Cemetery, Middletown, CT
**References:** George W. Cullum. *Biographical Register of the Officers and Graduates of the US Military Academy.* Boston and New York, 1891. *Who Was Who in America, 1897-1942.* Obituary, *Boston Daily Globe*, Feb. 20, 1928.

*Samuel Mather Mansfield*
*US Military Academy Library, West Point, NY. Burrows & Bundy Photograph Gallery, No. 136 Main Street, Middletown, CT.*

*Samuel Mather Mansfield*
*US Military Academy Library, West Point, NY. W.F. Burrows, Successor to Bundy & Williams, No. 158 Main Street, Middletown, CT.*

*Samuel Mather Mansfield (1862)*
*US Military Academy Library, West Point, NY.*

*Samuel Mather Mansfield (postwar)*
*Massachusetts MOLLUS Collection, USAMHI.*

## Dwight Morris

Colonel, 14 CT Infantry, May 23, 1862. Commanded 2 Brigade, 3 Division, 2 Army Corps, Army of the Potomac, Sept. 12-Dec. 13, 1862 and Jan. 24-Feb. 12, 1863. Shell wound left side of head, Antietam, MD, Sept. 17, 1862. Discharged for disability, Aug. 14, 1863, due to chronic diarrhea.

**Born:** Nov. 22, 1817 Morris, CT
**Died:** Sept. 26, 1894 Bridgeport, CT
**Education:** Attended Yale University, New Haven, CT. Graduated Union College, Schenectady, NY, 1838.
**Occupation:** Lawyer
**Offices/Honors:** Connecticut House of Representatives, 1845, 1864, and 1880. US Consul-General, Havre, France, 1866-69. Secretary of State of Connecticut, 1876.
**Miscellaneous:** Resided Bridgeport, Fairfield Co., CT.
**Buried:** Mountain Grove Cemetery, Bridgeport, CT (Section 2, Lot 1)

*Right:*
*Dwight Morris*
*History of the 14th Regiment Connecticut Volunteer Infantry.*

**References:** D. Hamilton Hurd, compiler. *History of Fairfield County, CT.* Philadelphia, PA, 1881. Julian K. Larke, editor. *Strong's Pictorial and Biographical Record of the Great Rebellion.* New York City, NY, 1866. Charles D. Page. *History of the 14th Regiment Connecticut Volunteer Infantry.* Meriden, CT, 1906. Pension File, National Archives.

## Warren Wightman Packer

Captain, Co. G, 5 CT Infantry, July 22, 1861. GSW right thigh, Cedar Mountain, VA, Aug. 9, 1862. Major, 5 CT Infantry, Aug. 9, 1862. Colonel, 5 CT Infantry, Jan. 28, 1863. Captured Chancellorsville, VA, May 2, 1863. Paroled May 23, 1863. Returned to regiment, June 12, 1863. Commanded 1 Brigade, 1 Division, 20 Army Corps, July 3-July 17, 1864; July 28-Aug. 28, 1864; and Sept. 22-Oct. 20, 1864. Honorably mustered out, Oct. 24, 1864.

**Born:** Feb. 1, 1835 Groton, CT
**Died:** July 12, 1912 Mystic, CT
**Occupation:** Mercantile clerk early in life. Later operated a newspaper and periodical shop.
**Offices/Honors:** Postmaster of Mystic, CT, for 17 years.
**Miscellaneous:** Resided Mystic, New London Co., CT.
**Buried:** Elm Grove Cemetery, Mystic, CT
**References:** Pension File and Military Service File, National Archives. Obituary, *Norwich Bulletin*, July 15, 1912. Edwin E. Marvin. *The 5th Regiment Connecticut Volunteers.* Hartford, CT, 1889.

*Warren Wightman Packer*
*Roger D. Hunt Collection, USAMHI.*

## Ira Welch Pettibone

Major, 10 CT Infantry, Oct. 30, 1861. Lieutenant Colonel, 10 CT Infantry, Feb. 8, 1862. Colonel, 10 CT Infantry, June 6, 1862. Discharged for disability, Nov. 15, 1862, due to "impaired health."

**Born:** July 27, 1833 Whitesboro, NY
**Died:** Sept. 29, 1917 Chicago, IL
**Education:** Attended Williston Seminary, Easthampton, MA. Attended Amherst (MA) College. Graduated Yale University, New Haven, CT, 1854.

*Right:*
*Warren Wightman Packer*
*Courtesy of Henry Deeks.*

**Occupation:** School principal and teacher, being connected with the Winchester (CT) Institute, Beloit (WI) College, and for 19 years with North Division High School in Chicago, IL

**Offices/Honors:** Connecticut House of Representatives, 1868

**Miscellaneous:** Resided Winchester, Litchfield Co., CT, until 1871; Beloit, Rock Co., WI, 1871-81; Morgan Park, Cook Co., IL, 1881-84; and Chicago, IL, 1884-1917.

**Buried:** Center Cemetery, Norfolk, CT

**References:** *Obituary Record of Graduates of Yale University Deceased During the Year Ending July 1, 1918.* Pension File, National Archives.

*Randall Hopkins Rice*
*An Illustrated History of Pawtucket, Central Falls and Vicinity.*

## Randall Hopkins Rice

Private, Co. E, 1 RI Detached Militia, May 2, 1861. Honorably mustered out, Aug. 2, 1861. 1 Sergeant, Co. G, 11 CT Infantry, Nov. 12, 1861. 2 Lieutenant, Co. G, 11 CT Infantry, March 28, 1862. 1 Lieutenant, Co. I, 11 CT Infantry, Oct. 27, 1862. Captain, Co. G, 11 CT Infantry, Jan. 1, 1863. GSW left arm, Providence Church Road, VA, May 3, 1863. GSW abdomen, Petersburg, VA, June 18, 1864. Discharged for disability, Oct. 31, 1864, due to wounds. Major, 11 CT Infantry, Nov. 25, 1864. Lieutenant Colonel, 11 CT Infantry, Dec. 10, 1864. Colonel, 11 CT Infantry, May 14, 1865. Commanded 1 Brigade, 3 Division, 24 Army Corps, June-July 1865. Discharged for disability, Sept. 18, 1865, due to wounds.

**Born:** May 11, 1837 Coventry, RI

**Died:** July 2, 1907 Pawtucket, RI

**Education:** Attended Plainfield (CT) Academy

**Occupation:** Machinist and textile mill superintendent.

**Offices/Honors:** Chief of Police, Pawtucket, RI, 1874-82 and 1896-1907.

**Miscellaneous:** Resided Plainfield, CT; and Pawtucket, RI, after 1857.

**Buried:** Swan Point Cemetery, Providence, RI (Group 313, Lot 2)

**References:** Robert Grieve. *An Illustrated History of Pawtucket, Central Falls and Vicinity.* Pawtucket, RI, 1897. Obituary, *Providence Journal*, July 3, 1907. Pension File, National Archives.

*Charles Lambert Russell*
*Roger D. Hunt Collection, USAMHI.*

## Charles Lambert Russell

1 Lieutenant, Adjutant, 2 CT Infantry, May 7, 1861. Honorably mustered out, Aug. 7, 1861. Colonel, 10 CT Infantry, Oct. 26, 1861. GSW lung, Roanoke Island, NC, Feb. 8, 1862.

**Born:** July 25, 1828 Litchfield, CT
**Died:** Feb. 8, 1862 KIA Roanoke Island, NC
**Occupation:** Practiced the trade of a tack-maker.
**Offices/Honors:** Captain of the Derby Blues before the war.
**Miscellaneous:** Resided Derby, New Haven Co., CT.
**Buried:** Oakcliff Cemetery, Derby, CT
**References:** *The Connecticut War Record.* Vol. 1, No. 9 (April 1864). Samuel Orcutt and Ambrose Beardsley. *History of the Old Town of Derby, CT, 1642-1880.* Springfield, MA, 1880. *Addresses Delivered in the Senate and House of Representatives of Connecticut in Honor of Colonel Charles L. Russell.* New Haven, CT, 1862.

*Charles Leslie Upham*
*Massachusetts MOLLUS Collection, USAMHI. Brady's National Photographic Portrait Gallery.*

## Charles Leslie Upham

1 Sergeant, Co. B, 3 CT Infantry, May 14, 1861. Honorably mustered out, Aug. 12, 1861. Captain, Co. K, 8 CT Infantry, Sept. 23, 1861. GSW left shoulder, New Berne, NC, March 14, 1862. Temporarily commanded 16 CT Infantry, Dec. 3-26, 1862. Major, 8 CT Infantry, Dec. 23, 1862. Lieutenant Colonel, 8 CT Infantry, March 9, 1863. Colonel, 15 CT Infantry, April 18, 1863. Commanded Sub-District of New Berne, District of North Carolina, Sept.-Oct. 1864. Commanded 2 Brigade, 2 Division, District of Beaufort (NC), March 1, 1865-March 18, 1865. Honorably mustered out, June 27, 1865.

**Born:** May 24, 1839 Townshend, VT
**Died:** May 28, 1929 Meriden, CT
**Occupation:** Dry goods merchant.
**Miscellaneous:** Resided Meriden, New Haven Co., CT; and Hartford, CT.
**Buried:** Walnut Grove Cemetery, Meriden, CT (Section K, Lot 68)
**References:** F. K. Upham. *The Descendants of John Upham of Massachusetts.* Albany, NY, 1892. Obituary, *Meriden Record*, May 29, 1929. Pension File and Military Service File, National Archives. Sheldon B. Thorpe. *The History of the 15th Connecticut Volunteers in the War for the Defense of the Union.* New Haven, CT, 1893.

*Charles Leslie Upham*
*The History of the 15th Connecticut Volunteers.*

## John Edward Ward

Sergeant, Co. D, 3 CT Infantry, May 11, 1861. 1 Lieutenant, Co. D, 3 CT Infantry, May 20, 1861. Honorably mustered out, Aug. 12, 1861. Captain, Co. D, 8 CT Infantry, Sept. 21, 1861. Major, 8 CT Infantry, March 28, 1862. Lieutenant Colonel, 8 CT Infantry, Dec. 23, 1862. Colonel, 8 CT Infantry, March 9, 1863. Shell wound right shoulder, Walthall Junction, VA, May

7, 1864. Commanded 2 Brigade, 3 Division, 24 Army Corps, Feb. 6, 1865-March 14, 1865. Honorably mustered out, March 14, 1865.

**Baptized:** Sept. 24, 1837 Saybrook, CT
**Died:** Nov. 7, 1886 Sault Ste. Marie, MI
**Education:** Graduated College of the City of New York, 1856.
**Occupation:** Civil engineer before war. Lawyer, insurance agent, and US Treasury Department clerk after war.
**Offices/Honors:** Executive Secretary to Connecticut Governor William A. Buckingham, 1865-66. Treasurer of Marquette Co., MI, 1878-82.
**Miscellaneous:** Resided Norwich, New London Co., CT; Marquette, Marquette Co., MI; and Sault Ste. Marie, Chippewa Co., MI.
**Buried:** Cypress Cemetery, Old Saybrook, CT
**References:** Pension File, National Archives. *Register of the Associate Alumni of the College of the City of New York.* New York City, NY, 1924. Elizebeth B. Plimpton, editor. *The Vital Records of Saybrook Colony, 1635-1860.* Old Saybrook, CT, 1985.

## Leverette Ward Wessells

*Leverette Ward Wessells*
*Roger D. Hunt Collection, USAMHI.*

Colonel, 2 CT Heavy Artillery, Sept. 11, 1862. Commanded 2 Brigade, Defenses South of the Potomac, May 3, 1863-Sept. 15, 1863. Discharged for disability, Sept. 15, 1863, due to a "serious affection of the lungs." Provost Marshal, 4 District of Connecticut, Jan. 9, 1864. Honorably discharged, Oct. 5, 1865.

**Born:** July 28, 1819 Litchfield, CT
**Died:** April 4, 1895 Dover, DE
**Education:** Attended Litchfield (CT) Academy
**Occupation:** Member of the drug firm of Wessells & Gates
**Offices/Honors:** Postmaster, Litchfield, CT, 1850-54. Sheriff of Litchfield Co., CT, 1854-66. Connecticut House of Representatives, 1879 and 1887.
**Miscellaneous:** Resided Litchfield, Litchfield Co., CT. Brother of Brig. Gen. Henry W. Wessells. First cousin of Colonel John Ward Birge.
**Buried:** East Cemetery, Litchfield, CT
**References:** Obituary Circular, Whole No. 466, New York MOLLUS. Obituary, *Hartford Daily Courant*, April 6, 1895. *History of Litchfield County, CT.* Philadelphia, PA, 1881. Military Service File, National Archives. Theodore F. Vaill. *History of the 2nd Connecticut Volunteer Heavy Artillery.* Winsted, CT, 1868.

## Levi Woodhouse

Colonel, 4 CT Infantry (later 1 CT Heavy Artillery), May 23, 1861. Resigned Aug. 31, 1861.

**Born:** March 13, 1823 Hartford, CT
**Died:** Oct. 17, 1895 Albany, NY
**Other Wars:** Mexican War (1 Lieutenant, 9 US Infantry)
**Occupation:** Railroad superintendent and ticket agent.
**Offices/Honors:** Connecticut Paymaster General, 1854. Connecticut Quartermaster General, 1857-58. Hartford City Clerk, 1866-72.
**Miscellaneous:** Resided Hartford, CT.
**Buried:** Cedar Hill Cemetery, Hartford, CT (Section 6, Lot 23)
**References:** Obituary, *Hartford Courant*, Oct. 19, 1895. Military Service File, National Archives. John C. Taylor. *History of the 1st Connecticut Artillery and of the Siege Trains of the Armies Operating Against Richmond.* Hartford, CT, 1893.

## William Burr Wooster

Lieutenant Colonel, 20 CT Infantry, Sept. 8, 1862. Captured Chancellorsville, VA, May 3, 1863. Confined Libby Prison, Richmond, VA. Paroled May 23, 1863. Colonel, 29 CT Infantry, March 8, 1864. Resigned Aug. 21, 1865, for "personal reasons." His sword, taken from him upon his capture at Chancellorsville, was returned to him by Colonel Mark Finnicum (7 WI Infantry), who took it from a Mississippi officer he captured at Weldon Railroad. Bvt. Colonel, USV, March 13, 1865, for gallant conduct in command of his regiment at the battle of Chancellorsville, VA, May 3, 1863.

**Born:** Aug. 22, 1821 Oxford, CT
**Died:** Sept. 20, 1900 Ansonia, CT
**Education:** Graduated Yale University Law School, New Haven, CT, 1846
**Occupation:** Lawyer
**Offices/Honors:** Connecticut House of Representatives, 1858 and 1861. Connecticut Senate, 1859. Connecticut Paymaster General, 1867.
**Miscellaneous:** Resided Birmingham (now Derby), New Haven Co., CT; and Ansonia, New Haven Co., CT
**Buried:** Pine Grove Cemetery, Ansonia, CT
**References:** *Commemorative Biographical Record of New Haven County, CT.* Chicago, IL, 1902. Charles B. Todd. *A General History of the Burr Family.* New York City, NY, 1902. Pension File, National Archives. John W. Storrs. *The "Twentieth Connecticut," A Regimental History.* Naugatuck, CT, 1886.

*Levi Woodhouse*
*History of the First Connecticut Artillery.*

*William Burr Wooster*
*Massachusetts MOLLUS Collection, USAMHI.*

## Dexter Russell Wright

Colonel, 15 CT Infantry, Aug. 26, 1862. Commanded 1 Brigade, Casey's Division, Military District of Washington, Oct.-Dec. 1862. Discharged for disability, Feb. 17, 1863, due to back injuries received in an ambulance accident.

**Born:** June 27, 1821 Windsor, VT
**Died:** July 23, 1886 New Haven, CT
**Education:** Graduated Wesleyan University, Middletown, CT, 1845. Graduated Yale University Law School, New Haven, CT, 1848.
**Occupation:** Lawyer
**Offices/Honors:** Assistant US District Attorney for Connecticut, 1865-69. Police Commissioner, New Haven, CT, 1872-75. Connecticut House of Representatives, 1863 and 1879. Speaker, Connecticut House of Representatives, 1879.

**Miscellaneous:** Resided Meriden, New Haven Co., CT, to 1865; and New Haven, CT, after 1865.

**Buried:** Evergreen Cemetery, New Haven, CT (Western Avenue, Lot 92)

**References:** Charles F. Ritter and Jon L. Wakelyn. *American Legislative Leaders, 1850-1910.* Westport, CT, 1989. Pension File, National Archives. Obituary, *New Haven Evening Register*, July 23, 1886. Sheldon B. Thorpe. *The History of the 15th Connecticut Volunteers in the War for the Defense of the Union.* New Haven, CT, 1893.

*Right:*
*Dexter Russell Wright*
*Massachusetts MOLLUS Collection, USAMHI.*

*Chapter II*

# MAINE

**1st Cavalry**

| | | |
|---|---|---|
| John Goddard | Sept. 26, 1861 | Resigned March 1, 1862 |
| Samuel H. Allen | March 1, 1862 | Resigned Jan. 5, 1863 |
| Calvin S. Douty | March 2, 1863 | KIA June 17, 1863 |
| Charles H. Smith | July 24, 1863 | Mustered out Aug. 1, 1865 **Bvt. Brig. Gen.** |

**2nd Cavalry**

| | | |
|---|---|---|
| Ephraim W. Woodman | Dec. 18, 1863 | Mustered out Dec. 6, 1865 |

**1st Heavy Artillery**

| | | |
|---|---|---|
| Daniel Chaplin | July 11, 1862 | DOW Aug. 20, 1864 **Bvt. Brig. Gen.** |
| Thomas H. Talbot | Sept. 17, 1864 | Discharged Sept. 14, 1864 **Bvt. Brig. Gen.** |
| Russell B. Shepherd | Oct. 17, 1864 | Mustered out Sept. 11, 1865 **Bvt. Brig. Gen.** |

**1st Light Artillery**

| | | |
|---|---|---|
| Freeman McGilvery | Sept. 1, 1863 | DOW Sept. 2, 1864 |

**1st Infantry**

| | | |
|---|---|---|
| Nathaniel J. Jackson | April 29, 1861 | Mustered out Aug. 26, 1861 Later **Brig. Gen., USV** |

**1st Veteran Infantry**

| | | |
|---|---|---|
| Thomas W. Hyde | Oct. 6, 1864 | Mustered out June 28, 1865 **Bvt. Brig. Gen.** |

**2nd Infantry**

| | | |
|---|---|---|
| Charles D. Jameson | May 6, 1861 | Promoted **Brig. Gen., USV** Sept. 3, 1861 |
| Charles W. Roberts | Aug. 29, 1861 | Discharged Jan. 10, 1863 **Bvt. Brig. Gen.** |
| George Varney | Feb. 5, 1863 | Mustered out June 9, 1863 **Bvt. Brig. Gen.** |

**3rd Infantry**

| | | |
|---|---|---|
| Oliver O. Howard | May 29, 1861 | Promoted **Brig. Gen., USV** Sept. 7, 1861 |
| Henry G. Staples | Sept. 12, 1861 | Resigned Nov. 14, 1862 |
| Moses B. Lakeman | Nov. 28, 1862 | Mustered out June 28, 1864 |

**4th Infantry**

| | | |
|---|---|---|
| Hiram G. Berry | June 14, 1861 | Promoted **Brig. Gen., USV** March 17, 1862 |
| Elijah Walker | March 20, 1862 | Mustered out July 19, 1864 |

**5th Infantry**

| | | |
|---|---|---|
| Mark H. Dunnell | May 24, 1861 | Resigned Sept. 2, 1861 |
| Nathaniel J. Jackson | Sept. 2, 1861 | Promoted **Brig. Gen., USV** Sept. 24, 1862 |
| Edward A. Scamman | Nov. 1, 1862 | Discharged Jan. 8, 1863 |
| Clark S. Edwards | March 2, 1863 | Mustered out July 27, 1864 **Bvt. Brig. Gen.** |

**6th Infantry**

| | | |
|---|---|---|
| Abner Knowles | July 15, 1861 | Resigned Dec. 11, 1861 |
| Hiram Burnham | Dec. 23, 1861 | Promoted **Brig. Gen., USV** April 1, 1864 |

**7th Infantry**

| | | |
|---|---|---|
| Thomas H. Marshall | Sept. 5, 1861 | Died Oct. 25, 1861 |
| Edwin C. Mason | Nov. 5, 1861 | Mustered out Aug. 21, 1864 **Bvt. Brig. Gen.** |

**8th Infantry**

| | | |
|---|---|---|
| Lee Strickland | Sept. 7, 1861 | Resigned Dec. 13, 1861 |
| John D. Rust | Dec. 23, 1861 | Discharged Aug. 19, 1864 **Bvt. Brig. Gen.** |
| Henry Boynton | Aug. 23, 1864 | Resigned Feb. 26, 1865 **Bvt. Brig. Gen.** |
| William M. McArthur | March 8, 1865 | Mustered out Jan. 18, 1866 **Bvt. Brig. Gen.** |

**9th Infantry**

| | | |
|---|---|---|
| Rishworth Rich | Sept. 23, 1861 | Resigned May 27, 1863 |
| Horatio Bisbee, Jr. | Jan. 2, 1863 | Resigned March 19, 1863 |
| Sabine Emery | June 23, 1863 | Resigned May 25, 1864 |
| Zina H. Robinson | June 6, 1864 | Resigned Aug. 16, 1864 |
| George F. Granger | Sept. 13, 1864 | Mustered out July 13, 1865 **Bvt. Brig. Gen.** |

**10th Infantry**

| | | |
|---|---|---|
| George L. Beal | Oct. 3, 1861 | Mustered out May 8, 1863 Later **Brig. Gen., USV** |

**11th Infantry**

| | | |
|---|---|---|
| John C. Caldwell | Sept. 21, 1861 | Promoted **Brig. Gen., USV** April 28, 1862 |
| Harris M. Plaisted | May 12, 1862 | Discharged March 25, 1865 **Bvt. Brig. Gen.** |
| Jonathan A. Hill | April 5, 1865 | Mustered out Feb. 2, 1866 **Bvt. Brig. Gen.** |

**12th Infantry**

| | | |
|---|---|---|
| George F. Shepley | Sept. 27, 1861 | Promoted **Brig. Gen., USV** July 17, 1862 |
| William K. Kimball | July 31, 1862 | Mustered out March 17, 1866 **Bvt. Brig. Gen.** |

**13th Infantry**

| | | |
|---|---|---|
| Neal Dow | Oct. 5, 1861 | Promoted **Brig. Gen., USV** April 28, 1862 |
| Henry Rust, Jr. | June 3, 1862 | Mustered out Jan. 6, 1865 **Bvt. Brig. Gen.** |

**14th Infantry**

| | | |
|---|---|---|
| Frank S. Nickerson | Dec. 28, 1861 | Promoted **Brig. Gen., USV** Nov. 29, 1862 |
| Thomas W. Porter | May 11, 1863 | Mustered out Jan. 13, 1865 |
| Albion K. Bolan | March 25, 1865 | Mustered out Aug. 28, 1865 |

**15th Infantry**

| | | |
|---|---|---|
| John McCluskey | Feb. 19, 1862 | Resigned Aug. 15, 1862 |
| Isaac Dyer | Sept. 13, 1862 | Mustered out Sept. 9, 1865 **Bvt. Brig. Gen.** |

**16th Infantry**

| | | |
|---|---|---|
| Asa W. Wildes | Aug. 9, 1862 | Resigned Jan. 7, 1863 |
| Charles W. Tilden | Feb. 5, 1863 | Mustered out June 5, 1865 **Bvt. Brig. Gen.** |

**17th Infantry**

| | | |
|---|---|---|
| Thomas A. Roberts | Aug. 19, 1862 | Discharged June 2, 1863 |
| George W. West | Oct. 2, 1863 | Discharged April 17, 1865 **Bvt. Brig. Gen.** |
| Charles P. Mattocks | May 9, 1865 | Mustered out June 4, 1865 **Bvt. Brig. Gen.** |

**18th Infantry** (see 1st Heavy Artillery)

**19th Infantry**

| | | |
|---|---|---|
| Frederic D. Sewall | Aug. 25, 1862 | Resigned Feb. 19, 1863 **Bvt. Brig. Gen.** |
| Francis E. Heath | March 2, 1863 | Resigned Nov. 4, 1863 **Bvt. Brig. Gen.** |
| Selden Connor | Dec. 1, 1863 | Promoted **Brig. Gen., USV** July 1, 1864 |
| James W. Welch | Aug. 16, 1864 | Resigned Oct. 21, 1864 |
| William H. Fogler | Nov. 2, 1864 | Discharged Nov. 2, 1864 |
| Isaac W. Starbird | Nov. 11, 1864 | Discharged June 7, 1865 **Bvt. Brig. Gen.** |

**20th Infantry**

| | | |
|---|---|---|
| Adelbert Ames | Aug. 8, 1862 | Promoted **Brig. Gen., USV** May 20, 1863 |
| Joshua L. Chamberlain | June 13, 1863 | Promoted **Brig. Gen., USV** June 18, 1864 |
| Charles D. Gilmore | July 11, 1864 | Resigned May 29, 1865 |
| Ellis Spear | May 29, 1865 | Mustered out July 16, 1865 **Bvt. Brig. Gen.** |

**21st Infantry**

| | | |
|---|---|---|
| Elijah D. Johnson | Oct. 27, 1862 | Mustered out Aug. 25, 1863 |

**22nd Infantry**

| | | |
|---|---|---|
| Simon G. Jerrard | Oct. 21, 1862 | Discharged June 14, 1863 |

**23rd Infantry**

| | | |
|---|---|---|
| William W. Virgin | Oct. 17, 1862 | Mustered out July 15, 1863 |

**24th Infantry**

| | | |
|---|---|---|
| George M. Atwood | Oct. 27, 1862 | Mustered out Aug. 25, 1863 |

**25th Infantry**

| | | |
|---|---|---|
| Francis Fessenden | Oct. 14, 1862 | Mustered out July 10, 1863 Later **Brig. Gen., USV** |

**26th Infantry**

| | | |
|---|---|---|
| Nathaniel H. Hubbard | Oct. 23, 1862 | Mustered out Aug. 17, 1863 |

**27th Infantry**

| | | |
|---|---|---|
| Rufus P. Tapley | Oct. 17, 1862 | Discharged Jan. 23, 1863 |
| Mark F. Wentworth | Feb. 11, 1863 | Mustered out July 17, 1863 **Bvt. Brig. Gen.** |

**28th Infantry**

| | | |
|---|---|---|
| Ephraim W. Woodman | Nov. 3, 1862 | Mustered out Aug. 31, 1863 |

**29th Infantry**

| | | |
|---|---|---|
| George L. Beal | Dec. 17, 1863 | Promoted **Brig. Gen., USV** Nov. 28, 1864 |
| George H. Nye | Dec. 17, 1864 | Mustered out June 21, 1866 **Bvt. Brig. Gen.** |

**30th Infantry**

| | | |
|---|---|---|
| Francis Fessenden | Dec. 18, 1863 | Promoted **Brig. Gen., USV** May 12, 1864 |
| Thomas H. Hubbard | May 13, 1864 | Resigned July 23, 1865 **Bvt. Brig. Gen.** |
| Royal E. Whitman | Aug. 7, 1865 | Mustered out Aug. 20, 1865 |

**31st Infantry**

| | | |
|---|---|---|
| Thomas Hight | April 29, 1864 | Discharged July 2, 1864 |
| Daniel White | July 1, 1864 | Mustered out July 15, 1865 **Bvt. Brig. Gen.** |

**32nd Infantry**

| | | |
|---|---|---|
| Mark F. Wentworth | May 6, 1864 | Discharged Oct. 18, 1864 **Bvt. Brig. Gen.** |

## Samuel Henderson Allen

Samuel Henderson Allen
*Massachusetts MOLLUS Collection, USAMHI.*

Major, 1 ME Cavalry, Sept. 28, 1861. Colonel, 1 ME Cavalry, March 1, 1862. Military Governor, Frederick, MD, Sept. 13, 1862-Jan. 5, 1863. Discharged for disability, Jan. 5, 1863, due to chronic asthma.

**Born:** Oct. 17, 1826 Cushing, ME
**Died:** Sept. 19, 1905 Togus, ME
**Occupation:** Maine State Prison overseer and labor contractor before war. Hotelkeeper, 1867-77. Ice and lumber business, 1877-88.
**Offices/Honors:** US Customs Inspector, Thomaston, ME, 1861. Maine Senate, 1885-87. Warden, Maine State Prison, 1888-96. Governor, Eastern Branch NHDVS, Togus, ME, 1897-1905.
**Miscellaneous:** Resided Thomaston, Knox Co., ME; and New York City, NY, 1867-76.
**Buried:** Elm Grove Cemetery, Thomaston, ME
**References:** Obituary Circular, Whole No. 223, Maine MOLLUS. Joseph T. Woodward. *Historic Record and Complete Biographic Roster 21st Maine Volunteers.* Augusta, ME, 1907. Edward P. Tobie. *History of the 1st Maine Cavalry, 1861-65.* Boston, MA, 1887. Pension File, National Archives.

## George Marston Atwood

Colonel, 24 ME Infantry, Oct. 16, 1862. Honorably mustered out, Aug. 25, 1863.

**Born:** Sept. 11, 1817 Sandwich, NH
**Died:** May 22, 1889 South Boston, MA
**Occupation:** Bookseller before war. Real estate agent and auctioneer after war.
**Offices/Honors:** Adjutant General of Maine, 1856
**Miscellaneous:** Resided Gardiner, Kennebec Co., ME; Augusta, Kennebec Co., ME; and Boston, MA
**Buried:** Oak Grove Cemetery, Gardiner, ME
**References:** Obituary, *Boston Evening Transcript*, May 23, 1889. Pension File, National Archives.

*Right:*
*Samuel Henderson Allen*
*Courtesy of Henry Deeks.*

## Horatio Bisbee, Jr.

George Marston Atwood
Maine State Archives. J.S. Variell, Water Street, Gardiner, ME.

Private, Co. E, 5 MA Infantry, April 19, 1861. Honorably mustered out, Aug. 1, 1861. Captain, Co. F, 9 ME Infantry, Sept. 22, 1861. Lieutenant Colonel, 9 ME Infantry, Jan. 10, 1862. *Colonel,* 9 ME Infantry, Jan. 2, 1863. Resumed duties as Lieutenant Colonel, Feb. 5, 1863, when Colonel Rich was restored to his command. Honorably discharged, March 19, 1863, at his own request.

**Born:** May 1, 1839 Canton, ME
**Died:** March 27, 1916 Dixfield, ME
**Education:** Graduated Tufts College, Medford, MA, 1863
**Occupation:** Lawyer
**Offices/Honors:** US District Attorney, Northern District of Florida, 1869-73. US House of Representatives, 1877-79, 1881, 1882-85.
**Miscellaneous:** Resided Canton, Oxford Co., ME; Rockford, Winnebago Co., IL; and Jacksonville, Duvall Co., FL
**Buried:** Greenwood Cemetery, Dixfield, ME
**References:** Rowland H. Rerick. *Memoirs of Florida.* Atlanta, GA, 1902. Obituary, *Jacksonville Florida Times-Union*, March 28, 1916. Pension File and Military Service File, National Archives. *Biographical Directory of the American Congress.*

## Albion Keith Bolan

2 Lieutenant, Co. F, 14 ME Infantry, Dec. 28, 1861. Captain, Co. F, 14 ME Infantry, April 11, 1862. Major, 14 ME Infantry, May 25, 1863. Volunteered for the "Forlorn Hope" storming party at Port Hudson, LA, June 15, 1863. Lieutenant Colonel, 14 ME Veteran Infantry, Feb. 8, 1865. Colonel, 14 ME Veteran Infantry, March 25, 1865. Honorably mustered out, Aug. 28, 1865.

**Born:** Aug. 2, 1838 Madrid, ME
**Died:** June 27, 1905 Castine, ME
**Occupation:** Engaged in oil business in association with the Rockefeller family.
**Miscellaneous:** Resided New York City, NY; and Castine, Hancock Co., ME
**Buried:** Woodlawn Cemetery, New York City, NY (Section 103, Hazel Plot, Lot 11670)

*Right:*
*Horatio Bisbee, Jr. (postwar)*
*Florida State Archives.*

*Albion Keith Bolan*
*Maine State Archives.*

*Albion Keith Bolan*
*Fourteenth Regiment Maine Infantry Roster of Survivors.*

**References:** Obituary Circular, Whole No. 853, New York MOLLUS. Willard Carver. *Fourteenth Regiment Maine Infantry Roster of Survivors.* N.p., 1892.

## Calvin Sanger Douty

Major, 1 ME Cavalry, Oct. 5, 1861. Lieutenant Colonel, 1 ME Cavalry, May 9, 1862. Colonel, 1 ME Cavalry, March 26, 1863. Commanded 1 Brigade, 3 Division, Cavalry Corps, Army of the Potomac, May 13, 1863-June 7, 1863. GSW side, Aldie, VA, June 17, 1863.

**Born:** 1812? ME
**Died:** June 17, 1863 KIA Aldie, VA
**Education:** Attended Foxcroft (ME) Academy
**Occupation:** Farmer
**Offices/Honors:** Three terms as Sheriff of Piscataquis Co., ME
**Miscellaneous:** Resided Guilford, Piscataquis Co., ME; and later Dover, Piscataquis Co., ME.
**Buried:** Dover Cemetery, Dover, ME

*Right:*
*Calvin Sanger Douty*
*Maine State Archives. Bogardus, Photographer, 363 Broadway, New York, NY*

Calvin Sanger Douty
Maine State Archives.

*Right:*
*Calvin Sanger Douty*
*Courtesy of Richard F. Carlile.*

**References:** *The Northern Monthly,* Vol. 1 (October 1864). Edward P. Tobie. *History of the 1st Maine Cavalry, 1861-65.* Boston, MA, 1887. Pension File, National Archives.

## Mark Hill Dunnell

Colonel, 5 ME Infantry, May 24, 1861. Resigned Sept. 2, 1861, in order to resume duties as US Consul at Vera Cruz, Mexico.

**Born:** July 2, 1823 Buxton, ME
**Died:** Aug. 8, 1904 Owatonna, MN
**Education:** Graduated Waterville (now Colby) College, Waterville, ME, 1849
**Occupation:** Principal, Norway (ME) and Hebron (ME) Academies, 1849-54. Subsequently practiced law, but continued to take an active interest in education.
**Offices/Honors:** Maine Legislature, 1854-55. Maine Superintendent of Schools, 1855, 1857-59. US Consul, Vera Cruz,

*Right:*
*Mark Hill Dunnell*
*Courtesy of Henry Deeks. King, Portland, ME.*

*Right bottom:*
*Mark Hill Dunnell (postwar)*
*Frederick H. Meserve. Historical Portraits. Courtesy of New York State Library.*

Mexico, 1861-62. Minnesota Legislature, 1867. Minnesota Superintendent of Public Instruction, 1867-70. US House of Representatives, 1871-83 and 1889-91.

**Miscellaneous:** Resided Portland, ME; Winona, Winona Co., MN, 1865-67; and Owatonna, Steele Co., MN, 1867-1904

**Buried:** Forest Hill Cemetery, Owatonna, MN

**References:** *The United States Biographical Dictionary and Portrait Gallery of Eminent and Self-Made Men.* Minnesota Volume. Chicago and New York, 1879. Obituary, *Owatonna Journal*, Aug. 8, 1904. *Biographical Directory of the American Congress.*

## Sabine Emery

Captain, Co. A, 9 ME Infantry, Sept. 21, 1861. Major, 9 ME Infantry, Sept. 22, 1861. Lieutenant Colonel, 9 ME Infantry, April 10, 1863. Colonel, 9 ME Infantry, May 27, 1863. GSW left leg and shell wound left breast, Fort Wagner, SC, July 18, 1863. In arrest for intoxication in the presence of the enemy near Walthall Junction, VA, May 7, 1864, he resigned May 25, 1864, "not because I am unwilling to fight for my country at this or any time, but because I am unable to."

**Born:** Feb. 28, 1835 Eastport, ME

**Died:** March 24, 1868 Baltimore, MD

**Education:** Graduated Waterville (now Colby) College, Waterville, ME, 1858.

**Occupation:** School principal before war. Practiced law after the war in partnership with Colonel William L. Schley of Baltimore.

**Miscellaneous:** Resided Eastport, Washington Co., ME; and Baltimore, MD.

**Buried:** Originally Green Mount Cemetery, Baltimore, MD, but he may have been removed to Eastport, ME, at a later time

**References:** R. C. Emery, compiler. *Genealogical Notes on the Eastport, Maine, Branch of the Emery Family.* N.p., 1950. Obituary, *Baltimore American & Commercial Advertiser*, March 25, 1868. Pension File and Military Service File, National Archives. *An Obituary Record of the Colby University from 1822 to 1870.* Waterville, ME, 1870.

## William Henry Fogler

*William Henry Fogler*
*Massachusetts MOLLUS Collection, USAMHI.*

Captain, Co. D, 19 ME Infantry, Aug. 25, 1862. GSW right knee, Totopotomoy, VA, June 1, 1864. *Colonel,* 19 ME Infantry, Nov. 2, 1864. Discharged for disability, Nov. 2, 1864, due to the effects of the wound of his right knee. Provost Marshal, 5 District of Maine, Nov. 15, 1864. Resigned Jan. 26, 1865.

**Born:** Nov. 10, 1837 Lincolnville, ME
**Died:** Feb. 18, 1902 Rockland, ME
**Education:** Attended Waterville (now Colby) College, Waterville, ME.
**Occupation:** Lawyer and US Customs inspector.
**Offices/Honors:** Deputy Collector of Customs, Belfast, ME, 1866-67. Associate Justice, ME Supreme Court, 1898-1902.
**Miscellaneous:** Resided Belfast, Waldo Co., ME, to 1890; and Rockland, Knox Co., ME, after 1890.
**Buried:** Achorn Cemetery, Rockland, ME (Section D, Lot 289, Avenue G South)
**References:** Obituary Circular, Whole No. 183, Maine MOLLUS. Pension File and Military Service File, National Archives. John D. Smith. *The History of the 19th Regiment of Maine Volunteer Infantry.* Minneapolis, MN, 1909. Obituary, *Augusta Daily Kennebec Journal*, Feb. 18, 1902.

## Charles D. Gilmore

*Charles D. Gilmore*
*Massachusetts MOLLUS Collection, USAMHI.*

Captain, Co. C, 7 ME Infantry, Aug. 21, 1861. Shell wound head, Lee's Mill, VA, April 16, 1862. Major, 20 ME Infantry, Aug. 11, 1862. Lieutenant Colonel, 20 ME Infantry, May 20, 1863. Discharged for disability, Feb. 22, 1865, due to paralysis of left side caused by head wound. Colonel, 20 ME Infantry, March 16, 1865. Discharged for disability, May 29, 1865, due to paralysis of left side caused by head wound.

**Born:** July 1819 Newburgh, ME
**Died:** Nov. 25, 1884 Washington, DC
**Occupation:** Lawyer and patent solicitor. Late in life became manager of a mining company.
**Offices/Honors:** Sheriff of Penobscot Co., ME, 1854-55 and 1857-60.
**Miscellaneous:** Resided Newburgh, Penobscot Co., ME; Bangor, Penobscot Co., ME; and Washington, DC.
**Buried:** Arlington National Cemetery, Arlington, VA (Section 3, Lot 1474)
**References:** Pension File and Military Service File, National Archives. Obituary, *Bangor Daily Whig and Courier*, Nov. 27, 1884. Obituary, *Washington Post*, Nov. 27, 1884. R.

H. Stanley and George O. Hall. *Eastern Maine and the Rebellion.* Bangor, ME, 1887. John J. Pullen. *The 20th Maine, A Volunteer Regiment in the Civil War.* Philadelphia, PA, 1957.

John Goddard
Courtesy of Tom MacDonald. Butler & King, No. 84 Middle Street, Portland, ME.

## John Goddard

Colonel, 1 ME Cavalry, Sept. 26, 1861. Resigned March 1, 1862, due to "great pecuniary losses and reverses of fortune."

**Born:** Feb. 28, 1811 ME
**Died:** March 27, 1870 Cape Elizabeth, ME
**Occupation:** Lumber merchant
**Miscellaneous:** Resided Cape Elizabeth, Cumberland Co., ME.
**Buried:** Evergreen Cemetery, Portland, ME (Section M, Lot 91)

Left:
John Goddard
Courtesy of Richard F. Carlile. T.R. Burnham, Photographer, 90 Middle Street, Portland, ME.

**References:** Obituary, *Portland Daily Eastern Argus*, March 29, 1870. Edward P. Tobie. *History of the 1st Maine Cavalry, 1861-65.* Boston, MA, 1887. Military Service File, National Archives.

*John Goddard and Sons (Left to right: Charles W. Goddard, John H. Goddard, and John Goddard). Courtesy of Richard F. Carlile. T.R. Burnham, Photographer, 90 Middle Street, Portland, ME.*

## Thomas Hight

Captain, 2 US Cavalry, Aug. 3, 1861. Lieutenant Colonel, 1 ME Cavalry, Oct. 19, 1861. Resigned volunteer commission, March 14, 1862. Captured Germantown, VA, Aug. 31, 1862. Exchanged Sept. 21, 1862. Resigned regular commission, April 27, 1863. Lieutenant Colonel, 31 ME Infantry, March 12, 1864. Colonel, 31 ME Infantry, April 29, 1864. Discharged for disability, July 2, 1864, due to severe diarrhea.

**Born:** Dec. 29, 1829 Bloomington, IN
**Died:** Oct. 17, 1867 Augusta, ME
**Education:** Graduated US Military Academy, West Point, NY, 1853
**Occupation:** Regular Army (Captain, 2 US Cavalry, resigned April 27, 1863). Partner in an apothecary shop after war.
**Miscellaneous:** Resided Augusta, Kennebec Co., ME.
**Buried:** Forest Grove Cemetery, Augusta, ME (Lot 93A)
**References:** Pension File, National Archives. Obituary, *Augusta Kennebec Weekly Journal*, Oct. 25, 1867. Georgia H. Truslow. *Hight Families.* Biddeford, ME, 1979. George W. Cullum. *Biographical Register of the Officers and Graduates of the US Military Academy.* Boston and New York, 1891. Edward P. Tobie. *History of the 1st Maine Cavalry, 1861-65.* Boston, MA, 1887.

## Nathaniel Hobbs Hubbard

Colonel, 26 ME Infantry, Sept. 23, 1862. Honorably mustered out, Aug. 17, 1863.

**Born:** June 20, 1812 North Berwick, ME
**Died:** March 9, 1892 Boston, MA
**Education:** Attended Waterville (now Colby) College, Waterville, ME
**Occupation:** Lawyer and judge
**Offices/Honors:** Judge of Probate, Waldo Co., ME
**Miscellaneous:** Resided Winterport, Waldo Co., ME
**Buried:** Oak Hill Cemetery, Winterport, ME (Section 7, Lot 16)
**References:** Elden B. Maddocks, compiler. *History of the 26th Maine Regiment.* Bangor, ME, 1899. Obituary, *Bangor Daily Whig and Courier*, March 11, 1892. Obituary, *Boston Evening Transcript*, March 15, 1892.

## Simon G. Jerrard

Colonel, 22 ME Infantry, Sept. 10, 1862. Dismissed June 14, 1863, for having used discouraging and insubordinate language in the presence of a large number of officers and enlisted men when ordered at Port Hudson to take a portion of the enemy's works by assault. Commenting on the "foul wrong" done to Jerrard, the Maine Adjutant General concluded: "The testimony is abundant in justification of his conduct, and that the order he disobeyed was impracticable must be apparent."

**Born:** July 14, 1828 Plymouth, ME
**Died:** Jan. 28, 1909 Levant, ME
**Education:** Attended Waterville (ME) Institute
**Occupation:** Lumberman and farmer
**Offices/Honors:** Sheriff of Penobscot Co., ME, 1875-78
**Miscellaneous:** Resided Albion, Kennebec Co., ME; and Levant, Penobscot Co., ME
**Buried:** Village Cemetery, Pittsfield, ME
**References:** Obituary, *Bangor Daily News*, Jan. 30, 1909. *Report of the Adjutant General of the State of Maine, 1864-65.* Augusta, ME, 1866.

*Right:*
*Simon G. Jerrard (postwar)*
*Courtesy of Tom MacDonald. Roster of 22nd Regiment Infantry Maine Volunteers.*

## Elijah D. Johnson

1 Lieutenant, Co. K, 1 ME Infantry, May 3, 1861. 1 Lieutenant, Adjutant, 7 ME Infantry, Aug. 22, 1861. Resigned Dec. 4, 1861, due to "important private business." 2 Lieutenant, Co. K, 7 ME Infantry, Feb. 17, 1862. 1 Lieutenant, Co. K, 7 ME Infantry, July 31, 1862. Colonel, 21 ME Infantry, Sept. 18, 1862. Honorably mustered out, Aug. 25, 1863. Captain, Co. C, 2 ME Cavalry, Dec. 3, 1863. Honorably mustered out, Dec. 6, 1865.

**Born:** June 5, 1832 Mercer, Somerset Co., ME
**Died:** Jan. 30, 1890 Dundee, Geneva Co., AL
**Occupation:** Mechanic and millwright.
**Miscellaneous:** Resided Lewiston, Androscoggin Co., ME; and Milton, Santa Rosa Co., FL.
**Buried:** Milton Cemetery, Milton, FL (Section 6)
**References:** Joseph T. Woodward. *Historic Record and Complete Biographic Roster 21st Maine Volunteers.* Augusta, ME, 1907. Pension File, National Archives.

*Elijah D. Johnson*
*Maine State Archives.*

*Right:*
*Elijah D. Johnson*
*Courtesy of Tom MacDonald. Meade Brothers "Specialite," 233 Broadway, near Astor, New York City, NY.*

## Abner Knowles

Colonel, 6 ME Infantry, July 15, 1861. On Oct. 11, 1861 a Board of Examination found him "incompetent to command a regiment," but recommended, in view of his patriotism, to allow him to resign. Resigned Dec. 11, 1861.

**Born:** July 17, 1806 Unity, Waldo Co., ME
**Died:** March 31, 1878 Bangor, ME
**Occupation:** Lawyer. "One of the most effective criminal lawyers in the state, ... nothing but unfortunate infirmities of habit prevented him from reaping the highest distinctions at the Bar of Maine."
**Miscellaneous:** Resided Dexter, Penobscot Co., ME; Hampden, Penobscot Co., ME; and Bangor, Penobscot Co., ME
**Buried:** Riverview Cemetery, Bucksport, ME
**References:** Obituary, *Bangor Daily Whig and Courier*, April 1, 1878. Virginia K. Hufbauer. *Descendants of Richard Knowles, 1637-1973.* San Diego, CA, 1974. Pension File, National Archives. James H. Mundy. *No Rich Men's Sons: The 6th Maine Volunteer Infantry.* Cape Elizabeth, ME, 1994.

*Moses B. Lakeman*
*Courtesy of William Gladstone. J.W. Black, 173 Washington Street, Boston, MA.*

## Moses B. Lakeman

Captain, Co. I, 3 ME Infantry, June 4, 1861. GSW Fair Oaks, VA, June 1, 1862. Lieutenant Colonel, 3 ME Infantry, July 7, 1862. Colonel, 3 ME Infantry, Nov. 14, 1862. Better known in the 3 Army Corps as "Fighting Mose." GSW scrotum, North Anna River, VA, May 23, 1864. Honorably mustered out, June 28, 1864.

*Moses B. Lakeman*
*Massachusetts MOLLUS Collection, USAMHI.*

**Born:** Sept. 11, 1828 Boston, MA
**Died:** March 15, 1907 Malden, MA
**Occupation:** Provision dealer before war. Foreman, Malden (MA) Street Department, after war.
**Miscellaneous:** Resided Augusta, Kennebec Co., ME; and Malden, Middlesex Co., MA
**Buried:** Salem Street Cemetery, Malden, MA
**References:** Pension File and Military Service File, National Archives. Hannibal A. Johnson. *The Sword of Honor: A Story of the Civil War.* Worcester, MA, 1906. Obituary, *Boston Evening Transcript*, March 20, 1907. Obituary, *Augusta Daily Kennebec Journal*, March 16, 1907.

*Thomas Henry Marshall*
*Maine State Archives.*

## Thomas Henry Marshall

Lieutenant Colonel, 4 ME Infantry, June 14, 1861. Colonel, 7 ME Infantry, Sept. 5, 1861.

**Born:** Feb. 10, 1826 Belfast, ME
**Died:** Oct. 25, 1861 Baltimore, MD, of typhoid fever
**Education:** Attended Bowdoin College, Brunswick, ME
**Occupation:** Merchant
**Offices/Honors:** Maine Legislature, 1857-58. Maine Senate, 1859-60.
**Miscellaneous:** Resided Belfast, Waldo Co., ME
**Buried:** Grove Cemetery, Belfast, ME
**References:** Joseph Williamson. *History of the City of Belfast, ME.* Portland, ME, 1877. *General Catalogue of Bowdoin College, 1794-1950.* Brunswick, ME, 1950.

*John McCluskey*
*The Story of the Maine Fifteenth.*

## John McCluskey

Colonel, 15 ME Infantry, Jan. 23, 1862. Acquitted by court martial of charges of conduct unbecoming an officer and a gentleman, threatening subordinate officers, and neglect of duty while en route to Ship Island, MS, March-April, 1862, he subsequently resigned, Aug. 25, 1862, without giving any reason. On his resignation Major Gen. Benjamin F. Butler commented, "Accepted with pleasure."

**Born:** 1811 County Tyrone, Ireland
**Died:** Jan. 18, 1863 Virgin Bay, Nicaragua, of chronic diarrhea
**Other Wars:** Texas War for Independence, 1836.
**Occupation:** Lumber merchant.
**Offices/Honors:** Two terms in Maine Senate.
**Miscellaneous:** Resided Houlton, Aroostook Co., ME.
**Buried:** Virgin Bay, Nicaragua

**References:** Pension File and Military Service File, National Archives. Obituary, *Houlton Aroostook Times*, April 17, 1863. Cora M. Putnam. *Story of Houlton.* Portland, ME, 1958. Henry A. Shorey. *The Story of the Maine Fifteenth.* Bridgton, ME, 1890.

## Freeman McGilvery

Captain, 6 Battery, 1 ME Light Artillery, Jan. 1, 1862. Major, 1 ME Light Artillery, Feb. 5, 1863. Commanded 1 Volunteer Brigade, Artillery Reserve, Army of the Potomac, May 16, 1863-May 16, 1864. Lieutenant Colonel, 1 ME Light Artillery, June 23, 1863. *Colonel,* 1 ME Light Artillery, Sept. 1, 1863. Chief of Artillery, 10 Army Corps, Aug. 13-Sept. 2, 1864. GSW left hand, Deep Bottom, VA, Aug. 16, 1864.

**Born:** Oct. 29, 1823 Prospect, Waldo Co., ME
**Died:** Sept. 2, 1864 DOW near Petersburg, VA
**Occupation:** As captain of trading vessels, he transacted business throughout the world.
**Miscellaneous:** Resided Searsport, Waldo Co., ME.
**Buried:** Village Cemetery, Searsport, ME
**References:** *Report of the Maine Adjutant General for 1864-1865.* Augusta, ME, 1866. Pension File, National Archives. William E. S. Whitman and Charles H. True. *Maine in the War for the Union.* Lewiston, ME, 1865.

*Freeman McGilvery*
*Courtesy of Tom MacDonald. Brady's National Photographic Portrait Gallery, Broadway & Tenth Street, New York.*

*Freeman McGilvery*
*Massachusetts MOLLUS Collection, USAMHI.*

*Freeman McGilvery*
*Massachusetts MOLLUS Collection, USAMHI.*

## Thomas Whittier Porter

Thomas Whittier Porter
Maine State Archives.

Major, 14 ME Infantry, Dec. 31, 1861. Lieutenant Colonel, 14 ME Infantry, June 2, 1862. Colonel, 14 ME Infantry, May 11, 1863. Commanded 1 Brigade, 3 Division, 19 Army Corps, Aug. 15, 1863-Aug. 29, 1863. Commanded 1 Brigade, 2 Division, 19 Army Corps, Oct. 19, 1864-Nov. 10, 1864. Honorably mustered out, Jan. 13, 1865.

**Born:** Nov. 13, 1820 Mount Vernon, ME
**Died:** June 23, 1896 Chelsea, MA
**Occupation:** Lawyer and patent solicitor.
**Miscellaneous:** Resided Bangor, Penobscot Co., ME; and Chelsea, Suffolk Co., MA.
**Buried:** Woodlawn Cemetery, Everett, MA (Hillside Avenue, Lot 1942)
**References:** Charles C. Whittier, compiler. *The Descendants of Thomas Whittier and Ruth Green of Salisbury and Haverhill, MA*. Rutland, VT, 1937. Obituary, *Boston Evening Transcript*, June 24, 1896. Military Service File, National Archives.

## Rishworth Rich

Colonel, 9 ME Infantry, Sept. 22, 1861. Commanded Post of Fernandina, FL, Department of the South, April-Dec. 1862. Dismissed Dec. 27, 1862 for incompetency and refusal to recognize officers of the regiment commissioned by the Governor of the State. Restored to his command, March 3, 1863. Resigned May 27, 1863, due to long standing and increasing lameness. Dismissal revoked Aug. 1, 1867.

**Born:** Sept. 27, 1835 Portland, ME
**Died:** March 15, 1891 Old Orchard, ME
**Occupation:** Shoe manufacturer and commission merchant.
**Miscellaneous:** Resided Portland, ME; Baltimore, MD, 1867-68; Waterbury, CT, 1868-70; Boston, MA, 1873-85.
**Buried:** Evergreen Cemetery, Portland, ME (Section U, Lot 349)
**References:** Pension File and Military Service File, National Archives. Obituary, *Portland Daily Eastern Argus*, March 17, 1891.

*Right:*
*Rishworth Rich*
*Courtesy of Henry Deeks. King, Portland, ME.*

## Thomas A. Roberts

Thomas A. Roberts
Maine State Archives. Brown, 235 1/2 Middle Street, Portland, ME.

Colonel, 17 ME Infantry, Aug. 7, 1862. Commanded 3 Brigade, 1 Division, 3 Army Corps, Army of the Potomac, Jan. 29-Feb. 4, 1863. Discharged for disability, June 2, 1863, due to vertigo.

**Born:** July 7, 1817 Portland, ME
**Died:** Feb. 9, 1888 Portland, ME
**Occupation:** Painter and paper hanger.
**Miscellaneous:** Resided Portland, ME.
**Buried:** Evergreen Cemetery, Portland, ME (Section D, Lot 176)
**References:** Obituary, *Portland Daily Eastern Argus*, Feb. 10, 1888. Military Service File, National Archives. William B. Jordan, Jr. *Red Diamond Regiment: The 17th Maine Infantry.* Shippensburg, PA, 1996. Edwin B. Houghton. *The Campaigns of the 17th Maine.* Portland, ME, 1866.

## Zina H. Robinson

Captain, Co. B, 9 ME Infantry, Sept. 21, 1861. Major, 9 ME Infantry, April 10, 1863. Lieutenant Colonel, 9 ME Infantry, May 27, 1863. Commanded 2 Brigade, 3 Division, 18 Army Corps, June 1-5, 1864. *Colonel,* 9 ME Infantry, June 6, 1864. Discharged for disability, Aug. 16, 1864, due to chronic diarrhea and hamoptysis.

**Born:** March 29, 1825 Bath, ME
**Died:** April 3, 1910 Los Angeles, CA
**Occupation:** Shipbuilder and lumber surveyor.
**Miscellaneous:** Resided Bath, Sagadahoc Co., ME; San Francisco, CA; and Los Angeles, CA.
**Buried:** Los Angeles National Cemetery, Los Angeles, CA (Section 16, Row J, Grave 17)
**References:** *Annual Report of the Maine Adjutant General for the Year Ending Dec. 31, 1866.* Augusta, ME, 1867. Pension File, National Archives.

*Right:*
*Thomas A. Roberts*
*Massachusetts MOLLUS Collection, USAMHI. Brady's National Photographic Portrait Gallery.*

## Edward A. Scamman

Henry Genet Staples
Courtesy Massachusetts Historical Society, Boston, MA. J.W. Black, 173 Washington Street, Boston, MA.

Captain, Co. H, 5 ME Infantry, June 24, 1861. Major, 5 ME Infantry, Sept. 25, 1861. Lieutenant Colonel, 5 ME Infantry, July 25, 1862. Colonel, 5 ME Infantry, Sept. 24, 1862. Resigned Jan. 8, 1863, due to "the state of his private affairs at home."

**Born:** Aug. 28, 1825 Gorham, ME
**Died:** Oct. 26, 1864 Beaufort, NC, of yellow fever
**Occupation:** Clerk
**Miscellaneous:** Resided Gorham, Cumberland Co., ME; and Portland, ME.
**Buried:** Eastern Cemetery, Gorham, ME
**References:** Hugh D. McLellan. *History of Gorham, ME.* Portland, ME, 1903. Military Service File, National Archives. George W. Bicknell. *History of the 5th Regiment Maine Volunteers.* Portland, ME, 1871.

## Henry Genet Staples

Major, 3 ME Infantry, May 30, 1861. Colonel, 3 ME Infantry, Sept. 7, 1861. Commanded 2 Brigade, 1 Division, 3 Army Corps, Army of the Potomac, Oct. 10-12, 1862. Resigned Nov. 14, 1862, due to "family affairs."

**Born:** Nov. 30, 1835 Portland, ME
**Died:** March 3, 1906 Augusta, ME
**Education:** Attended Yarmouth (ME) Institute
**Occupation:** Grocer, window shade manufacturer, real estate developer and capitalist.
**Offices/Honors:** Founder of the Augusta Building and Loan Association. President of the Maine Mutual Fire Insurance Co. Founder of the Augusta Board of Trade. Promoter and director of the Augusta, Winthrop & Gardiner Electric Railway.
**Miscellaneous:** Resided Augusta, Kennebec Co., ME
**Buried:** Hallowell Cemetery, Hallowell, ME
**References:** Obituary Circular, Whole No. 230, Maine MOLLUS. Obituary, *Augusta Daily Kennebec Journal*, March 5, 1906. P. W. McIntyre and W. F. Blanding, editors. *Men of Progress State of Maine.* Boston, MA, 1897. Pension File, National Archives.

*Right:*
*Henry Genet Staples (postwar)*
*Men of Progress State of Maine.*

## Lee Strickland

Colonel, 8 ME Infantry, Sept. 7, 1861. Resigned Dec. 13, 1861, due to "reasons personal to myself."

**Born:** Jan. 14, 1806 ME
**Died:** Sept. 28, 1873 Livermore, ME
**Occupation:** Merchant and railroad promoter
**Offices/Honors:** Maine Senate. Sheriff of Oxford Co., ME, 1853. Sheriff of Androscoggin Co., ME, 1856.
**Miscellaneous:** Resided North Turner, Androscoggin Co., ME; and Livermore, Androscoggin Co., ME
**Buried:** Lakeside Cemetery, Livermore, ME
**References:** Pension File and Military Service File, National Archives. Georgia Drew Merrill, editor. *History of Androscoggin County, ME.* Boston, MA, 1891. Obituary, *Augusta Kennebec Weekly Journal*, Oct. 1, 1873.

## Rufus Preston Tapley

Colonel, 27 ME Infantry, Sept. 19, 1862. Facing discharge upon "adverse report of a Board of Examination," he was allowed to resign, Jan. 23, 1863.

**Born:** Jan. 2, 1823 Danvers, MA
**Died:** April 10, 1893 Saco, ME
**Occupation:** Lawyer and judge
**Offices/Honors:** Maine Legislature, 1858, 1864-65 and 1874. Associate Justice, Maine Supreme Court, 1866-72.
**Miscellaneous:** Resided Saco, York Co., ME
**Buried:** Laurel Hill Cemetery, Saco, ME (New Avenue, Lot 625, family monument)
**References:** W. W. Clayton. *History of York County, ME.* Philadelphia, PA, 1880. James M. Stone. *The History of the 27th Regiment Maine Volunteer Infantry.* Portland, ME, 1895. Pension File and Military Service File, National Archives.

*Rufus Preston Tapley*
*Massachusetts MOLLUS Collection, USAMHI.*

## William Wirt Virgin

Colonel, 23 ME Infantry, Sept. 29, 1862. Honorably mustered out, July 15, 1863.

**Born:** Sept. 18, 1823 Rumford, ME
**Died:** Jan. 23, 1893 Portland, ME
**Education:** Graduated Bowdoin College, Brunswick, ME, 1844
**Occupation:** Lawyer and judge

**Offices/Honors:** Major Gen., Maine State Militia, 1859-61. Maine Senate, 1865-66. Associate Justice, Maine Supreme Court, 1872-93.

**Miscellaneous:** Resided Norway, Oxford Co., ME; and Portland, ME

**Buried:** Evergreen Cemetery, Portland, ME (Section R, Lot 317)

**References:** Obituary Circular, Whole No. 105, Maine MOLLUS. W. Woodford Clayton. *History of Cumberland County, ME.* Philadelphia, PA, 1880. Pension File, National Archives. *General Catalogue of Bowdoin College, 1794-1950.* Brunswick, ME, 1950.

*William Wirt Virgin*
*Massachusetts MOLLUS Collection, USAMHI.*

## Elijah Walker

Captain, Co. B, 4 ME Infantry, June 15, 1861. Major, 4 ME Infantry, Nov. 30, 1861. Colonel, 4 ME Infantry, March 17, 1862. GSW left leg, Gettysburg, PA, July 2, 1863. Commanded 2 Brigade, 1 Division, 3 Army Corps, Army of the Potomac, Dec. 29, 1863-Jan. 17, 1864 and Jan. 28-Feb. 17, 1864. Commanded 2 Brigade, 3 Division, 2 Army Corps, Army of the Potomac, May 18-23, 1864. Honorably mustered out, July 19, 1864.

**Born:** July 2, 1818 Union, ME

**Died:** March 20, 1905 Somerville, MA

**Occupation:** Carpenter and builder.

**Miscellaneous:** Resided Rockland, Knox Co., ME; and Somerville, Middlesex Co., MA.

**Buried:** Cambridge Cemetery, Cambridge, MA (Arbutus Path, Lot 840)

**References:** *American Series of Popular Biographies.* Massachusetts Edition. Boston, MA, 1901. Pension File, National Archives. Obituary, *Boston Evening Transcript*, March 21, 1905.

*Elijah Walker*
*Maine State Archives.*

## James William Welch

Captain, Co. G, 19 ME Infantry, Aug. 25, 1862. Major, 19 ME Infantry, Feb. 21, 1863. GSW head, Gettysburg, PA, July 2, 1863. GSW left thigh, Spotsylvania, VA, May 12, 1864. Captured the colors of the 33rd Virginia, Spotsylvania, VA, May 12, 1864. Colonel, 19 ME Infantry, Sept. 16, 1864. Commanded 1 Brigade, 2 Division, 2 Army Corps, Army of the Potomac, Oct. 1864. Discharged for disability, Oct. 21, 1864, due to wounds.

**Born:** July 4, 1827 Bath, ME
**Died:** Nov. 23, 1895 New York City, NY
**Occupation:** Paint manufacturer. Associated with the paint manufacturing firm of F. W. Devoe & Co. of New York as its chemist and colorist, he later became a member of the firm.
**Miscellaneous:** Resided Augusta, Kennebec Co., ME; and New York City, NY
**Buried:** Forest Grove Cemetery, Augusta, ME (Lot 83)
**References:** Obituary, *Augusta Daily Kennebec Journal*, Nov. 25, 1895. Pension File, National Archives. John D. Smith. *The History of the 19th Regiment of Maine Volunteer Infantry.* Minneapolis, MN, 1909.

*James W. Welch*
*Maine State Archives.*

## Royal Emerson Whitman

Sergeant Major, 23 ME Infantry, Sept. 10, 1862. Captain, Co. G, 23 ME Infantry, March 1, 1863. Honorably mustered out, July 15, 1863. Major, 30 ME Infantry, Dec. 29, 1863. GSW both thighs, Sabine Cross Roads, LA, April 8, 1864. Lieutenant Colonel, 30 ME Infantry, Sept. 1, 1864. Colonel, 30 ME Infantry, Aug. 14, 1865. Honorably mustered out, Aug. 20, 1865.

*Royal Emerson Whitman*
*Roger D. Hunt Collection, USAMHI. Brady's National Photographic Portrait Gallery, 352 Pennsylvania Avenue, Washington, DC.*

*Royal Emerson Whitman*
*Maine State Archives. Starbird, Photographer, A few doors north of the Stanley House, Augusta, ME.*

**Born:** May 11, 1833 Turner, ME
**Died:** Feb. 12, 1913 Washington, DC
**Occupation:** Regular Army (1 Lieutenant, 3 US Cavalry, retired March 20, 1879). Wine merchant later in life.
**Miscellaneous:** Resided Turner, Androscoggin Co., ME; Portland, ME; Columbus, OH; and Washington, DC. Invented Whitman saddle.
**Buried:** Arlington National Cemetery, Arlington, VA (Section 1, Lot 49-A)
**References:** Charles H. Farnam. *History of the Descendants of John Whitman of Weymouth, MA.* New Haven, CT, 1889. Constance Wynn Altshuler. *Cavalry Yellow & Infantry Blue.* Tucson, AZ, 1991. ACP File, National Archives.

## Asa Waldo Wildes

*Asa Waldo Wildes (postwar)*
*Maine State Archives. Lamson, Portland, ME.*

Colonel, 16 ME Infantry, May 21, 1862. Discharged for disability, Jan. 7, 1863, suffering from "torpidity of the liver with consequent nephritic irritation."

**Born:** Aug. 2, 1822 Newburyport, MA
**Died:** Sept. 3, 1894 Augusta, ME
**Occupation:** Railroad construction engineer
**Offices/Honors:** Maine State Railroad Commissioner, 1862-94
**Miscellaneous:** Resided Skowhegan, Somerset Co., ME
**Buried:** North Cemetery, Skowhegan, ME
**References:** Walter G. Davis. *The Ancestry of Dudley Wildes, 1759-1820, of Topsfield, MA.* Portland, ME, 1959. George T. Little, editor. *Genealogical and Family History of the State of Maine.* New York City, NY, 1909. Pension File, National Archives. Abner R. Small. *The 16th Maine Regiment in the War of the Rebellion.* Portland, ME, 1886.

## Ephraim Warren Woodman

*Ephraim Warren Woodman*
*Massachusetts MOLLUS Collection, USAMHI. C.H. Williamson's Photographic Portrait Gallery, 245 Fulton Street, Brooklyn, NY.*

Colonel, 28 ME Infantry, Oct. 6, 1862. Honorably mustered out, Aug. 31, 1863. Colonel, 2 ME Cavalry, Dec. 28, 1863. Commanded 2 Brigade, 1 Division, District of West Florida, Sept. 3, 1864-Jan. 23, 1865. Commanded 3 Brigade, 1 Division, District of West Florida, Jan. 25, 1865-March 10, 1865. Honorably mustered out, Dec. 6, 1865.

**Born:** Aug. 17, 1822 Wilton, ME
**Died:** 1869 Vernon, AL
**Occupation:** Farmer
**Miscellaneous:** Resided Colusa Township, Colusa Co., CA (1860); Wilton, Franklin Co., ME; and Vernon, Lamar Co., AL.
**Buried:** Probably Vernon, Lamar Co., AL
**References:** John A. Woodman. *Genealogy and History of the Descendants of Mr. Edward Woodman.* N.p., 1995. Cyrus Woodman. *The Woodmans of Buxton, Maine.* Boston, MA, 1874. Military Service File, National Archives.

## *Chapter III*

# MASSACHUSETTS

| | | |
|---|---|---|
| **1st Cavalry** | | |
| Robert Williams | Oct. 7, 1861 | Resigned Oct. 29, 1862 **Bvt. Brig. Gen.** |
| Horace B. Sargent | Oct. 30, 1862 | Discharged Sept. 29, 1864 **Bvt. Brig. Gen.** |
| Samuel E. Chamberlain | Sept. 30, 1864 | To 5th MA Cavalry July 26, 1865 **Bvt. Brig. Gen.** |
| **2nd Cavalry** | | |
| Charles R. Lowell | April 15, 1863 | Promoted **Brig. Gen., USV** Oct. 19, 1864 |
| Caspar Crowninshield | Oct. 21, 1864 | Resigned June 16, 1865 **Bvt. Brig. Gen.** |
| **3rd Cavalry** | | |
| Thomas E. Chickering | Sept. 15, 1862 | Resigned Sept. 1, 1864 **Bvt. Brig. Gen.** |
| Lorenzo D. Sargent | Sept. 2, 1864 | Discharged March 10, 1865 |
| Burr B. Porter | March 21, 1865 | Mustered out July 21, 1865 |
| Frederick G. Pope | Oct. 5, 1865 | Mustered out Sept. 28, 1865 |
| **4th Cavalry** | | |
| Arnold A. Rand | Jan. 22, 1864 | Resigned Feb. 3, 1865 |
| Francis Washburn | Feb. 4, 1865 | DOW April 22, 1865 **Bvt. Brig. Gen.** |
| Horatio Jenkins, Jr. | April 23, 1865 | Mustered out Nov. 14, 1865 **Bvt. Brig. Gen.** |
| **5th Cavalry** | | |
| Henry S. Russell | April 5, 1864 | Resigned Feb. 14, 1865 **Bvt. Brig. Gen.** |
| Charles F. Adams, Jr. | Feb. 15, 1865 | Resigned Aug. 1, 1865 **Bvt. Brig. Gen.** |
| Samuel E. Chamberlain | July 26, 1865 | Mustered out Oct. 31, 1865 **Bvt. Brig. Gen.** |
| **1st Heavy Artillery** | | |
| William B. Greene | July 5, 1861 | Resigned Oct. 11, 1862 |
| Thomas R. Tannatt | Nov. 28, 1862 | Resigned July 18, 1864 |
| Levi P. Wright | Jan. 26, 1865 | Mustered out May 16, 1865 |
| Nathaniel Shatswell | Jan. 27, 1865 | Mustered out Aug. 16, 1865 |
| **2nd Heavy Artillery** | | |
| Jones Frankle | May 13, 1863 | Mustered out Sept. 3, 1865 **Bvt. Brig. Gen.** |
| Augustus B. R. Sprague | Sept. 18, 1865 | Mustered out Sept. 3, 1865 **Bvt. Brig. Gen.** |
| **3rd Heavy Artillery** | | |
| William S. Abert | Nov. 16, 1864 | Mustered out Sept. 18, 1865 **Bvt. Brig. Gen.** |
| **4th Heavy Artillery** | | |
| William S. King | Nov. 14, 1864 | Mustered out June 17, 1865 **Bvt. Brig. Gen.** |
| **1st Infantry** | | |
| Robert Cowdin | May 22, 1861 | Promoted **Brig. Gen., USV** Sept. 30, 1862 |
| Napoleon B. McLaughlen | Oct. 1, 1862 | Mustered out May 28, 1864 **Bvt. Brig. Gen.** |
| **2nd Infantry** | | |
| George H. Gordon | May 24, 1861 | Promoted **Brig. Gen., USV** June 12, 1862 |
| George L. Andrews | June 13, 1862 | Promoted **Brig. Gen., USV** Nov. 9, 1862 |
| Samuel M. Quincy | Nov. 9, 1862 | Resigned June 6, 1863 **Bvt. Brig. Gen.** |
| William Cogswell | June 6, 1863 | Mustered out July 24, 1865 **Bvt. Brig. Gen.** |
| Charles F. Morse | July 24, 1865 | Mustered out July 14, 1865 |
| **3rd Infantry (3 Months)** | | |
| David W. Wardrop | April 23, 1861 | Mustered out July 22, 1861 |
| **3rd Infantry (9 Months)** | | |
| Silas P. Richmond | Oct. 7, 1862 | Mustered out June 26, 1863 |
| **4th Infantry (3 Months)** | | |
| Abner B. Packard | April 22, 1861 | Mustered out July 22, 1861 |
| **4th Infantry (9 Months)** | | |
| Henry Walker | Dec. 6, 1862 | Mustered out Sept. 3, 1863 |

**5th Infantry (3 Months)**

| | | |
|---|---|---|
| Samuel C. Lawrence | May 1, 1861 | Mustered out July 31, 1861 |

**5th Infantry (9 Months)**

| | | |
|---|---|---|
| George H. Peirson | June 26, 1862 | Mustered out July 2, 1863 |

**5th Infantry (100 Days)**

| | | |
|---|---|---|
| George H. Peirson | July 28, 1864 | Mustered out Nov. 16, 1864 |

**6th Infantry (3 Months)**

| | | |
|---|---|---|
| Edward F. Jones | April 22, 1861 | Mustered out Aug. 2, 1861 **Bvt. Brig. Gen.** |

**6th Infantry (9 Months)**

| | | |
|---|---|---|
| Albert S. Follansbee | May 27, 1862 | Mustered out June 3, 1863 |

**6th Infantry (100 Days)**

| | | |
|---|---|---|
| Albert S. Follansbee | July 20, 1864 | Mustered out Oct. 27, 1864 |

**7th Infantry**

| | | |
|---|---|---|
| Darius N. Couch | June 15, 1861 | Promoted **Brig. Gen., USV** Sept. 3, 1861 |
| Nelson H. Davis | Sept. 4, 1861 | Discharged Nov. 2, 1861 **Bvt. Brig. Gen.** |
| Joseph H. Wheelock | Nov. 20, 1861 | Resigned Jan. 30, 1862 |
| David A. Russell | Feb. 1, 1862 | Promoted **Brig. Gen., USV** Dec. 27, 1862 |
| Thomas D. Johns | Feb. 23, 1863 | Mustered out June 27, 1864 **Bvt. Brig. Gen.** |

**8th Infantry (3 Months)**

| | | |
|---|---|---|
| Timothy Munroe | April 17, 1861 | Resigned May 15, 1861 |
| Edward W. Hinks | May 16, 1861 | Mustered out Aug. 1, 1861 Later **Brig. Gen., USV** |

**8th Infantry (9 Months)**

| | | |
|---|---|---|
| Frederic J. Coffin | May 26, 1862 | Mustered out Aug. 7, 1863 |

**8th Infantry (100 Days)**

| | | |
|---|---|---|
| Benjamin F. Peach, Jr. | July 22, 1864 | Mustered out Nov. 10, 1864 |

**9th Infantry**

| | | |
|---|---|---|
| Thomas Cass | June 11, 1861 | DOW July 12, 1862 |
| Patrick R. Guiney | July 26, 1862 | Mustered out June 21, 1864 **Bvt. Brig. Gen.** |

**10th Infantry**

| | | |
|---|---|---|
| Henry S. Briggs | June 21, 1861 | Promoted **Brig. Gen., USV** July 28, 1862 |
| Henry L. Eustis | Aug. 15, 1862 | Promoted **Brig. Gen., USV** Sept. 15, 1863 |

**11th Infantry**

| | | |
|---|---|---|
| George Clark, Jr. | June 13, 1861 | Resigned Oct. 11, 1861 |
| William Blaisdell | Oct. 11, 1861 | KIA June 23, 1864 **Bvt. Brig. Gen.** |
| Thomas H. Dunham, Jr. | July 11, 1865 | Mustered out July 14, 1865 **Bvt. Brig. Gen.** |

**12th Infantry**

| | | |
|---|---|---|
| Fletcher Webster | June 26, 1861 | KIA Aug. 30, 1862 |
| James L. Bates | Sept. 9, 1862 | Mustered out July 8, 1864 **Bvt. Brig. Gen.** |

**13th Infantry**

| | | |
|---|---|---|
| Samuel H. Leonard | July 16, 1861 | Mustered out Aug. 1, 1864 |

**14th Infantry** (see 1st Heavy Artillery)

**15th Infantry**

| | | |
|---|---|---|
| Charles Devens | July 24, 1861 | Promoted **Brig. Gen., USV** April 26, 1862 |
| George H. Ward | April 29, 1862 | DOW July 3, 1863 **Bvt. Brig. Gen.** |
| George C. Joslin | July 4, 1863 | Mustered out July 29, 1864 |

**16th Infantry**

| | | |
|---|---|---|
| Powell T. Wyman | July 13, 1861 | KIA June 30, 1862 |
| Thomas R. Tannatt | July 14, 1862 | To 1st MA Heavy Artillery Nov. 28, 1862 |
| Gardner Banks | Nov. 28, 1862 | Discharged Sept. 4, 1863 |

**17th Infantry**

| | | |
|---|---|---|
| Thomas I. C. Amory | Sept. 2, 1861 | Died of disease Oct. 7, 1864 **Bvt. Brig. Gen.** |
| John F. Fellows | Oct. 9, 1864 | Not Mustered |
| Henry Splaine | June 16, 1865 | Mustered out July 11, 1865 |

**18th Infantry**

| | | |
|---|---|---|
| James Barnes | July 26, 1861 | Promoted **Brig. Gen., USV** Nov. 29, 1862 |
| Joseph Hayes | Nov. 30, 1862 | Promoted **Brig. Gen., USV** June 14, 1864 |

**19th Infantry**

| | | |
|---|---|---|
| Edward W. Hinks | Aug. 3, 1861 | Promoted **Brig. Gen., USV** Nov. 29, 1862 |
| Arthur F. Devereux | Nov. 29, 1862 | Resigned Feb. 27, 1864 **Bvt. Brig. Gen.** |
| Ansel D. Wass | Feb. 28, 1864 | Discharged July 27, 1864 **Bvt. Brig. Gen.** |
| Edmund Rice | July 28, 1864 | Mustered out June 30, 1865 |

**20th Infantry**

| | | |
|---|---|---|
| William R. Lee | July 1, 1861 | Discharged Dec. 17, 1862 **Bvt. Brig. Gen.** |
| Francis W. Palfrey | Dec. 18, 1862 | Discharged April 13, 1863 **Bvt. Brig. Gen.** |
| Paul J. Revere | April 14, 1863 | DOW July 4, 1863 **Bvt. Brig. Gen.** |
| George N. Macy | July 5, 1863 | Mustered out July 27, 1865 **Bvt. Brig. Gen.** |

**21st Infantry**

| | | |
|---|---|---|
| Augustus Morse | Aug. 23, 1861 | Resigned May 15, 1862 |
| William S. Clark | May 16, 1862 | Resigned April 22, 1863 |

**22nd Infantry**

| | | |
|---|---|---|
| Henry Wilson | Sept. 2, 1861 | Resigned Oct. 29, 1861 |
| Jesse A. Gove | Oct. 30, 1861 | KIA June 27, 1862 |
| Charles E. Griswold | June 28, 1862 | Discharged Oct. 16, 1862 |
| William S. Tilton | Oct. 17, 1862 | Mustered out Oct. 17, 1864 **Bvt. Brig. Gen.** |

**23rd Infantry**

| | | |
|---|---|---|
| John Kurtz | Oct. 23, 1861 | Resigned Nov. 25, 1862 |
| Andrew Elwell | Nov. 26, 1862 | Discharged Sept. 20, 1864 |
| John W. Raymond | Sept. 20, 1864 | Mustered out June 25, 1865 |

**24th Infantry**

| | | |
|---|---|---|
| Thomas G. Stevenson | Aug. 31, 1861 | Promoted **Brig. Gen., USV** Dec. 26, 1862 |
| Francis A. Osborn | Dec. 28, 1862 | Mustered out Nov. 14, 1864 **Bvt. Brig. Gen.** |
| Charles H. Hooper | Nov. 15, 1864 | Mustered out March 18, 1865 |
| Albert Ordway | May 7, 1865 | Mustered out Feb. 10, 1866 **Bvt. Brig. Gen.** |

**25th Infantry**

| | | |
|---|---|---|
| Edwin Upton | Sept. 9, 1861 | Discharged Oct. 28, 1862 |
| Josiah Pickett | Oct. 29, 1862 | Mustered out Jan. 10, 1865 **Bvt. Brig. Gen.** |
| James Tucker | Jan. 10, 1865 | Mustered out July 13, 1865 |

**26th Infantry**

| | | |
|---|---|---|
| Edward F. Jones | Aug. 28, 1861 | Resigned July 27, 1862 **Bvt. Brig. Gen.** |
| Alpha B. Farr | July 28, 1862 | Mustered out Nov. 7, 1864 |
| William H. Chapman | Dec. 11, 1864 | Mustered out Aug. 26, 1865 |

**27th Infantry**

| | | |
|---|---|---|
| Horace C. Lee | Sept. 3, 1861 | Mustered out Sept. 27, 1864 **Bvt. Brig. Gen.** |
| Walter G. Bartholomew | Sept. 21, 1864 | Mustered out May 15, 1865 |

**28th Infantry**

| | | |
|---|---|---|
| William Monteith | Nov. 25, 1861 | Resigned Aug. 12, 1862 |
| Richard Byrnes | Sept. 29, 1862 | DOW June 12, 1864 |
| George W. Cartwright | July 21, 1864 | Mustered out Dec. 19, 1864 |

**29th Infantry**

| | | |
|---|---|---|
| Ebenezer W. Peirce | Dec. 13, 1861 | Discharged Nov. 8, 1864 |
| Thomas W. Clarke | Nov. 8, 1864 | Commission revoked Mustered out July 29, 1865 |

**30th Infantry**

| | | |
|---|---|---|
| Nathan A. M. Dudley | Feb. 8, 1862 | Mustered out Feb. 16, 1865 **Bvt. Brig. Gen.** |
| Francis H. Whittier | Feb. 17, 1865 | Mustered out July 5, 1866 **Bvt. Brig. Gen.** |

**31st Infantry**

| | | |
|---|---|---|
| Oliver P. Gooding | Feb. 8, 1862 | Mustered out Nov. 26, 1864 **Bvt. Brig. Gen.** |
| Edward P. Nettleton | June 7, 1865 | Mustered out Sept. 9, 1865 |

**32nd Infantry**

| | | |
|---|---|---|
| Francis J. Parker | Aug. 6, 1862 | Resigned Dec. 27, 1862 |
| George L. Prescott | Dec. 28, 1862 | DOW June 19, 1864 **Bvt. Brig. Gen.** |
| J. Cushing Edmands | June 30, 1864 | Mustered out July 1, 1865 **Bvt. Brig. Gen.** |

**33rd Infantry**

| | | |
|---|---|---|
| Alberto C. Maggi | June 26, 1862 | Resigned April 1, 1863 |
| Adin B. Underwood | April 3, 1863 | Promoted **Brig. Gen., USV** Jan. 21, 1864 |
| Elisha Doane | Jan. 23, 1864 | Mustered out June 11, 1865 |

**34th Infantry**

| | | |
|---|---|---|
| George D. Wells | July 11, 1862 | KIA Oct. 13, 1864 **Bvt. Brig. Gen.** |
| William S. Lincoln | Oct. 14, 1864 | Mustered out June 16, 1865 **Bvt. Brig. Gen.** |

**35th Infantry**

| | | |
|---|---|---|
| Edward A. Wild | Aug. 11, 1862 | Promoted **Brig. Gen., USV** April 24, 1863 |
| Sumner Carruth | April 25, 1863 | Mustered out June 9, 1865 **Bvt. Brig. Gen.** |

**36th Infantry**

| | | |
|---|---|---|
| Henry Bowman | Aug. 22, 1862 | Resigned July 27, 1863 |
| Thaddeus L. Barker | Nov. 13, 1864 | Mustered out June 8, 1865 |

**37th Infantry**

| | | |
|---|---|---|
| Oliver Edwards | Aug. 27, 1862 | Promoted **Brig. Gen., USV** May 19, 1865 |
| Rufus P. Lincoln | May 19, 1865 | To 20th MA Infantry June 19, 1865 |
| Mason W. Tyler | June 26, 1865 | Mustered out June 21, 1865 |

**38th Infantry**

| | | |
|---|---|---|
| Timothy Ingraham | Aug. 18, 1862 | Discharged Oct. 3, 1865 **Bvt. Brig. Gen.** |

**39th Infantry**

| | | |
|---|---|---|
| P. Stearns Davis | Aug. 29, 1862 | KIA July 11, 1864 |
| Charles L. Peirson | July 13, 1864 | Discharged Jan. 4, 1865 **Bvt. Brig. Gen.** |
| Henry M. Tremlett | Jan. 5, 1865 | DOW June 6, 1865 |

**40th Infantry**

| | | |
|---|---|---|
| Burr B. Porter | Sept. 7, 1862 | Resigned July 21, 1863 |
| Guy V. Henry | Oct. 28, 1863 | Mustered out June 30, 1865 **Bvt. Brig. Gen.** |

**41st Infantry** (see 3rd Cavalry)

**42nd Infantry (9 Months)**

| | | |
|---|---|---|
| Isaac S. Burrell | Nov. 6, 1862 | Mustered out Aug. 10, 1864 |

**42nd Infantry (100 Days)**

| | | |
|---|---|---|
| Isaac S. Burrell | Aug. 10, 1864 | Mustered out Nov. 11, 1864 |

**43rd Infantry**

| | | |
|---|---|---|
| Charles L. Holbrook | Oct. 13, 1862 | Mustered out July 30, 1863 |

**44th Infantry**

| | | |
|---|---|---|
| Francis L. Lee | Aug. 25, 1862 | Mustered out June 18, 1863 |

**45th Infantry**

| | | |
|---|---|---|
| Charles R. Codman | Oct. 8, 1862 | Mustered out July 7, 1863 |

**46th Infantry**

| | | |
|---|---|---|
| George Bowler | Oct. 27, 1862 | Discharged Jan. 23, 1863 |
| William S. Shurtleff | Feb. 5, 1863 | Mustered out July 29, 1863 |

**47th Infantry**

| | | |
|---|---|---|
| Lucius B. Marsh | Oct. 31, 1862 | Mustered out Sept. 1, 1863 |

**48th Infantry**

| | | |
|---|---|---|
| Eben F. Stone | Dec. 6, 1862 | Mustered out Sept. 3, 1863 |

**49th Infantry**

| | | |
|---|---|---|
| William F. Bartlett | Nov. 10, 1862 | Mustered out Sept. 1, 1863 Later **Brig. Gen., USV** |

**50th Infantry**

| | | |
|---|---|---|
| Carlos P. Messer | Nov. 7, 1862 | Mustered out Aug. 24, 1863 |

**51st Infantry**

| | | |
|---|---|---|
| Augustus B. R. Sprague | Oct. 29, 1862 | Mustered out July 27, 1863 **Bvt. Brig. Gen.** |

**52nd Infantry**

| | | |
|---|---|---|
| Halbert S. Greenleaf | Oct. 13, 1862 | Mustered out Aug. 14, 1863 |

**53rd Infantry**

| | | |
|---|---|---|
| John W. Kimball | Nov. 8, 1862 | Mustered out Sept. 2, 1863 **Bvt. Brig. Gen.** |

**54th Infantry (Colored)**

| | | |
|---|---|---|
| Robert G. Shaw | April 17, 1863 | KIA July 18, 1863 |
| Edward N. Hallowell | July 18, 1863 | Mustered out Aug. 20, 1865 **Bvt. Brig. Gen.** |

**55th Infantry (Colored)**

| | | |
|---|---|---|
| Norwood P. Hallowell | May 30, 1863 | Discharged Nov. 2, 1863 |
| Alfred S. Hartwell | Nov. 3, 1863 | Mustered out April 30, 1866 **Bvt. Brig. Gen.** |

**56th Infantry**

| | | |
|---|---|---|
| Charles E. Griswold | July 14, 1863 | KIA May 6, 1864 |
| Stephen M. Weld, Jr. | May 6, 1864 | Mustered out July 12, 1865 **Bvt. Brig. Gen.** |

**57th Infantry**

| | | |
|---|---|---|
| William F. Bartlett | Aug. 17, 1863 | Promoted **Brig. Gen., USV** June 27, 1864 |
| Napoleon B. McLaughlen | July 21, 1864 | Mustered out Aug. 10, 1865 **Bvt. Brig. Gen.** |

**58th Infantry**

| | | |
|---|---|---|
| John C. Whiton | Aug. 31, 1864 | Mustered out July 14, 1865 |

**59th Infantry**

| | | |
|---|---|---|
| Jacob P. Gould | April 25, 1864 | DOW Aug. 21, 1864 |
| Joseph Colburn | Aug. 22, 1864 | Discharged April 28, 1865 |
| Joseph W. Gelray | Feb. 8, 1865 | Not mustered |

**60th Infantry**

| | | |
|---|---|---|
| Ansel D. Wass | July 30, 1864 | Mustered out Dec. 29, 1864 **Bvt. Brig. Gen.** |

**61st Infantry**

| | | |
|---|---|---|
| Charles F. Walcott | Nov. 9, 1864 | Mustered out June 4, 1865 **Bvt. Brig. Gen.** |

**62nd Infantry**

| | | |
|---|---|---|
| Ansel D. Wass | March 2, 1865 | Not Mustered **Bvt. Brig. Gen.** |

## Gardner Banks

Gardner Banks
Massachusetts MOLLUS Collection, USAMHI.

Captain, Co. H, 16 MA Infantry, June 29, 1861. Major, 16 MA Infantry, July 23, 1862. Lieutenant Colonel, 16 MA Infantry, Sept. 30, 1862. Colonel, 16 MA Infantry, Nov. 28, 1862. Discharged for disability, Sept. 2, 1863, due to inflammatory rheumatism, chronic diarrhea, and malarial poisoning.

**Born:** May 10, 1830 Waltham, MA
**Died:** July 9, 1871 Waltham, MA
**Occupation:** Carpenter before war. Cotton planter and broker after war.
**Miscellaneous:** Resided Waltham, Middlesex Co., MA, to 1864; and New Orleans, LA, after 1864. Brother of Major General Nathaniel P. Banks.
**Buried:** Grove Hill Cemetery, Waltham, MA
**References:** Pension File, National Archives. Obituary, *Boston Morning Journal*, July 11, 1871. Obituary, *New Orleans Daily Picayune*, July 11, 1871. James G. Hollandsworth, Jr. *Pretense of Glory: The Life of Gen. Nathaniel P. Banks*. Baton Rouge, LA, 1998. *The American Annual Cyclopedia and Register of Important Events of the Year 1871*. New York City, NY, 1872.

## Thaddeus Lyscom Barker

Captain, Co. A, 36 MA Infantry, Aug. 19, 1862. GSW right ankle, Campbell's Station, TN, Nov. 16, 1863. Major, 36 MA Infantry, May 6, 1864. GSW left arm, Cold Harbor, VA, June 3, 1864. Lieutenant Colonel, 36 MA Infantry, Oct. 12, 1864. *Colonel*, 36 MA Infantry, Nov. 13, 1864. Honorably mustered out, June 8, 1865.

**Born:** June 17, 1826 Nelson, NH
**Died:** Jan. 18, 1903 Acton, MA
**Occupation:** Machinist and toolmaker.
**Miscellaneous:** Resided Fitchburg, Worcester Co., MA; and Waltham, Middlesex Co., MA.
**Buried:** Mount Feake Cemetery, Waltham, MA (Brewer Path, Lot 1648)
**References:** Pension File, National Archives. Henry S. Burrage. *History of the 36th Regiment Massachusetts Volunteers*. Boston, MA, 1884.

*Right:*
*Thaddeus Lyscom Barker*
*Massachusetts MOLLUS Collection, USAMHI.*

## Walter Gustin Bartholomew

Captain, Co. H, 27 MA Infantry, Oct. 16, 1861. Major, 27 MA Infantry, Dec. 7, 1861. Lieutenant Colonel, 27 MA Infantry, May 29, 1863. Captured Drewry's Bluff, VA, May 16, 1864. Confined at Macon, GA, and Charleston, SC. Paroled Aug. 3, 1864. Exchanged Sept. 12, 1864. *Colonel,* 27 MA Infantry, Sept. 21, 1864. GSW left leg, Southwest Creek, near Kinston, NC, March 8, 1865. Captured Southwest Creek, near Kinston, NC, March 8, 1865. Released May 1, 1865. Honorably mustered out May 15, 1865.

**Born:** June 26, 1826 Colchester, CT
**Died:** Oct. 3, 1912 Tampa, FL
**Occupation:** Corporal, Co. A, Sappers and Miners, US Engineers, 1849-54. Employed in the office of the Thompson Express Co. before war. Orange grower later in life.
**Offices/Honors:** Assistant US Internal Revenue Collector.
**Miscellaneous:** Resided Springfield, Hampden Co., MA, to 1869, and Tampa, FL, after 1869.
**Buried:** Oaklawn Cemetery, Tampa, FL
**References:** William P. Derby. *Bearing Arms in the 27th Massachusetts Regiment.* Boston, MA, 1883. George W. Bartholomew. *Record of the Bartholomew Family.* Austin, TX, 1885. Pension File, National Archives. Wiley Sword. "The Saga of Walter G. Bartholomew," *The Gun Report,* Vol. 16, No. 6 (Nov. 1970).

*Thaddeus Lyscom Barker (1900)*
*Massachusetts MOLLUS Collection, USAMHI.*

*Walter Gustin Bartholomew*
*Courtesy of Everitt Bowles.*

*Right:*
*Walter Gustin Bartholomew*
*Roger D. Hunt Collection, USAMHI.*

## George Bowler

Colonel, 46 MA Infantry, Oct. 27, 1862. Discharged for disability, Jan. 23, 1863, due to debilitating illness.

**Born:** Sept. 23, 1821 Lynn, MA
**Died:** March 26, 1869 Nashua, NH
**Occupation:** Methodist clergyman
**Miscellaneous:** Resided Lynn, Essex Co., MA; Westfield, Hampden Co., MA; and Nashua, Hillsboro Co., NH.
**Buried:** Pine Grove Cemetery, Lynn, MA (Tupelo Avenue, Lot 46)
**References:** Obituary, *Boston Evening Transcript*, March 26, 1869. Military Service File, National Archives.

*George Bowler*
*Massachusetts MOLLUS Collection, USAMHI.*

*George Bowler*
*Roger D. Hunt Collection, USAMHI. Silsbee, Case & Co., Photographic Artists, 299 1/2 Washington Street, Boston, MA.*

## Henry Bowman

Captain, Co. C, 15 MA Infantry, July 12, 1861. Captured Ball's Bluff, VA, Oct. 21, 1861. Confined Richmond, VA. Paroled Feb. 22, 1862. Major, 34 MA Infantry, Aug. 6, 1862. Colonel, 36 MA Infantry, Aug. 22, 1862. Commanded 1 Brigade, 1 Division, 9 Army Corps, June 1, 1863-July 27, 1863. Resigned July 27, 1863, "to accept a position in Massachusetts." *Colonel* 36 MA Infantry, Oct. 1863. Chief of Staff to Brig.Gen. Orlando B. Willcox, Nov. 21, 1863-Dec. 25, 1863. Captain, AQM, USV, Feb. 29, 1864. Major, Quartermaster, USV, assigned Aug. 2, 1864-Nov. 10, 1864. Chief Quartermaster, 1 Division, 9 Army Corps, Oct.-Nov. 1864. Honorably mustered out, Aug. 15, 1866.

**Born:** Sept. 9, 1834 Lancaster, MA
**Died:** April 12, 1908 Denver, CO
**Occupation:** Bookkeeper before war. Book agent, school superintendent, and US Government agent after war.
**Miscellaneous:** Resided Clinton, Worcester Co., MA; Philadelphia, PA; New York City, NY; Idaho Springs, Clear Creek Co., CO; and Denver, CO.
**Buried:** Woodlawn Cemetery, Clinton, MA (Section 16, Jewett Avenue, Lot 250)
**References:** Pension File, National Archives. Obituary, *Denver Rocky Mountain News*, April 13, 1908. Circular, Whole No. 148, California MOLLUS. Henry S. Burrage. *History of the 36th Regiment Massachusetts Volunteers.* Boston, MA, 1884.

*Henry Bowman*
*Massachusetts MOLLUS Collection, USAMHI.*

## Isaac Sanderson Burrell

Colonel, 42 MA Infantry, Nov. 6, 1862. Captured Galveston, TX, Jan. 1, 1863. Confined at Houston, TX; Huntsville, TX; Camp Groce, Hempstead, TX; and Camp Ford, near Tyler, TX. Paroled July 22, 1864. Honorably mustered out, Nov. 11, 1864.

**Born:** Oct. 14, 1820 Dorchester, MA
**Died:** Sept. 13, 1895 Roxbury, MA
**Occupation:** Carriage maker and Roxbury postmaster before war. Roxbury city marshal, Roxbury postmaster and Boston street commissioner after war.
**Offices/Honors:** Brigadier General, Massachusetts Volunteer Militia, 1865-75. Three years in Massachusetts Legislature.

*Right:*
*Henry Bowman*
*Massachusetts MOLLUS Collection, USAMHI.*

**Miscellaneous:** Resided Roxbury, Suffolk Co., MA

**Buried:** Forest Hills Cemetery, Jamaica Plain, MA (Lavender Path, Lot 2871)

**References:** Oliver A. Roberts. *History of the Ancient and Honorable Artillery Company of Massachusetts, 1637-1888.* Vol. 4. Boston, MA, 1901. Pension File, National Archives. Obituary, *Boston Evening Transcript*, Sept. 13, 1895. Charles P. Bosson. *History of the 42nd Regiment Infantry Massachusetts Volunteers.* Boston, MA, 1886.

*Isaac Sanderson Burrell*
*Massachusetts MOLLUS Collection, USAMHI.*

*Isaac Sanderson Burrell*
*Courtesy of Chaf. J.W. Black, 173 Washington Street, Boston, MA.*

*Right:*
*Isaac Sanderson Burrell (postwar)*
*Massachusetts MOLLUS Collection, USAMHI.*

## Richard Byrnes

2 Lieutenant, 17 US Infantry, May 14, 1861. 2 Lieutenant, 5 US Cavalry, Sept. 21, 1861. 1 Lieutenant, 5 US Cavalry, July 17, 1862. Colonel, 28 MA Infantry, Sept. 29, 1862. Commanded 2 Brigade, 1 Division, 2 Army Corps, Jan. 12-Feb. 14, 1864 and May 17-June 3, 1864. GSW back, Cold Harbor, VA, June 3, 1864.

**Born:** 1833 County Cavan, Ireland
**Died:** June 12, 1864 DOW Washington, DC
**Occupation:** Regular Army enlisted man (Sergeant Major, 1 US Cavalry, March 17, 1860).
**Miscellaneous:** Resided Jersey City, Hudson Co., NJ.
**Buried:** Calvary Cemetery, Long Island City, NY (Section 3, Range 23, Plot W)

Isaac Sanderson Burrell (postwar)
Massachusetts MOLLUS Collection, USAMHI.

*Richard Byrnes*
*USAMHI. C.H. Williamson's Photographic Portrait Gallery, 245 Fulton Street, Brooklyn, NY.*

*Right:*
*Richard Byrnes*
*Courtesy of Thomas Harris. J.W. Black, 173 Washington Street, Boston, MA.*

**References:** Barry L. Spink. *From Cavan to Cold Harbor: The Life of Colonel Richard Byrnes.* N.p., 1994. Pension File, National Archives. David P. Conyngham. *The Irish Brigade and Its Campaigns.* Boston, MA, 1869.

## George W. Cartwright

*George W. Cartwright*
*USAMHI. Black & Case, Photographic Artists, 163 & 173 Washington Street, Boston, MA.*

Sergeant, Co. H, 12 NY State Militia, April 19, 1861. 1 Lieutenant, Co. F, 12 NY State Militia, Oct. 3, 1861. Major, 28 MA Infantry, Oct. 8, 1861. Lieutenant Colonel, 28 MA Infantry, July 26, 1862. GSW 2nd Bull Run, VA, Aug. 30, 1862. GSW left shoulder, Wilderness, VA, May 6, 1864. *Colonel,* 28 MA Infantry, July 21, 1864. Honorably mustered out, Dec. 13, 1864.

**Born:** 1828 Dublin, Ireland
**Died:** March 20, 1868 Charleston, SC
**Occupation:** Printer
**Miscellaneous:** Resided Newark, NJ
**Buried:** Fairmount Cemetery, Newark, NJ (Section S, Lot 12, unmarked)
**References:** Pension File and Military Service File, National Archives. Obituary, *Newark Daily Advertiser,* March 27, 1868. David P. Conyngham. *The Irish Brigade and Its Campaigns.* Boston, MA, 1869.

## Thomas Cass

Colonel, 9 MA Infantry, June 11, 1861. GSW face, Malvern Hill, VA, July 1, 1862.

**Born:** 1821 Farmly, County Queens, Ireland
**Died:** July 12, 1862 DOW Boston, MA
**Occupation:** Learned the currier's trade. Later engaged in commercial pursuits with his father and became a real estate broker.
**Miscellaneous:** Resided Boston, MA
**Buried:** Mount Auburn Cemetery, Cambridge, MA (Chestnut Avenue, Lot 1049)
**References:** Daniel G. Macnamara. *History of the 9th Regiment Massachusetts Volunteer Infantry.* Boston, MA, 1899. Oliver A. Roberts. *History of the Ancient and Honorable Artillery Company of Massachusetts, 1637-1888.* Vol. 3. Boston, MA, 1898.

*Right:*
*Thomas Cass*
*Massachusetts MOLLUS Collection, USAMHI.*

*Thomas Cass*
*Massachusetts MOLLUS Collection, USAMHI.*

*Thomas Cass*
*Massachusetts MOLLUS Collection, USAMHI. Brady's National Photographic Portrait Gallery.*

*Thomas Cass*
*Massachusetts MOLLUS Collection, USAMHI.*

*Thomas Cass*
*Civil War Library & Museum, Philadelphia, PA.*

*Left:*
*Thomas Cass*
*Massachusetts MOLLUS Collection, USAMHI.*

## William Henry Chapman

1 Lieutenant, Co. E, 6 MA Infantry, April 22, 1861. Honorably mustered out, Aug. 2, 1861. Captain, Co. E, 26 MA Infantry, Aug. 31, 1861. GSW head, Winchester, VA, Sept. 19, 1864. Major, 26 MA Infantry, Nov. 15, 1864. Lieutenant Colonel, 26 MA Infantry, Nov. 16, 1864. *Colonel,* 26 MA Infantry, Dec. 11, 1864. Honorably mustered out, Aug. 26, 1865.

**Born:** March 31, 1829 New York City, NY
**Died:** April 24, 1891 Everett, MA
**Occupation:** Farmer before war. Livery stable keeper, undertaker, and mail contractor after war.
**Miscellaneous:** Resided Acton, Middlesex Co., MA; Charlestown, Suffolk Co., MA; and Everett, Middlesex Co., MA, after 1874.
**Buried:** Woodlawn Cemetery, Acton, MA
**References:** Obituary, *Boston Herald*, April 25, 1891. Obituary, *Concord Enterprise*, May 1, 1891. Pension File and Military Service File, National Archives.

## George Clark, Jr.

Colonel, 11 MA Infantry, June 13, 1861. Discharged for disability, Oct. 11, 1861, on account of "debilitated condition, loss of appetite, and inability to take ordinary exercise without great fatigue."

**Born:** Sept. 28, 1823 Boston, MA
**Died:** May 5, 1895 Boston, MA
**Occupation:** Real estate agent with a large interest in the business affairs of a land company at Vineyard Haven, MA
**Offices/Honors:** Brigade-Major and Inspector, 2 Brigade, 1 Division, Massachusetts Volunteer Militia, 1861
**Miscellaneous:** Resided Boston, MA
**Buried:** Forest Hills Cemetery, Jamaica Plain, MA (Clover Path, Lot 2158)
**References:** Oliver A. Roberts. *History of the Ancient and Honorable Artillery Company of Massachusetts, 1637-1888.* Vol. 3. Boston, MA, 1898. Pension File, National Archives. Obituary, *Boston Evening Transcript*, May 7, 1895. Gustavus B. Hutchinson. *A Narrative of the Formation and Services of the 11th Massachusetts Volunteers.* Boston, MA, 1893.

*George Clark, Jr.*
*USAMHI.*

## William Smith Clark

Major, 21 MA Infantry, July 19, 1861. Lieutenant Colonel, 21 MA Infantry, Feb. 28, 1862. Colonel, 21 MA Infantry, May 16, 1862. Resigned April 22, 1863, due to the "reduced condition of my regiment and my belief that I can be more useful at home than in the army under existing circumstances."

**Born:** July 31, 1825 Ashfield, MA
**Died:** March 9, 1886 Amherst, MA
**Education:** Attended Williston Seminary, Easthampton, MA. Graduated Amherst (MA) College, 1848. Ph.D., University of Gottingen, Germany, 1852.

**Occupation:** Professor of chemistry and zoology, Amherst College, 1852-58. Professor of chemistry, Amherst College, 1858-67. Engaged in unsuccessful mining operations, 1880-83.

**Offices/Honors:** Massachusetts Legislature, 1864, 1865, 1867. President, Massachusetts Agricultural College, 1867-79.

**Miscellaneous:** Resided Amherst, Hampshire Co., MA

**Buried:** West Cemetery, Amherst, MA

**References:** *Dictionary of American Biography.* Robert S. Fletcher and Malcolm O. Young, editors. *Amherst College Biographical Record.* Centennial Edition. Amherst, MA, 1927. Charles F. Walcott. *History of the 21st Regiment Massachusetts Volunteers.* Boston, MA, 1882.

*William Smith Clark*
*Courtesy of Henry Deeks. J. L. Lovell, Amherst MA.*

*William Smith Clark*
*Massachusetts MOLLUS Collection, USAMHI.*

## Thomas William Clarke

Captain, Co. A, 29 MA Infantry, May 21, 1861. Acting AAG, 2 Brigade, 1 Division, 9 Army Corps and 3 Brigade, 1 Division, 9 Army Corps, June 1, 1864-June 5, 1865. *Colonel,* 29 MA Infantry, Nov. 8, 1864. Commission revoked. Honorably mustered out, July 29, 1865.

**Born:** Dec. 1, 1834 Boston, MA

**Died:** Feb. 17, 1895 Roxbury, MA

**Education:** Graduated Harvard University, Cambridge, MA, 1855. Graduated Harvard University Law School, Cambridge, MA, 1858.

**Occupation:** Lawyer, dealing primarily in patent, copyright, and trademark cases.

**Miscellaneous:** Resided Boston, MA; and Roxbury, Suffolk Co., MA.

**Buried:** Central Cemetery, Cohasset, MA (unmarked)

**References:** William T. Davis, editor. *Professional and Industrial History of Suffolk County, MA.* Boston, MA, 1894. Obituary, *Boston Evening Transcript*, Feb. 18, 1895. Military Service File, National Archives. William H. Osborne. *The History of the 29th Regiment of Massachusetts Volunteer Infantry.* Boston, MA, 1877.

*Thomas William Clarke (1855)*
*Harvard College Portraits, Class of 1855, 1851-1905.*

*Thomas William Clarke (postwar)*
*Massachusetts MOLLUS Collection, USAMHI.*

## Charles Russell Codman

Captain, Adjutant, 1 Corps of Cadets, MA Volunteer Militia, May 26, 1852. Honorably mustered out, July 2, 1862. Colonel, 45 MA Infantry, Oct. 8, 1862. Honorably mustered out, July 7, 1863.

**Born:** Oct. 28, 1829 Paris, France
**Died:** Oct. 5, 1918 Cotuit, MA
**Education:** Graduated Harvard University, Cambridge, MA, 1849. Graduated Harvard University Law School, Cambridge, MA, 1852.
**Occupation:** Lawyer, but practiced law for only a short time, after which he devoted his attention to the management of his father's property and engaged in politics
**Offices/Honors:** Massachusetts Senate, 1864-65. Massachusetts House of Representatives, 1872-76.
**Miscellaneous:** Resided Boston, MA; and Brookline, Norfolk Co., MA

*Right*
*Charles Russell Codman*
*Massachusetts MOLLUS Collection, USAMHI. Whipple, 96 Washington Street, Boston, MA*

**Buried:** Forest Hills Cemetery, Jamaica Plain, MA (Hawthorn Path, Lot 1734)

**References:** William V. Kellen. "Memoir of Charles Russell Codman." *Proceedings of the Massachusetts Historical Society*, Volume 53 (April 1920). Obituary, *Boston Evening Transcript*. Oct. 5, 1918. Albert W. Mann. *History of the 45th Regiment Massachusetts Volunteer Militia*. Boston, MA, 1908. *National Cyclopedia of American Biography*.

*Right:*
*Charles Russell Codman*
*Massachusetts MOLLUS Collection, USAMHI.*

*Charles Russell Codman*
*Massachusetts MOLLUS Collection, USAMHI. J.W. Black, 173 Washington Street, Boston, MA*

*Charles Russell Codman*
*Massachusetts MOLLUS Collection, USAMHI.*

## Frederic Jones Coffin

Colonel, 8 MA Infantry, May 26, 1862. Honorably mustered out Aug. 7, 1863.

**Born:** Oct. 17, 1807 Newburyport, MA
**Died:** July 26, 1880 Lynn, MA
**Occupation:** Architect and contractor for work on large buildings, including cotton mills, the Northampton Insane Asylum, and the Newburyport City Hall
**Offices/Honors:** Massachusetts General Court, 1841 and 1845. Postmaster of Newburyport, MA, 1850-53. Colonel, 8 Massachusetts Volunteer Militia, 1855-61.
**Miscellaneous:** Resided Newburyport, Essex Co., MA. Father-in-law of Colonel Benjamin F. Peach, Jr.
**Buried:** Oak Hill Cemetery, Newburyport, MA (Section 3, Lot 627)
**References:** Obituary, *Boston Morning Journal*, July 28, 1880. *The Eighth Regiment of Massachusetts at Chickamauga Park: Historical and Pictorial.* Beverly, MA, 1898(?).

## Joseph Colburn

1 Lieutenant, Co. E, 13 MA Infantry, July 16, 1861. GSW 2nd Bull Run, VA, Aug. 30, 1862. Captain, Co. E, 13 MA Infantry, Feb. 2, 1863. Major, 59 MA Infantry, Oct. 23, 1863. GSW left breast Petersburg, VA, June 17, 1864. Lieutenant Colonel, 59 MA Infantry, Aug. 4, 1864. *Colonel,* 59 MA Infantry, Aug. 22, 1864. Discharged for disability, April 28, 1865, due to "hypertrophy of the heart."

**Born:** Feb. 23, 1831 Dresden, ME
**Died:** March 29, 1900 Denver, CO
**Occupation:** Market keeper before war. Engaged primarily in mining after moving to Colorado in 1865. Also employed as merchant and postmaster in early 1870's. Bookkeeper late in life.
**Miscellaneous:** Resided Roxbury, Suffolk Co., MA, to 1865; Gilpin and Boulder Counties, CO, 1865-82; and Denver, CO, after 1882.
**Buried:** Fairmount Cemetery, Denver, CO (Block 11, Lot 28)
**References:** Silas R. Coburn, editor. *Genealogy of the Descendants of Edward Colburn/Coburn.* Lowell, MA, 1913. Pension File and Military Service File, National Archives. Charles E. Davis, Jr. *Three Years in the Army, The Story of the 13th Massachusetts Volunteers.* Boston, MA, 1894.

*Charles Russell Codman (postwar)*
*Massachusetts MOLLUS Collection, USAMHI.*

*Right*
*Frederic Jones Coffin*
*Massachusetts MOLLUS Collection, USAMHI.*

Joseph Colburn
Massachusetts MOLLUS Collection, USAMHI.

Joseph Colburn
Massachusetts MOLLUS Collection, USAMHI.

Left:
Joseph Colburn
Ed Italo Collection, USAMHI. J.R. Aull, 105 1/2 and 107 1/2 Washington Street, Roxbury, MA.

## Phineas Stearns Davis

Phineas Stearns Davis
Massachusetts MOLLUS Collection, USAMHI.

Colonel, 39 MA Infantry, Aug. 29, 1862. Commanded Independent Brigade, Defenses of Washington, Nov. 11, 1862-Jan. 5, 1863. Shell wound right thigh, Petersburg, VA, July 11, 1864.

**Born:** June 23, 1818 Brookline, MA
**Died:** July 11, 1864 KIA Petersburg, VA
**Occupation:** Book publisher and stationer.
**Offices/Honors:** Brigadier General, Massachusetts Volunteer Militia, 1861.
**Miscellaneous:** Resided Boston, MA; and Cambridge, Middlesex Co., MA.
**Buried:** Mount Auburn Cemetery, Cambridge, MA (Chestnut Avenue, Lot 2320)
**References:** Alfred S. Roe. *The 39th Regiment Massachusetts Volunteers, 1862-1865.* Worcester, MA, 1914. Pension File, National Archives. Obituary, *Boston Post*, July 18, 1864.

## Elisha Doane

Sergeant, Co. L, 3 MA Infantry, May 8, 1861. Honorably mustered out, July 22, 1861. Captain, Co. I, 33 MA Infantry, Aug. 1, 1862. Resigned Aug. 8, 1863, due to the continued ill health of his wife. *Colonel,* 33 MA Infantry, Jan. 23, 1864. Captain, Co. I, 33 MA Infantry, Feb. 9, 1864. Major, 33 MA Infantry, March 9, 1864. Lieutenant Colonel, 33 MA Infantry, Sept. 18, 1864. Bvt. Colonel, USV, March 13, 1865, for gallant and meritorious services during the recent campaign in Georgia and the Carolinas. Honorably mustered out, June 11, 1865.

**Born:** Nov. 22, 1826 Harwich, MA
**Died:** Aug. 13, 1899 Taunton, MA
**Occupation:** Engaged in whaling before war. Fish merchant after war.
**Miscellaneous:** Resided New Bedford, Bristol Co., MA; and Taunton, Bristol Co., MA.
**Buried:** Oak Grove Cemetery, New Bedford, MA (Section U, Lot 56)
**References:** Obituary, *Taunton Daily Gazette*, Aug. 14, 1899. Pension File and Military Service File, National Archives. Adin B. Underwood. *The Three Years' Service of the 33rd Massachusetts Infantry Regiment.* Boston, MA, 1881.

*Right:*
*Elisha Doane*
*Roger D. Hunt Collection, USAMHI. Bierstadt Brothers, Photographers, China Hall, 35 Purchase Street, New Bedford, MA.*

*Opposite:*
*Elisha Doane*
*Massachusetts MOLLUS Collection, USAMHI.*

## Andrew Elwell

Major, 8 MA Infantry, April 30, 1861. Lieutenant Colonel, 8 MA Infantry, May 16, 1861. Honorably mustered out, Aug. 1, 1861. Major, 23 MA Infantry, Oct. 24, 1861. Lieutenant Colonel, 23 MA Infantry, March 15, 1862. Colonel, 23 MA Infantry, Nov. 25, 1862. Discharged for disability, Sept. 20, 1864, due to general debility resulting from sunstroke and diarrhea.

**Born:** Oct. 23, 1817 Gloucester, MA
**Died:** May 16, 1903 Gloucester, MA
**Occupation:** Engaged in tailoring and clothing business.
**Miscellaneous:** Resided Gloucester, Essex Co., MA; Manchester, Essex Co., MA; and Chelsea, Suffolk Co., MA.
**Buried:** Oak Grove Cemetery, Gloucester, MA
**References:** Elizabeth S. Versailles. *Elwelliana: Memorabilia of Levi H. Elwell (1854-1916).* Williamsburg, MA, 1974. James A. Emmerton. *A Record of the 23rd Regiment Massachusetts Volunteer Infantry in the War of the Rebellion.* Boston, MA, 1886. Pension File, National Archives.

*Andrew Elwell*
*Massachusetts MOLLUS Collection, USAMHI.*

*Left:*
*Andrew Elwell*
*Massachusetts MOLLUS Collection, USAMHI.*

*Opposite, bottom left:*
*Andrew Elwell*
*Massachusetts MOLLUS Collection, USAMHI.*

*Opposite, bottom right:*
*Andrew Elwell*
*Massachusetts MOLLUS Collection, USAMHI.*

## Alpha Burnham Farr

1 Lieutenant, Adjutant, 6 MA Infantry, April 22, 1861. Honorably mustered out, Aug. 3, 1861. Lieutenant Colonel, 26 MA Infantry, Aug. 28, 1861. Colonel, 26 MA Infantry, July 28, 1862. Commanded 2 Brigade, 2 Division, 19 Army Corps, Jan. 15-May 12, 1863. Commanded 2 Brigade, 3 Division, 19 Army Corps, Aug. 29-Oct. [illegible], 1863 and Nov. 2-Dec. 3, 1863. Commanded 1 Brigade, 2 Division, 19 Army Corps, June 1864. Honorably mustered out, Nov. 7, 1864.

**Born:** March 22, 182[illegible] Littleton, NH

**Died:** July 4, 1879 Rumney, NH

**Occupation:** Police officer and city marshal before war. US Customs official after war.

**Miscellaneous:** Resided Lowell, Middlesex Co., MA; and Rumney, Grafton Co., NH, 1877-79.

**Buried:** Rumney Cemetery, Rumney, NH

**References:** Pension File, National Archives. James R. Jackson. *History of Littleton, NH.* Cambridge, MA, 1905. Obituary, *Lowell Daily Courier*, July 5, 1879.

*Right:*
*Alpha Burnham Farr*
*National Archives*

## John Foster Fellows

Lieutenant Colonel, 17 MA Infantry, Aug. 21, 1861. Captured Batchelder's Creek, NC, Feb. 1, 1864. Confined at Richmond, VA; Macon, GA; and Charleston, SC. Paroled Aug. 3, 1864. Honorably mustered out, Aug. 9, 1864. *Colonel,* 17 MA Infantry, Oct. 9, 1864. The reduced strength of the regiment prevented his muster as colonel.

**Born:** Jan. 8, 1815 Ipswich, MA
**Died:** July 6, 1887 Chelsea, MA
**Occupation:** Early in life bookkeeper for several Boston newspapers and in 1861 merchant dealing in fireproof safes. Bookkeeper and savings bank treasurer after war.
**Offices/Honors:** Deputy Collector of Internal Revenue.
**Miscellaneous:** Resided Salem, Essex Co., MA; Boston, MA; and Chelsea, Suffolk Co., MA.
**Buried:** Harmony Grove Cemetery, Salem, MA (Crocus Path, Lot 1393)
**References:** Thomas Kirwan and Henry Splaine. *Memorial History of the 17th Regiment Massachusetts Volunteer Infantry.* Salem, MA, 1911. Obituary, *Boston Evening Transcript,* July 7, 1887. Pension File, National Archives.

*Alpha Burnham Farr*
*Courtesy of Gil Barrett. E. Jacobs, New Orleans, LA.*

*Left:*
*John Foster Fellows*
*Massachusetts MOLLUS Collection, USAMHI.*

*Opposite:*
*John Foster Fellows*
*Massachusetts MOLLUS Collection, USAMHI.*

## Albert S. Follansbee

Captain, Co. C, 6 MA Infantry, April 22, 1861. Honorably mustered out, Aug. 2, 1861. Colonel, 6 MA Infantry, Aug. 15, 1862. Honorably mustered out, June 3, 1863. Colonel, 6 MA Infantry, July 20, 1864. Honorably mustered out, Oct. 27, 1864.

**Born:** April 7, 1824 MA
**Died:** March 31, 1891 Chicago, IL
**Occupation:** Engaged in tannery business.
**Miscellaneous:** Resided Lowell, Middlesex Co., MA; and Chicago, IL
**Buried:** Mount Prospect Cemetery, Amesbury, MA
**References:** Obituary, *Lowell Daily Courier*, March 31, 1891. Obituary, *Boston Evening Transcript*, April 1, 1891. Obituary, *Chicago Times*, April 1, 1891. John W. Hanson. *Historical Sketch of the Old 6th Regiment of Massachusetts Volunteers.* Boston, MA, 1866.

*Albert S. Follansbee*
*Courtesy of Gil Barrett. Warren, 100 Merrimack Street, Lowell, MA.*

*Albert S. Follansbee*
*Massachusetts MOLLUS Collection, USAMHI.*

*Right:*
*Albert S. Follansbee*
*Massachusetts MOLLUS Collection, USAMHI.*

## Joseph Wiley Gelray

Corporal, Co. A, 2 MA Infantry, May 25, 1861. Sergeant, Co. H, 2 MA Infantry, Dec. 22, 1861. GSW right shoulder and right thigh, Antietam, MD, Sep. 17, 1862. 2 Lieutenant, Co. A, 2 MA Infantry, Dec. 25, 1862. GSW right arm (amputated), Gettysburg, PA, July 3, 1863. 1 Lieutenant, Co. A, 2 MA Infantry, July 4, 1863. Captain, Co. B, 57 MA Infantry, July 25, 1864. Major, 4 MA Heavy Artillery, Nov. 14, 1864. *Colonel,* 59 MA Infantry, Feb. 8, 1865. Reduced strength of the regiment preventing his muster as colonel, he never joined regiment. Honorably mustered out, June 17, 1865.

**Born:** Feb. 28, 1837 Manchester, England
**Died:** March 10, 1900 Boston, MA
**Occupation:** Printer and weaver before war. Regular Army (Captain, 45 US Infantry, retired Dec. 15, 1870). Later engaged in coal shipping.

*Joseph Wiley Gelray*
*Massachusetts MOLLUS Collection, USAMHI.*

*Joseph Wiley Gelray (postwar)*
*Massachusetts MOLLUS Collection, USAMHI.*

*Right:*
*Joseph Wiley Gelray*
*Massachusetts MOLLUS Collection, USAMHI.*

**Miscellaneous:** Resided Lowell, Middlesex Co., MA; and Boston, MA

**Buried:** Arlington National Cemetery, Arlington, VA (Section 1, Lot 475)

**References:** Obituary, *Boston Evening Transcript*, March 12, 1900. Alonzo H. Quint. *The Record of the 2nd Massachusetts Infantry.* Boston, MA, 1867. Pension File, National Archives. John Anderson. *The 57th Regiment of Massachusetts Volunteers in the War of the Rebellion.* Boston, MA, 1896.

## Jacob Parker Gould

Major, 13 MA Infantry, July 16, 1861. Colonel, 59 MA Infantry, April 25, 1864. Commanded 1 Brigade, 1 Division, 9 Army Corps, May 6-8, 1864 and June 9-July 23, 1864. GSW left leg, Petersburg, VA, July 30, 1864.

*Jacob Parker Gould*
*Massachusetts MOLLUS Collection, USAMHI.*

**Born:** May 15, 1822 Stoneham, MA

**Died:** Aug. 21, 1864 DOW Philadelphia, PA

**Education:** Graduated Norwich (VT) University, 1849.

**Occupation:** Civil engineer engaged in railroad construction.

**Offices/Honors:** Massachusetts General Court, 1855 and 1859.

**Miscellaneous:** Resided Stoneham, Middlesex Co., MA

**Buried:** Lindenwood Cemetery, Stoneham, MA

**References:** William A. Ellis, editor. *History of Norwich University, 1819-1911.* Montpelier, VT, 1911. Obituary, *Boston Daily Advertiser*, Aug. 23, 1864. William B. Stevens. *History of Stoneham, MA.* Stoneham, MA, 1891. Charles E. Davis, Jr. *Three Years in the Army, The Story of the 13th Massachusetts Volunteers.* Boston, MA, 1894.

*Left:*
*Jacob Parker Gould*
*Massachusetts MOLLUS Collection, USAMHI.*

## Jesse Augustus Gove

Captain, 10 US Infantry, March 3, 1855. Colonel, 22 MA Infantry, Oct. 30, 1861. GSW heart, Gaines' Mill, VA, June 27, 1862.

**Born:** Dec. 5, 1824 Weare, NH
**Died:** June 27, 1862 KIA Gaines' Mill, VA
**Education:** Graduated Norwich (VT) University, 1849.
**Other Wars:** Mexican War (1 Lieutenant, 9 US Infantry)
**Occupation:** Practiced law until 1855 when he accepted a commission as captain in the Regular Army.
**Offices/Honors:** Deputy Secretary of State of NH, 1850-55.
**Miscellaneous:** Resided Concord, NH. "He was a fine botanist and mineralogist, an accomplished draughtsman and painter, and every inch a soldier." Parker
**Buried:** Gaines' Mill, VA (Body never recovered). Cenotaph in Blossom Hill Cemetery, Concord, NH.
**References:** Jane Eames. *Colonel Jesse A. Gove, USA.* Concord, NH, 1870. Otis G. Hammond, editor. *The Utah Expedition, 1857-1858.* New Hampshire Historical Society Collections, Vol. 12. Concord, NH, 1928. William A. Ellis, editor. *History of Norwich University, 1819-1911.* Montpelier, VT, 1911. John L. Parker. *History of the 22nd Massachusetts Infantry.* Boston, MA, 1887.

*Jesse Augustus Gove*
*Courtesy of Robert C. Trownsell.*

*Jesse Augustus Gove*
*Massachusetts MOLLUS Collection, USAMHI.*

*Jesse Augustus Gove*
*The Utah Expedition, 1857-1858.*

## William Batchelder Greene

Colonel, 1 MA Heavy Artillery, July 5, 1861. Resigned Oct. 11, 1862, claiming that he was "the victim of an unmerited, unmerciful, and unrelenting persecution on the part of influential members of the Republican Party in Massachusetts and on the part of the political influences which prevail in Washington."

**Born:** April 4, 1819 Haverhill, MA

**Died:** May 30, 1878 Weston-Super-Mare, England

**Education:** Attended US Military Academy, West Point, NY (Class of 1839). Graduated Harvard Divinity School, Cambridge, MA, 1845.

**Other Wars:** Florida Indian Wars (2 Lieutenant, 7 US Infantry, resigned Nov. 20, 1841)

**Occupation:** Briefly a Unitarian clergyman, he turned to scholarly pursuits, becoming a writer of note on mathematical, philosophical and historical subjects.

**Miscellaneous:** Resided Boston, MA; Paris, France; and Weston-Super-Mare, England. Described as "one of the most powerful and original of American metaphysicians." Uncle of Colonel Robert Gould Shaw.

*William Batchelder Greene*
*Courtesy of Dave Zullo. R.W. Addis, Photographer, McClees' Gallery, 308 Penna. Avenue, Washington, DC.*

*William Batchelder Greene*
*Massachusetts MOLLUS Collection, USAMHI.*

*Left:*
*William Batchelder Greene (1876)*
*Massachusetts MOLLUS Collection, USAMHI.*

**Buried:** Forest Hills Cemetery, Jamaica Plain, MA (Green Brier Path, Lot 38)

**References:** *National Cyclopedia of American Biography.* Alfred S. Roe and Charles Nutt. *History of the 1st Regiment of Heavy Artillery Massachusetts Volunteers.* Worcester, MA, 1917. Obituary. *Boston Daily Advertiser*, June 3-4, 1878.

Halbert Stevens Greenleaf
Massachusetts MOLLUS Collection, USAMHI. E.C. Ely, Photographic Artist, Greenfield, MA.

## Halbert Stevens Greenleaf

Captain, Co. E, 52 MA Infantry, Sept. 10, 1862. Colonel, 52 MA Infantry, Oct. 13, 1862. Honorably mustered out, Aug. 14, 1863.

**Born:** April 12, 1827 Guilford, VT
**Died:** Aug. 25, 1906 Greece, NY
**Occupation:** Lock manufacturer (junior partner in the well known firm of Sargent & Greenleaf)
**Offices/Honors:** US House of Representatives, 1883-85, 1891-93
**Miscellaneous:** Resided Shelburne Falls, Franklin Co., MA, 1852-59, 1861-67; Philadelphia, PA, 1859-61; and Rochester, NY, 1867-1906
**Buried:** Mount Hope Cemetery, Rochester, NY (Section C, Lot 194)
**References:** *Dictionary of American Biography.* James E. Greenleaf, compiler. *Genealogy of the Greenleaf Family.* Boston, MA, 1896. *Encyclopedia of Contemporary Biography of New York.* New York City, NY, 1884. Pension File, National Archives. John F. Moors. *History of the 52nd Regiment Massachusetts Volunteers.* Boston, MA, 1893.

Charles Edward Griswold
Massachusetts MOLLUS Collection, USAMHI.

## Charles Edward Griswold

Major, 22 MA Infantry, Sept. 12, 1861. Lieutenant Colonel, 22 MA Infantry, Oct. 4, 1861. Colonel, 22 MA Infantry, June 28, 1862. Discharged for disability, Oct. 16, 1862, due to chronic diarrhea. Colonel, 56 MA Infantry, July 14, 1863. GSW neck, Wilderness, VA, May 6, 1864.

**Born:** Nov. 16, 1834 Boston, MA
**Died:** May 6, 1864 KIA Wilderness, VA
**Education:** Attended Norwich (VT) University
**Occupation:** Commission merchant
**Miscellaneous:** Resided Boston, MA
**Buried:** Mount Auburn Cemetery, Cambridge, MA (Linden Path, Lot 157

**References:** Anna Griswold. *Colonel Griswold.* Brookline, MA, 1866. William A. Ellis, editor. *History of Norwich University, 1819-1911.* Montpelier, VT, 1911. John L. Parker. *History of the 22nd Massachusetts Infantry.* Boston, MA, 1887.

*Right:*
*Charles Edward Griswold*
*Massachusetts MOLLUS Collection, USAMHI.*

*Charles Edward Griswold*
*Massachusetts MOLLUS Collection, USAMHI. J.W. Black, 173 Washington Street, Boston, MA.*

*Right: Charles Edward Griswold, with Major Horatio D. Jarves (left) and Lt. Col. Stephen M. Weld, Jr. (right). Massachusetts MOLLUS Collection, USAMHI. Whipple, 96 Washington Street, Boston, MA.*

*Charles Edward Griswold, with Major Horatio D. Jarves (left) and Lt. Col. Stephen M. Weld, Jr. (right). Courtesy of Richard F. Carlile. Whipple, 96 Washington Street, Boston, MA.*

## Norwood Penrose Hallowell

Private, 4 Battalion, MA Militia, April 25, 1861. 1 Lieutenant, Co. H, 20 MA Infantry, July 10, 1861. Captain, Co. D, 20 MA Infantry, Nov. 26, 1861. GSW left arm, Antietam, MD, Sept. 17, 1862. Lieutenant Colonel, 54 MA Infantry, April 17, 1863. Colonel, 55 MA Infantry, May 30, 1863. Discharged for disability, Nov. 2, 1863, on account of the continuing effects of the wound of his left arm.

**Born:** April 13, 1839 Philadelphia, PA
**Died:** April 11, 1914 West Medford, MA
**Education:** Graduated Harvard University, Cambridge, MA, 1861.
**Occupation:** Wool commission merchant and bank president.
**Miscellaneous:** Resided West Medford, Middlesex Co., MA. Brother of Bvt. Brig. Gen. Edward N. Hallowell.
**Buried:** Mount Auburn Cemetery, Cambridge, MA (Indian Ridge Path, Lot 4124)
**References:** *National Cyclopedia of American Biography.* William P. Hallowell, compiler. *Record of a Branch of the Hallowell Family.* Philadelphia, PA, 1893. Pension File, National Archives. Charles B. Fox. *Record of the Service of the 55th Regiment of Massachusetts Volunteer Infantry.* Cambridge, MA, 1868. George A. Bruce. *The 20th Regiment of Massachusetts Volunteer Infantry, 1861-1865.* Boston, MA, 1906.

*Norwood Penrose Hallowell*
*Massachusetts MOLLUS Collection, USAMHI.*

*Norwood Penrose Hallowell*
*Massachusetts MOLLUS Collection, USAMHI.*

Norwood Penrose Hallowell
Massachusetts MOLLUS Collection, USAMHI.

## Charles L. Holbrook

Colonel, 43 MA Infantry, Oct. 13, 1862. Commanded 1 Brigade, 1 Division, 18 Army Corps, May 23, 1863-June 24, 1863. Honorably mustered out, July 30, 1863.

**Born:** May 5, 1816 Boston, MA
**Died:** Sept. 13, 1887 Boston, MA
**Occupation:** Commission merchant early in life. Bookkeeper in the Suffolk National Bank for more than 30 years.
**Miscellaneous:** Resided Boston, MA.
**Buried:** Mount Auburn Cemetery, Cambridge, MA (Cypress Avenue, Lot 1733)
**References:** Obituary, *Boston Evening Transcript*, Sept. 14, 1887. Oliver A. Roberts. *History of the Ancient and Honorable Artillery Company of Massachusetts, 1637-1888.* Vol. 3. Boston, MA, 1898. Edward H. Rogers. *Reminiscences of Military Service in the 43rd Regiment Massachusetts Infantry.* Boston, MA, 1883.

*Charles L. Holbrook*
*Massachusetts MOLLUS Collection, USAMHI.*

*Charles L. Holbrook, with Field and Staff of the 43rd Massachusetts Infantry. Left to right: Adjutant James M. Whitney, Lieutenant Colonel John C. Whiton, Quartermaster Henry A. Turner, Colonel Charles L. Holbrook, Chaplain Jacob M. Manning, and Major Everett Lane. Courtesy of the author.*

## Charles Holden Hooper

Captain, Co. E, 24 MA Infantry, Sept. 2, 1861. Major, 24 MA Infantry, Dec. 28, 1862. Lieutenant Colonel, 24 MA Infantry, June 1, 1864. Captured July 24, 1864, Deep Bottom, VA. Confined in Libby Prison, Richmond, VA; Danville (VA) Prison; and Salisbury (NC) Prison. *Colonel,* 24 MA Infantry, Nov. 15, 1864. Paroled Feb. 22, 1865. Honorably mustered out, March 18, 1865.

**Born:** 1836 MA
**Died:** June 25, 1899 Boston, MA (accidental asphyxiation by gas)
**Occupation:** Partner in a stationery firm.
**Miscellaneous:** Resided Brookline, Norfolk Co., MA.
**Buried:** Mount Auburn Cemetery, Cambridge, MA (Hemlock Path, Lot 463)
**References:** Obituary, *Boston Evening Transcript*, June 26, 1899. Obituary, *Boston Globe*, June 26, 1899. Alfred S. Roe. *The 24th Regiment Massachusetts Volunteers.* Worcester, MA, 1907.

*Charles Holden Hooper*
*Massachusetts MOLLUS Collection, USAMHI.*

*Charles L. Holbrook*
*Massachusetts MOLLUS Collection, USAMHI.*

*Right:*
*Charles Holden Hooper*
*Massachusetts MOLLUS Collection, USAMHI. Whipple, 96 Washington Street, Boston, MA.*

*Charles Holden Hooper (postwar)*
*Massachusetts MOLLUS Collection, USAMHI.*

## George Clesson Joslin

2 Lieutenant, Co. A, 3 Battalion MA Rifles, April 17, 1861. Honorably mustered out, Aug. 3, 1861. Captain, Co. I, 15 MA Infantry, Aug. 5, 1861. GSW right wrist, Antietam, MD, Sept. 17, 1862. Major, 15 MA Infantry, Nov. 13, 1862. Lieutenant Colonel, 15 MA Infantry, April 17, 1863. *Colonel,* 15 MA Infantry, July 4, 1863. Captured Nov. 27, 1863, Mine Run, VA. Confined at Richmond, VA; Macon, GA; and Charleston, SC. Paroled Aug. 3, 1864. Honorably mustered out, Aug. 9, 1864.

**Born:** Aug. 19, 1839 Leominster, MA
**Died:** Nov. 21, 1916 Dorchester, MA
**Occupation:** Salesman before war. Furniture merchant and US Customs appraiser after war.
**Miscellaneous:** Resided Worcester, MA, to 1865; Chicago, IL, 1865-68; and Boston, MA, 1868-1916.
**Buried:** Evergreen Cemetery, Leominster, MA (Section 11, Lot 254)
**References:** Pension File, National Archives. Andrew E. Ford. *The Story of the 15th Regiment Massachusetts Volunteer Infantry.* Clinton, MA, 1898. Obituary, *Boston Evening Transcript*, Nov. 22, 1916.

*George Clesson Joslin*
*Massachusetts MOLLUS Collection, USAMHI.*

*George Clesson Joslin*
*Massachusetts MOLLUS Collection, USAMHI.*

*George Clesson Joslin*
*Massachusetts MOLLUS Collection, USAMHI.*

*George Clesson Joslin (postwar)*
*Massachusetts MOLLUS Collection, USAMHI.*

## John Kurtz

Captain, Co. C, 13 MA Infantry, July 16, 1861. Lieutenant Colonel, 23 MA Infantry, Sept. 25, 1861. Colonel, 23 MA Infantry, Oct. 23, 1861. Provost Marshal, New Berne, NC, June-Nov. 1862. Resigned Nov. 25, 1862, due to "dissatisfaction relative to rank."

**Born:** Oct. 2, 1813 Boston, MA
**Died:** Nov. 10, 1881 Boston, MA
**Occupation:** Railroad employee and hotelkeeper before war. Inspector in the Boston Custom House after war.
**Offices/Honors:** Chief of Police, Boston, MA, 1863-70
**Miscellaneous:** Resided Boston, MA
**Buried:** Forest Hills Cemetery, Jamaica Plain, MA (Pilgrim Path, Lot 3524)
**References:** James A. Emmerton. *A Record of the 23rd Regiment Massachusetts Volunteer Infantry.* Boston, MA, 1886. Pension File, National Archives. Obituary, *Boston Evening Transcript*, Nov. 10, 1881.

*John Kurtz*
*USAMHI. Silsbee, Case & Co., Photographic Artists, 299 1/2 Washington Street, Boston, MA.*

*John Kurtz*
*Massachusetts MOLLUS Collection, USAMHI.*

*Left:*
*John Kurtz*
*Massachusetts MOLLUS Collection, USAMHI.*

## Samuel Crocker Lawrence

Samuel Crocker Lawrence (1855)
Harvard College Portraits, Class of 1855, 1851-1905.

Colonel, 5 MA Infantry, May 1, 1861. GSW side, 1st Bull Run, VA, July 21, 1861. Honorably mustered out, July 31, 1861. Brigadier General, Massachusetts Volunteer Militia, 1862-64.

**Born:** Nov. 22, 1832 Medford, MA
**Died:** Sept. 24, 1911 Medford, MA
**Education:** Graduated Harvard University, Cambridge, MA, 1855.
**Occupation:** Engaged in the distilling business with his father. Later served as director of various financial and railroad corporations.
**Offices/Honors:** Mayor of Medford, MA, 1892-94.
**Miscellaneous:** Resided Medford, Middlesex Co., MA. Prominent in Free Masonry being Grand Master of Massachusetts Masons, 1881-83.
**Buried:** Mount Auburn Cemetery, Cambridge, MA (Central Avenue, Lot 2214)
**References:** Oliver A. Roberts. *History of the Ancient and Honorable Artillery Company of Massachusetts, 1637-1888.* Vol. 4. Boston, MA, 1901. Obituary, *Boston Evening Transcript*, Sept. 25, 1911. Richard Herndon, compiler. *Men of Progress: Massachusetts.* Boston, MA, 1896.

Samuel Crocker Lawrence
History of the Ancient and Honorable Artillery Company of Massachusetts, Vol. 4.

Samuel Crocker Lawrence (1880)
Massachusetts MOLLUS Collection, USAMHI.

## Francis L. Lee

Major, 4 Battalion, MA Militia, May 26, 1862. Honorably mustered out, May 31, 1862. Colonel, 44 MA Infantry, Aug. 29, 1862. Commanded 2 Brigade, 4 Division, 18 Army Corps, March 1863. Commanded Independent Brigade, 18 Army Corps, May-June 1863. Honorably mustered out, June 18, 1863.

**Born:** Dec. 10, 1823 Boston, MA
**Died:** Sept. 2, 1886 Westport, NY
**Education:** Graduated Harvard University, Cambridge, MA, 1843.
**Occupation:** Gentleman of leisure. He gave largely to charity and occupied himself with landscape gardening at his country place at Westport, NY.
**Miscellaneous:** Resided Newton, Middlesex Co., MA; and Westport, Essex Co., NY. His first cousin, Anna Cabot Jackson, was the mother of Brig. Gen. Charles R. Lowell. Another first cousin, George Cabot Lee, was the father-in-law of President Theodore Roosevelt. Another first cousin, Amelia Lee Jackson, married the noted poet Oliver Wendell Holmes.

*Samuel Crocker Lawrence (1895)*
*Massachusetts MOLLUS Collection, USAMHI.*

*Right:*
*Francis L. Lee*
*Massachusetts MOLLUS Collection, USAMHI. J.W. Black, 173 Washington Street, Boston, MA.*

*Below:*
*Francis L. Lee*
*USAMHI. J.W. Black, 173 Washington Street, Boston, MA.*

**Buried:** Hillside Cemetery, Westport, NY

**References:** Obituary, *Boston Evening Transcript*, Sept. 2, 1886. *New England Historical and Genealogical Register.* Vol. 76 (July 1922). Mary Lee. *A History of the Chestnut Hill Chapel.* Waltham, MA, 1937. *Record of the Service of the 44th Massachusetts Volunteer Militia in North Carolina.* Boston, MA, 1887.

## Samuel Haven Leonard

Colonel, 13 MA Infantry, July 16, 1861. Commanded 3 Brigade, 2 Division, 1 Army Corps, Dec. 13-30, 1862; Jan. 23-Feb. 17, 1863; and April 10-May 20, 1863. Commanded 1 Brigade, 2 Division, 1 Army Corps, May 21-June 17, 1863; July 1, 1863; Nov. 1863; and Jan. 21-March 24, 1864. GSW left arm, Gettysburg, PA, July 1, 1863. Commanded 1 Brigade, 2 Division, 5 Army Corps, March 24-May 6, 1864. Honorably mustered out, Aug. 1, 1864.

*Francis L. Lee*
*Massachusetts MOLLUS Collection, USAMHI. J.W. Black, 173 Washington Street, Boston, MA.*

*Left:*
*Samuel Haven Leonard*
*Massachusetts MOLLUS Collection, USAMHI. J.W. Black, 173 Washington Street, Boston, MA.*

**Born:** July 10, 1825 Bolton, MA
**Died:** Dec. 27, 1902 West Newton, MA
**Occupation:** Engaged in the express business.
**Offices/Honors:** Brigadier General, Massachusetts Volunteer Militia, 1856-60.
**Miscellaneous:** Resided Worcester, MA; Boston, MA; and West Newton, Middlesex Co., MA.
**Buried:** Rural Cemetery, Worcester, MA (Section 14, Lot I)
**References:** *Circular No. 16, 13th Massachusetts Regiment.* Boston, MA, 1903. Oliver A. Roberts. *History of the Ancient and Honorable Artillery Company of Massachusetts, 1637-1888.* Vol. 4. Boston, MA, 1901. Pension File, National Archives. Charles E. Davis, Jr. *Three Years in the Army, The Story of the 13th Massachusetts Volunteers.* Boston, MA, 1894.

*Samuel Haven Leonard*
*Massachusetts MOLLUS Collection, USAMHI.*

*Samuel Haven Leonard*
*Massachusetts MOLLUS Collection, USAMHI.*

*Right:*
*Samuel Haven Leonard*
*Massachusetts MOLLUS Collection, USAMHI.*

Samuel Haven Leonard
Massachusetts MOLLUS Collection, USAMHI.

Samuel Haven Leonard, with John G. Hovey (left) and Charles H. Hovey (right).
Massachusetts MOLLUS Collection, USAMHI.

## Rufus Pratt Lincoln

2 Lieutenant, Co. C, 37 MA Infantry, Aug. 27, 1862. Captain, Co. C, 37 MA Infantry, Oct. 15, 1862. GSW side, Wilderness, VA, May 6, 1864. GSW left breast, Spotsylvania, VA, May 12, 1864. Major, 37 MA Infantry, July 27, 1864. Major, Acting AIG, 1 Division, 6 Army Corps, Aug. 1864-June 21, 1865. Lieutenant Colonel, 37 MA Infantry, March 4, 1865. Bvt. Colonel, USV, April 6, 1865, for gallant and meritorious services before Petersburg and at the battle of Little Sailor's Creek, VA. *Colonel*, 37 MA Infantry, May 19, 1865. Lieutenant Colonel, 20 MA Infantry, June 19, 1865. Honorably mustered out, July 16, 1865.

**Born:** April 27, 1840 Belchertown, MA
**Died:** Nov. 27, 1900 New York City, NY
**Education:** Attended Williston Seminary, Easthampton, MA. Graduated Amherst (MA) College, 1862. Graduated Harvard Medical School, Cambridge, MA, 1868.
**Occupation:** Physician specializing in the treatment of diseases of the throat, lungs and air passages.
**Miscellaneous:** Resided Boston, MA; New York City, NY; and Plainfield, Union Co. NJ.
**Buried:** Hillside Cemetery, Plainfield, NJ (Section A, Division 5, Lot 34)

Rufus Pratt Lincoln
Massachusetts MOLLUS Collection, USAMHI. J.L. Lovell, Amherst, MA.

**References:** Obituary Circular, Whole No. 658, New York MOLLUS. Robert S. Fletcher and Malcolm O. Young, editors. *Amherst College Biographical Record.* Centennial Edition. Amherst, MA, 1927. Pension File, National Archives. James L. Bowen. *History of the 37th Regiment Massachusetts Volunteers.* Holyoke, MA, 1884.

*Rufus Pratt Lincoln*
*Massachusetts MOLLUS Collection, USAMHI. George C. Rockwood, Photographer, 839 Broadway, New York.*

## Alberto Camillo Maggi

Sergeant Major, 3 MA Infantry, April 23, 1861. Honorably mustered out, July 22, 1861. Lieutenant Colonel, 21 MA Infantry, Sept. 2, 1861. Resigned Feb. 27, 1862, charges of "gross insubordination" pending, citing "ingratitude" and the feeling that his "services would be injurious to the welfare of the regiment." Colonel, 33 MA Infantry, June 26, 1862. Discharged for disability, April 1, 1863, due to the reopening of an old wound in his right leg.

**Born:** Oct. 1824 Florence, Italy
**Died:** May 23, 1880 Medford, MA
**Education:** Educated as professional soldier at Turin, Italy
**Other Wars:** Served as an officer under Garibaldi in campaigns against the Austrians in 1848 and against the French in 1849. Condemned, sentenced to die, and banished to America for espousing cause of the Republic in revolt against Italy.

*Alberto Camillo Maggi*
*Massachusetts MOLLUS Collection, USAMHI.*

*Alberto Camillo Maggi*
*Massachusetts MOLLUS Collection, USAMHI.*

**Occupation:** Teacher of languages, eventually becoming professor of languages at the New England Conservatory of Music.

**Miscellaneous:** Resided New Bedford, Bristol Co., MA; and Medford, Middlesex Co., MA.

**Buried:** Oak Grove Cemetery, Medford, MA

**References:** Pension File and Military Service File, National Archives. Charles F. Walcott. *History of the 21st Regiment Massachusetts Volunteers.* Boston, MA, 1882. Adin B. Underwood. *The Three Years' Service of the 33rd Massachusetts Infantry Regiment.* Boston, MA, 1881. Obituary, *Boston Post*, May 25, 1880.

*Alberto Camillo Maggi*
*Massachusetts MOLLUS Collection, USAMHI.*

## Lucius Bolles Marsh

Colonel, 47 MA Infantry, Oct. 31, 1862. Honorably mustered out, Sept. 1, 1863.

**Born:** April 18, 1818 Danvers, MA
**Died:** Aug. 14, 1901 North Scituate, MA
**Occupation:** Merchant dealing in woollen goods.
**Miscellaneous:** Resided Boston, MA. Received thanks from the State of Massachusetts, Nov. 8, 1861, "for his very valuable services to the State in the procurement of Arms and Military Equipments."
**Buried:** Mount Auburn Cemetery, Cambridge, MA (Pearl Avenue, Lot 4890)
**References:** Lucius B. Marsh and Harriet F. Parker, compilers. *Bronsdon and Box Families.* Lynn, MA, 1902. Obituary, *Boston Evening Transcript*, Aug. 14, 1901.

*Lucius Bolles Marsh*
*Roger D. Hunt Collection, USAMHI.*

*Above right:*
*Lucius Bolles Marsh*
*Massachusetts MOLLUS Collection, USAMHI.*

*Right:*
*Lucius Bolles Marsh*
*Massachusetts MOLLUS Collection, USAMHI.*

Lucius Bolles Marsh
Massachusetts MOLLUS Collection, USAMHI.

Lucius Bolles Marsh
Massachusetts MOLLUS Collection, USAMHI.

Lucius Bolles Marsh (1890)
Massachusetts MOLLUS Collection, USAMHI.

Lucius Bolles Marsh (postwar)
Massachusetts MOLLUS Collection, USAMHI.

## Archibald McKendry

Archibald McKendry
Massachusetts MOLLUS Collection, USAMHI.

1 Lieutenant, Co. A, 2 MA Cavalry, Dec. 10, 1862. Captain, Co. A, 2 MA Cavalry, April 10, 1863. Major, 2 MA Cavalry, Aug. 31, 1864. Commanded Reserve Brigade, 1 Cavalry Division, Middle Military Division, Dec. 1864-Jan. 15, 1865. *Colonel,* 2 MA Cavalry, June 17, 1865. Honorably mustered out, July 20, 1865.

**Born:** Oct. 26, 1829 Milton, MA
**Died:** June 8, 1885 near Santa Cruz, CA
**Occupation:** Farmer and capitalist
**Miscellaneous:** Resided San Francisco, CA; Menlo Park, San Mateo Co., CA; and San Jose, CA.
**Buried:** Oak Hill Memorial Park, San Jose, CA (Section I, Block 207, Lot 1)
**References:** Pension File, National Archives. Obituary, *San Francisco Examiner*, June 10, 1885.

## Carlos Page Messer

Captain, Co. D, 5 MA Infantry, May 1, 1861. Honorably mustered out, July 31, 1861. Colonel, 50 MA Infantry, Nov. 7, 1862. Honorably mustered out, Aug. 24, 1863.

**Born:** Oct. 3, 1833 New London, NH
**Died:** Feb. 11, 1907 Los Angeles, CA
**Education:** Attended New London (NH) Academy.
**Occupation:** Conducted a grocery business in Haverhill, MA, until 1896.
**Miscellaneous:** Resided Haverhill, Essex Co., MA; Boston, MA; and Los Angeles, CA.
**Buried:** Inglewood Park Cemetery, Inglewood, CA (Sequoia Plot, Lot 461)
**References:** Pension File, National Archives. Oliver A. Roberts. *History of the Ancient and Honorable Artillery Company of Massachusetts, 1637-1888.* Vol. 3. Boston, MA, 1898. William B. Stevens. *History of the 50th Regiment of Infantry Massachusetts Volunteer Militia in the Late War of the Rebellion.* Boston, MA, 1907. Myra B. Lord, compiler. *A History of the Town of New London, Merrimack Co., NH.* Concord, NH, 1899.

*Right:*
*Carlos Page Messer*
*History of the 50th Regiment of Infantry Massachusetts Volunteer Militia.*
*Higgins & Collier, 109 Washington Street, Boston, MA.*

## William Monteith

2 Lieutenant, Co. C, 12 NY State Militia, April 19, 1861. Honorably mustered out, Aug. 5, 1861. Colonel, 28 MA Infantry, Oct. 7, 1861. Dismissed Aug. 3, 1862, for "neglect of duty" and "conduct unbecoming an officer and gentleman – drinking in his tent with privates of the 76th Pennsylvania regiment." Dismissal revoked and his resignation accepted to date, Aug. 12, 1862.

**Born:** 1827 Ireland
**Died:** Feb. 28, 1869 New York City, NY
**Occupation:** Builder before war. Hatter after war.
**Miscellaneous:** Resided New York City, NY.
**Buried:** Green-Wood Cemetery, Brooklyn, NY (Section 33, Lot 4800)
**References:** Pension File and Military Service File, National Archives.

*William Monteith*
*Courtesy Massachusetts Historical Society, Boston, MA. J.W. Black, 173 Washington Street, Boston, MA.*

## Augustus Morse

Colonel, 21 MA Infantry, July 19, 1861. Commanded Post of Annapolis, MD, Oct.1861-March 1862. Resigned May 15, 1862. Captain, AQM, USV, July 14, 1862. Assigned to 3 Division, 3 Army Corps, Nov. 15, 1862-May 23, 1863. Resigned June 10, 1863. "Though of a kindly disposition, he was of a lazy habit, entirely destitute of soldierly enthusiasm or spirit, wonderfully ignorant of military drill and maneuvers, and a wretched disciplinarian." Walcott

**Born:** May 16, 1817 Leominster, MA
**Died:** Nov. 25, 1888 Brooklyn, NY
**Occupation:** Comb maker before war. Commission merchant after war.
**Offices/Honors:** Major General, Massachusetts Volunteer Militia, 1861
**Miscellaneous:** Resided Leominster, Worcester Co., MA; and Brooklyn, NY
**Buried:** Evergreen Cemetery, Leominster, MA (Section 1, Lot 104)
**References:** Obituary, *Brooklyn Daily Eagle*, Nov. 27, 1888. Charles F. Walcott. *History of the 21st Regiment Massachusetts Volunteers*. Boston, MA, 1882. Military Service File, National Archives. Letters Received, Volunteer Service Branch, Adjutant General's Office, File E59VS1862, National Archives.

*William Monteith (seated center) with officers of Co. C, 12th NGSNY: Captain William Fowler (standing), 1st Lieutenant Charles Whitlock (left), and Sergeant William H. Devens (right). Annual Reunion of the Old Guard Association, 12th Regiment, NGSNY, 1894.*

## Charles Fessenden Morse

1 Lieutenant, Co. B, 2 MA Infantry, May 25, 1861. Captain, Co. B, 2 MA Infantry, July 11, 1862. Provost Marshal, Staff of Major Gen. Henry W. Slocum, Feb. 25, 1863-May 1863. Major, 2 MA Infantry, June 6, 1863. Lieutenant Colonel, 2 MA Infantry, July 4, 1863. Provost Marshal and Acting AAG, Staff of Major Gen. Henry W. Slocum, Oct. 11, 1863-April 10, 1864. GSW left shoulder, Averasborough, NC, March 16, 1865. Bvt. Colonel, USV, March 13, 1865, for gallant and meritorious services during the recent campaign in Georgia and the Carolinas. *Colonel,* 2 MA Infantry, July 24, 1865. Honorably mustered out, July 14, 1865.

**Born:** Sept. 22, 1839 Boston, MA
**Died:** Dec. 1, 1926 Boston, MA
**Education:** Graduated Lawrence Scientific School, Harvard University, Cambridge, MA, 1858.
**Occupation:** Architect before war. Cotton planter, railroad superintendent, and President of Kansas City Stockyards after war.
**Miscellaneous:** Resided Boston, MA; Savannah, GA; Burlington, IA; Plattsmouth, NE; Topeka, KS; and Kansas City, MO.
**Buried:** Oak Grove Cemetery, Falmouth, MA
**References:** Alonzo H. Quint. *The Record of the 2nd Massachusetts Infantry.* Boston, MA, 1867. Military Service File, National Archives. Obituary, *Boston Evening Transcript*, Dec. 1, 1926. *The United States Biographical Dictionary.* Kansas Volume. Chicago & Kansas City, 1879. Charles F. Morse. *Letters Written During the Civil War, 1861-1865.* Boston, MA, 1898.

*Charles Fessenden Morse*
*Massachusetts MOLLUS Collection, USAMHI.*

*Charles Fessenden Morse*
*Letters Written During the Civil War, 1861-1865.*

*Left:*
*Charles Fessenden Morse*
*Roger D. Hunt Collection, USAMHI. J.W. Black, 173 Washington Street, Boston, MA.*

*Charles Fessenden Morse*
*Massachusetts MOLLUS Collection, USAMHI.*

## Timothy Munroe, Jr.

Colonel, 8 MA Infantry, April 17, 1861. Resigned May 15 1861, due to physical debility.

**Born:** Dec. 13, 1800 Lynn, MA
**Died:** May 25, 1873 Lynn, MA
**Occupation:** Engaged in the shoe business. Later became an inspector and weigher in the Boston Custom House, and finally Collector of the Port of Marblehead, MA.
**Miscellaneous:** Resided Lynn, Essex Co., MA
**Buried:** Pine Grove Cemetery, Lynn, MA (Linden Avenue, Lot 117)
**References:** Richard S. Munroe, compiler. *History and Genealogy of the Lexington, Mass., Munroes.* Holyoke, MA, 1966. Charles W. Hall, editor. *Regiments and Armories of Massachusetts.* Boston, MA, 1899-1901. Death notice, *Boston Post*, May 27, 1873.

*Timothy Munroe, Jr.*
*Massachusetts MOLLUS Collection, USAMHI.*

## Edward Payson Nettleton

Captain, Co. E, 31 MA Infantry, Oct. 30, 1861. Acting AIG, 2 Brigade, 1 Division, 19 Army Corps, Aug. 22, 1863-Sept. 1, 1863. Ordnance Officer, 1 Division, 19 Army Corps, Sept. 1, 1863-Dec. 1863. Lieutenant Colonel, 31 MA Infantry, April 15, 1864. GSW right thigh, Alexandria, LA, May 1, 1864. *Colonel,* 31 MA Infantry, June 7, 1865. Provost Marshal General, Department of Alabama, July 19-Sept. 9, 1865. Honorably mustered out, Sept. 9, 1865. Bvt. Colonel, USV, March 13, 1865, for gallant and meritorious conduct at the capture of Port Hudson, LA, in the fight at Shreveport, Pinewood, and Alexandria, and also in the taking of Mobile, AL.

**Born:** Nov. 7, 1834 Chicopee, MA
**Died:** April 17, 1889 Boston, MA
**Education:** Graduated Yale University, New Haven, CT, 1856. Attended Harvard Law School, Cambridge, MA.
**Occupation:** School principal and law student before war. Lawyer after war.

*Edward Payson Nettleton*
*Massachusetts MOLLUS Collection, USAMHI.*

*Edward Payson Nettleton (postwar)*
*Massachusetts MOLLUS Collection, USAMHI.*

*Left:*
*Edward Payson Nettleton (postwar)*
*Massachusetts MOLLUS Collection, USAMHI.*

**Offices/Honors:** Corporation counsel for the city of Boston, MA, 1882-88. Judge Advocate General, Staff of Governor George D. Robinson, 1884-87.
**Miscellaneous:** Resided Chicopee, Hampden Co., MA; and Boston, MA.
**Buried:** East Street Cemetery, Chicopee, MA
**References:** *Obituary Record of Graduates of Yale College Deceased During the Academical Year Ending in June 1889.* Obituary, *Boston Evening Transcript*, April 18, 1889. Obituary, *Springfield Daily Republican*, April 18, 1889. Military Service File, National Archives. Anna Nettleton Miles. *Edward Payson Nettleton: A Book of Remembrance.* N.p., 1939.

## Abner Butterfield Packard

Colonel, 4 MA Infantry, April 22, 1861. Honorably mustered out, July 22, 1861.

**Born:** Nov. 9, 1822 Quincy, MA
**Died:** Oct. 17, 1902 Quincy, MA
**Occupation:** Merchant before war. Metal refiner after war, supplying nearly all the metal used for stereotyping and linotyping by the newspapers of New England and New York.
**Miscellaneous:** Resided Quincy, Norfolk Co., MA.
**Buried:** Hancock Cemetery, Quincy, MA
**References:** Obituary, *Boston Evening Transcript*, Oct. 17, 1902. Pension File, National Archives. George W. Nason. *Minute Men of '61.* Boston, MA, 1910.

*Abner Butterfield Packard*
*Massachusetts MOLLUS Collection, USAMHI.*

## Francis Jewett Parker

Major, 1 Battalion, MA Infantry, Dec. 2, 1861. Discharged May 22, 1862. Lieutenant Colonel, 32 MA Infantry, May 25, 1862. Colonel, 32 MA Infantry, Aug. 6, 1862. Resigned Dec. 27, 1862, due to "the excessive loss occasioned by my absence from business."

**Born:** March 3, 1825 Boston, MA
**Died:** Jan. 20, 1909 Boston, MA
**Occupation:** Merchant and manufacturer, long associated with the business of cotton manufacturing and the sale of mill products

*Right:*
*Francis Jewett Parker*
*Roger D. Hunt Collection, USAMHI. F.L. Lay's Photographic Atelier, 31 Winter Street, Boston, MA.*

**Offices/Honors:** Massachusetts General Court, 1861. Massachusetts Senate, 1858 and 1876.

**Miscellaneous:** Resided Boston, MA; and Newton, Middlesex Co., MA, where he was active in civic and church activities. Author of a history of the 32nd MA Infantry and also several genealogical works. Uncle of Bvt. Brig. Gen. Charles G. Sawtelle.

**Buried:** Mount Auburn Cemetery, Cambridge, MA (Elder Path, Lot 1250)

**References:** Obituary, *Boston Evening Transcript*, Jan. 21, 1909. *New England Historical and Genealogical Register.* Vol. 63 (July 1909). Francis J. Parker. *The Story of the 32nd Regiment Massachusetts Infantry.* Boston, MA, 1880.

*Right:*
*Francis Jewett Parker*
*Massachusetts MOLLUS Collection, USAMHI.*

*Francis Jewett Parker*
*Massachusetts MOLLUS Collection, USAMHI.*

*Right:*
*Francis Jewett Parker (postwar)*
*Massachusetts MOLLUS Collection, USAMHI.*

## Benjamin Franklin Peach, Jr.

1 Sergeant, Co. C, 8 MA Infantry, April 16, 1861. Honorably mustered out, Aug. 1, 1861. 1 Lieutenant, Adjutant, 8 MA Infantry, Sept. 12, 1862. Acting AAG, 2 Brigade, 5 Division, 18 Army Corps, Feb. 1863. Honorably mustered out, Aug. 7, 1863. Colonel, 8 MA Infantry, July 26, 1864. Honorably mustered out, Nov. 10, 1864.

**Born:** Oct. 17, 1838 Marblehead, MA
**Died:** May 26, 1927 Swampscott, MA
**Occupation:** Foreman in shoe manufacturing firm before war. Becoming a partner in that firm after the war and retiring in 1879, he later served as treasurer and trustee of various corporations.
**Offices/Honors:** Treasurer, City of Lynn, MA, 1879-85. Brigadier General, Massachusetts State Militia, 1882-97, retiring with the rank of Major General. US Pension Agent, Boston, MA, 1885-89.
**Miscellaneous:** Resided Marblehead, Essex Co., MA; Lynn, Essex Co., MA; and Boston, MA. Son-in-law of Colonel Frederic J. Coffin.

*Benjamin Franklin Peach, Jr.*
*Massachusetts MOLLUS Collection, USAMHI. Dampf, 105 W. Baltimore Street, Next to Sun Building, Baltimore, MD.*

*Benjamin Franklin Peach, Jr.*
*Courtesy of Gil Barrett.*

*Right:*
*Benjamin Franklin Peach, Jr.*
*Massachusetts MOLLUS Collection, USAMHI.*

**Buried:** Oak Hill Cemetery, Newburyport, MA (Section 3, Lot 627)

**References:** Charles W. Hall, editor. *Regiments and Armories of Massachusetts.* Boston, MA, 1899-1901. Obituary, *Boston Evening Transcript*, May 26, 1927. Pension File, National Archives.

*Benjamin Franklin Peach, Jr. (postwar)*
*Massachusetts MOLLUS Collection, USAMHI.*

*Opposite:*
*Ebenezer Weaver Peirce*
*Courtesy of Dennis Keesee. J.W. Black, 173 Washington Street, Boston, MA.*

## Ebenezer Weaver Peirce

Brigadier General, Massachusetts Volunteer Militia, April 22, 1861. Honorably mustered out, July 22, 1861. Colonel, 29 MA Infantry, Dec. 13, 1861. Right arm torn off by cannon ball, White Oak Swamp, VA, June 30, 1862. Commanded 2 Brigade, 1 Division, 9 Army Corps, Aug. 18-Sept. 18, 1863; Jan. 10-March 16, 1864; and June 4-July 23, 1864. Discharged for disability, Nov. 8, 1864, due to the loss of his right arm and also due to general nervous debility resulting from miasmatic diseases.

**Born:** April 5, 1822 Assonet, MA

**Died:** Aug. 14, 1902 Assonet, MA

**Education:** Attended Peirce Academy, Middleboro, MA; Bacon Academy, Colchester, CT; and Durham (NH) Academy

**Occupation:** Gentleman farmer, real estate speculator and author of historical and genealogical works.

**Miscellaneous:** Resided Assonet, Bristol Co., MA.

**Buried:** Assonet Burying Ground, Assonet, MA

**References:** Ebenezer W. Peirce. *The Peirce Family of the Old Colony.* Boston, MA, 1870. *History of Freetown, MA.* Fall River, MA, 1902. *New England Historical and Genealogical Register.* Vol. 57 (Jan. 1903). Military Service File, National Archives. William H. Osborne. *The History of the 29th Regiment of Massachusetts Volunteer Infantry.* Boston, MA, 1877.

*George Henry Peirson*
*Massachusetts MOLLUS Collection, USAMHI.*

## George Henry Peirson

Captain, Co. A, 5 MA Infantry, May 1, 1861. Lieutenant Colonel, 5 MA Infantry, July 5, 1861. Honorably mustered out, July 31, 1861. Colonel, 5 MA Infantry, Oct. 8, 1862. Commanded 2 Brigade, 1 Division, 18 Army Corps, May 12-June 7, 1863. Honorably mustered out, July 2, 1863. Colonel, 5 MA Infantry, July 28, 1864. Honorably mustered out, Nov. 16, 1864.

**Born:** June 16, 1816 Salem, MA

**Died:** Feb. 8, 1881 Salem, MA

**Occupation:** Blacksmith and mechanic

**Offices/Honors:** Brigadier General, Massachusetts Volunteer Militia, 1866-76. Massachusetts Legislature, 1867-68. Postmaster, Salem, MA, 1869-81.

**Miscellaneous:** Resided Salem, Essex Co., MA. Joined the Salem Light Infantry in 1834 and was identified with the Massachusetts State Militia from that time until 1876. Name changed from George W. Honeycomb by act of the Massachusetts Legislature, May 10, 1848.

**Buried:** Harmony Grove Cemetery, Salem, MA (Halidon Avenue, Lot 858)

**References:** Alfred S. Roe. *The 5th Regiment Massachusetts Volunteer Infantry.* Boston, MA, 1911. Oliver A. Roberts. *History of the Ancient and Honorable Artillery Company of Massachusetts, 1637-1888.* Vol. 3. Boston, MA, 1898. Obituary, *Boston Post*, Feb. 9, 1881.

## Frederick G. Pope

Captain, Co. D, 41 MA Infantry, Sept. 2, 1862. Major, 3 MA Cavalry, Dec. 12, 1864. Lieutenant Colonel, 3 MA Cavalry, Aug. 15, 1865. *Colonel,* 3 MA Cavalry, Oct. 5, 1865. Honorably mustered out, Sept. 28, 1865.

*Frederick G. Pope (postwar)*
*The Third Massachusetts Cavalry in the War for the Union.*

*George Henry Peirson*
*Massachusetts MOLLUS Collection, USAMHI.*

Frederick G. Pope (seated 2nd from left) with officers of the 3rd Massachusetts Cavalry. The Third Massachusetts Cavalry in the War for the Union.

**Born:** Oct. 6, 1824 Kennebunkport, ME

**Died:** Feb. 16, 1884 Boston, MA

**Occupation:** Employed with his brothers as a mason before the war. Held an office in the Boston Custom House after the war.

**Miscellaneous:** Resided Boston, MA.

**Buried:** Forest Hills Cemetery, Jamaica Plain, MA (Honeysuckle Path, Lot 3600)

**References:** James K. Ewer. *The Third Massachusetts Cavalry in the War for the Union.* Maplewood, MA, 1903. Obituary, *Boston Evening Transcript*, Feb. 18, 1884. Pension File, National Archives.

## Burr Baldwin Porter

Major, Additional ADC, USV, June 2, 1862. Assistant to Chief of Staff, Staff of Major General John C. Fremont, June 1862. Colonel, 40 MA Infantry, Sept. 7, 1862. Commanded 2 Brigade, Abercrombie's Division, 22 Army Corps, Department of Washington, March 31-April 17, 1863. Commanded Porter's Brigade, Gurney's Division, 7 Army Corps, Department of Virginia, April 17-May 4, 1863. Commanded 2 Brigade, 2 Division, 4 Army Corps, Department of Virginia, May 4-July 15, 1863. Resigned July 21, 1863, due to "discontent unfitting me for a command, and pressing reasons of a family and private

*Burr Baldwin Porter*
*Massachusetts MOLLUS Collection, USAMHI.*

*Burr Baldwin Porter*
*Massachusetts MOLLUS Collection, USAMHI.*

*Burr Baldwin Porter*
*Massachusetts MOLLUS Collection, USAMHI.*

nature." Colonel, 26 NY Cavalry, Feb. 13, 1865. Colonel, 3 MA Cavalry, March 21, 1865. Commanded 1 Cavalry Brigade, 22 Army Corps, Department of Washington, June 1865. Honorably mustered out, July 21, 1865.

**Born:** Oct. 26, 1829 Montrose, PA
**Died:** Dec. 10, 1870 Josnes, France (KIA, Franco-Prussian War)
**Education:** Graduated Rutgers College, New Brunswick, NJ, 1849.
**Other Wars:** Crimean War on staff of Omar Pasha of Turkey. Franco-Prussian War on staff of Gen. Chanzy of France.
**Occupation:** Lawyer
**Miscellaneous:** Resided Newark, NJ; and Boston, MA. Born Burr Baldwin, he was adopted by his uncle, P. H. Porter.
**Buried:** Forest Hills Cemetery, Jamaica Plain, MA (Rhododendron Path, Lot 1558)
**References:** Charles C. Baldwin. *The Baldwin Genealogy From 1500 to 1881.* Cleveland, OH, 1881. James K. Ewer. *The Third Massachusetts Cavalry in the War For the Union.* Maplewood, MA, 1903. Military Service File, National Archives.

## Arnold Augustus Rand

Private, 4 Battalion, MA Militia, April 14, 1861. 2 Lieutenant, Co. F, 1 MA Cavalry, Dec. 19, 1861. Captain, Co. F, 1 MA Cavalry, Feb. 4, 1862. Captain, AAG, USV, June 3, 1863. Assigned to Staff of Brig. Gen. Rufus Saxton. Lieutenant Colonel, 4 MA Cavalry, Dec. 3, 1863. Colonel, 4 MA Cavalry, Jan. 22, 1864. Commanded Provisional Brigade, 18 Army Corps, May 27-June 19, 1864. Commanded Post of Deep Bottom, VA, Oct.-Nov. 1864. Resigned Feb. 3, 1865.

**Born:** March 25, 1837 Boston, MA
**Died:** Dec. 23, 1917 Brookline, MA
**Education:** After attending Mr. Dixwell's school in Boston, he finished his early education in Vevay, Switzerland. After war attended Boston University Law School.
**Occupation:** Employed by a shipping firm and a banking house before war. After war practiced real estate law, managed a title insurance company, and became a life insurance executive.
**Offices/Honors:** In 1898 became Vice President and General Counsel of the John Hancock Mutual Life Insurance Company. Commander-in-Chief, MOLLUS, 1912-13.
**Miscellaneous:** Resided Boston, MA; and Brookline, Norfolk Co., MA. As Recorder of the Massachusetts Commandery,

*Arnold Augustus Rand (1864)*
*Massachusetts MOLLUS Collection, USAMHI. Black & Case, Photographic Artists, Boston & Newport, RI.*

MOLLUS, 1881-1906, devoted much time and energy to the development of the MOLLUS Library at the Cadet Armory in Boston.

**Buried:** Mount Auburn Cemetery, Cambridge, MA (Spruce Avenue, Lot 750)

**References:** Obituary, *Boston Evening Transcript*, Dec. 24, 1917. Obituary Circular, Whole No. 548, Massachusetts MOLLUS. Pension File, National Archives. Benjamin W. Crowninshield. *A History of the 1st Regiment of Massachusetts Cavalry Volunteers.* Boston, MA, 1891.

*Arnold Augustus Rand (1861)*
*Massachusetts MOLLUS Collection, USAMHI. Seaver & Lothrop, Photographic Artists, 27 Tremont Row, Boston, MA.*

*Left:*
*Arnold Augustus Rand (1862)*
*Massachusetts MOLLUS Collection, USAMHI.*

*Arnold Augustus Rand (1862)*
*Massachusetts MOLLUS Collection, USAMHI.*

*Arnold Augustus Rand (1863)*
*Massachusetts MOLLUS Collection, USAMHI.*

*Arnold Augustus Rand (1882)*
*Massachusetts MOLLUS Collection, USAMHI.*

*Arnold Augustus Rand (1895)*
*Massachusetts MOLLUS Collection, USAMHI.*

*Arnold Augustus Rand (1865)*
*Massachusetts MOLLUS Collection, USAMHI.*

*Arnold Augustus Rand (1880)*
*Massachusetts MOLLUS Collection, USAMHI.*

Arnold Augustus Rand (1880)
Massachusetts MOLLUS Collection, USAMHI.

Arnold Augustus Rand (1900)
Massachusetts MOLLUS Collection, USAMHI.

## John William Raymond

1 Lieutenant, Co. E, 8 MA Infantry, April 30, 1861. Honorably mustered out, Aug. 1, 1861. Captain, Co. G, 23 MA Infantry, Oct. 8, 1861. GSW head, Drewry's Bluff, VA, May 16, 1864. GSW right arm, Cold Harbor, VA, June 3, 1864. Lieutenant Colonel, 23 MA Infantry, July 14, 1864. *Colonel,* 23 MA Infantry, Sept. 20, 1864. Honorably mustered out, June 25, 1865.

**Born:** Sept. 25, 1827 Beverly, MA
**Died:** April 1, 1902 Beverly, MA
**Occupation:** Farmer and probation officer.
**Offices/Honors:** Massachusetts Legislature, 1865-66.
**Miscellaneous:** Resided Beverly, Essex Co., MA; and Gordon, Walton Co., FL.
**Buried:** North Beverly Cemetery, North Beverly, MA
**References:** James A. Emmerton. *A Record of the 23rd Regiment Massachusetts Volunteer Infantry.* Boston, MA, 1886. Pension File, National Archives.

*John William Raymond*
*Courtesy of Henry Deeks. William H. Barnes, Photographer, Fort Totten, NC.*

*Right:*
*John William Raymond*
*Massachusetts MOLLUS Collection, USAMHI.*

*John William Raymond*
*Massachusetts MOLLUS Collection, USAMHI.*

*John William Raymond*
*Massachusetts MOLLUS Collection, USAMHI.*

## Edmund Rice

Captain, Co. F, 19 MA Infantry, Aug. 22, 1861. Major, 19 MA Infantry, Sept. 7, 1862. Shell wound right leg, Antietam, MD, Sept. 17, 1862. Two GSW right thigh, Gettysburg, PA, July 3, 1863. Lieutenant Colonel, 19 MA Infantry, Feb. 28, 1864. Captured Spotsylvania, VA, May 12, 1864. Escaped while being transported south and walked over 300 miles to the Union lines. *Colonel,* 19 MA Infantry, July 28, 1864. Honorably mustered out, June 30, 1865.

**Born:** Dec. 2, 1842 Cambridge, MA
**Died:** July 20, 1906 Wakefield, MA
**Education:** Attended Norwich (VT) University
**Other Wars:** Spanish American War (Colonel, 6 MA Infantry). Philippine Insurrection (Colonel, 26 US Volunteer Infantry).

*Right:*
*Edmund Rice (postwar)*
*Massachusetts MOLLUS Collection, USAMHI.*

**Occupation:** Regular Army (Brigadier General, retired Aug. 14, 1903).

**Offices/Honors:** Medal of Honor, Gettysburg, PA, July 3, 1863. "Conspicuous bravery on the third day of the battle in the countercharge against Pickett's Division where he fell severely wounded within the enemy's lines."

**Miscellaneous:** Resided Cambridge, Middlesex Co., MA; Boston, MA; and Wakefield, Middlesex Co., MA. Invented a trowel bayonet, a knife entrenching tool, a stacking swivel, and an improved blanket roll and shelter tent, all of which were adopted by the US Army.

**Buried:** Arlington National Cemetery, Arlington, VA (Section 3, Lot 1875)

**References:** William A. Ellis, editor. *History of Norwich University, 1819-1911*. Montpelier, VT, 1911. William H. Powell and Edward Shippen, editors. *Officers of the Army and Navy (Regular) Who Served in the Civil War*. Philadelphia, PA, 1892. Ernest L. Waitt. *History of the 19th Regiment Massachusetts Volunteer Infantry*. Salem, MA, 1906. Pension File, National Archives.

*Edmund Rice*
*Massachusetts MOLLUS Collection, USAMHI.*

*Right:*
*Edmund Rice*
*Massachusetts MOLLUS Collection, USAMHI.*

## Silas Peirce Richmond

Captain, ADC, Massachusetts Volunteer Militia, May 28, 1861. Assigned to Staff of Brig. Gen. Ebenezer W. Peirce. Honorably mustered out, July 24, 1861. Colonel, 3 MA Infantry, Oct. 7, 1862. Honorably mustered out, June 26, 1863. Assistant Provost Marshal General, Department of the South, July 19, 1864. Honorably mustered out, Sept. 1865.

**Born:** June 19, 1831 Freetown, MA
**Died:** April 24, 1915 Assonet, MA
**Education:** Attended Peirce Academy, Middleboro, MA
**Occupation:** Farmer and lumber merchant until 1871, after which time he found employment successively as a prison guard, a traveling agent and a deputy sheriff
**Offices/Honors:** Massachusetts Legislature, 1892
**Miscellaneous:** Resided Freetown, Bristol Co., MA, to 1867; Newport, Vermilion Co., IN, 1867-69; Decatur, Van Buren Co., MI, 1869-70; Assonet, Bristol Co., MA, 1870-72, 1882-1915; Charlestown, Suffolk Co., MA, 1872-79; New Bedford, Bristol Co., MA, 1880-82
**Buried:** Richmond Cemetery, Assonet, MA
**References:** *History of Freetown, MA.* Fall River, MA, 1902. George W. Nason. *Minute Men of '61.* Boston, MA, 1910. Obituary, *Providence Journal,* April 25, 1915. Pension File, National Archives. John G. Gammons. *The 3rd Massachusetts Regiment Volunteer Militia in the War of the Rebellion.* Providence, RI, 1906.

*Silas Peirce Richmond*
*Massachusetts MOLLUS Collection, USAMHI. J.W. Black, 173 Washington Street, Boston, MA*

*Silas Peirce Richmond*
*Massachusetts MOLLUS Collection, USAMHI.*

*Silas Peirce Richmond (1903)*
*Massachusetts MOLLUS Collection, USAMHI.*

## Lorenzo Dow Sargent

Major, 41 MA Infantry, Aug. 22, 1862. Lieutenant Colonel, 41 MA Infantry, Feb. 1, 1863. GSW right shoulder, Muddy Bayou, LA, April 15, 1864. Colonel, 3 MA Cavalry, Sept. 2, 1864. GSW Cedar Creek, VA, Oct. 19, 1864. Discharged for disability, March 10, 1865, due to failing eyesight.

**Born:** Dec. 8, 1825 Nottingham, NH
**Died:** Sept. 19, 1882 Oakdale, CA
**Occupation:** Overseer of weaving department of the Atlantic Mills of Lawrence, MA, before war. Engaged in box manufacturing after war.
**Miscellaneous:** Resided Lawrence, Essex Co., MA; and Oakdale, Stanislaus Co., CA.
**Buried:** Bellevue Cemetery, Lawrence, MA (Group 6, Lot 45)
**References:** Pension File and Military Service File, National Archives. Obituary, *Boston Evening Transcript*, Sept. 22, 1882. James K. Ewer. *The 3rd Massachusetts Cavalry in the War for the Union*. Maplewood, MA, 1903.

*Silas Peirce Richmond*
*Massachusetts MOLLUS Collection, USAMHI.*

## Nathaniel Shatswell

Captain, Co. A, 1 MA Heavy Artillery, July 5, 1861. Major, 1 MA Heavy Artillery, Dec. 31, 1862. Shell wound head, Spotsylvania, VA, May 19, 1864. Contused wound right side, Petersburg, VA, June 18, 1864. Lieutenant Colonel, 1 MA Heavy Artillery, Jan. 26, 1865. *Colonel,* 1 MA Heavy Artillery, Jan. 27, 1865. Bvt. Colonel, USV, March 13, 1865, for faithful and meritorious services. Honorably mustered out, Aug. 16, 1865.

*Lorenzo Dow Sargent (seated 2nd from right) with officers of the 3rd Massachusetts Cavalry. The Third Massachusetts Cavalry in the War for the Union.*

*Right:*
*Lorenzo Dow Sargent (postwar).*
*The Third Massachusetts Cavalry in the War for the Union.*

**Born:** Nov. 26, 1834 Ipswich, MA
**Died:** Dec. 14, 1905 Ipswich, MA
**Occupation:** Farmer and overseer in County Receptacle for Insane.
**Miscellaneous:** Resided Ipswich, Essex Co., MA; and Washington, DC.
**Buried:** Highland Cemetery, Ipswich, MA
**References:** Alfred S. Roe and Charles Nutt. *History of the 1st Regiment of Heavy Artillery Massachusetts Volunteers.* Worcester, MA, 1917. D. Hamilton Hurd. *History of Essex County, MA.* Philadelphia, PA, 1888. Pension File, National Archives.

*Nathaniel Shatswell*
*Massachusetts MOLLUS Collection, USAMHI.*

*Nathaniel Shatswell (1893)*
*District of Columbia MOLLUS Collection, USAMHI. Taylor & Preston, Artistic Photographers, 188 Essex Street, Salem, MA.*

*Nathaniel Shatswell*
*Massachusetts MOLLUS Collection, USAMHI.*

## Robert Gould Shaw

Private, Co. F, 7 NY State Militia, April 19, 1861. 2 Lieutenant, Co. H, 2 MA Infantry, May 25, 1861. 1 Lieutenant, Co. H, 2 MA Infantry, July 8, 1861. Acting ADC, Staff of Brig. Gen. George H. Gordon July-Aug. 1862. Captain, Co. H, 2 MA Infantry, Aug. 10, 1862. Major, 54 MA Infantry, March 31, 1863. Colonel, 54 MA Infantry, April 17, 1863. GSW Fort Wagner, SC, July 18, 1863.

**Born:** Oct. 10, 1837 Boston, MA
**Died:** July 18, 1863 KIA Fort Wagner, SC
**Education:** Attended St. John's College, Fordham, NY. Attended Harvard University, Cambridge, MA.
**Occupation:** Mercantile clerk in New York City.
**Miscellaneous:** Resided Boston, MA; and New York City, NY. Brother-in-law of Brig. Gen. Charles R. Lowell. Brother-in-law of Brig. Gen. Francis C. Barlow. Nephew of Colonel William B. Greene. First cousin of Bvt. Brig. Gen. Henry S. Russell.

*Robert Gould Shaw*
*Massachusetts MOLLUS Collection, USAMHI.*

*Right:*
*Robert Gould Shaw*
*Courtesy of Henry Deeks.*

**Buried:** Fort Wagner, Morris Island, SC (Body never recovered). Cenotaph in Moravian Cemetery, New Dorp, Staten Island, NY.

**References:** Russell Duncan, editor. *Blue-Eyed Child of Fortune: The Civil War Letters of Colonel Robert Gould Shaw.* Athens, GA, 1992. Thomas W. Higginson. *Harvard Memorial Biographies.* Cambridge, MA, 1866. *Memorial RGS.* Cambridge, MA, 1864. Luis F. Emilio. *History of the 54th Regiment of Massachusetts Volunteer Infantry.* Boston, MA, 1894.

*Right:*
*Robert Gould Shaw*
*Massachusetts MOLLUS Collection, USAMHI.*

*Robert Gould Shaw*
*Massachusetts MOLLUS Collection, USAMHI.*

## William Steele Shurtleff

1 Lieutenant, Co. A, 46 MA Infantry, Aug. 27, 1862. Lieutenant Colonel, 46 MA Infantry, Oct. 30, 1862. Colonel, 46 MA Infantry, Feb. 5, 1863. Honorably mustered out, July 29, 1863.

**Born:** Feb. 17, 1830 Newbury, VT

**Died:** Jan. 14, 1896 Longmeadow, MA

**Education:** Attended Williston Seminary, Easthampton, MA. Graduated Yale University, New Haven, CT, 1854. Attended Harvard University Law School, Cambridge, MA.

**Occupation:** Lawyer and judge

**Offices/Honors:** Judge of Probate, Hampden Co., MA, 1863-96

**Miscellaneous:** Resided Springfield, Hampden Co., MA

**Buried:** Springfield Cemetery, Springfield, MA (Section 15-R-20, Lot 228)

**References:** Obituary, *Springfield Daily Republican*, Jan. 15, 1896. Benjamin Shurtleff. *The Descendants of William Shurtleff.* Revised by Roy L. Shurtleff. San Francisco, CA, 1976.

*William Steele Shurtleff (postwar)*
*Massachusetts MOLLUS Collection, USAMHI.*

*Right:*
*William Steele Shurtleff*
*Roger D. Hunt Collection, USAMHI.*

## Henry Splaine

1 Lieutenant, Co. E, 17 MA Infantry, July 22, 1861. Captain, Co. E, 17 MA Infantry, Jan. 31, 1862. GSW left arm, Winton, NC, July 26, 1863. Major, 17 MA Infantry, Aug. 4, 1864. Lieutenant Colonel, 17 MA Infantry, Aug. 10, 1864. Commanded 3 Brigade, 2 Division, District of Beaufort (NC), March 1-March 18, 1865. *Colonel,* 17 MA Infantry, June 16, 1865. Honorably mustered out, July 11, 1865.

**Born:** Aug. 6, 1837 Muskerry, County Cork, Ireland
**Died:** Aug. 9, 1922 Hampton Beach, NH
**Occupation:** Shoemaker before war. Trader after war.
**Miscellaneous:** Resided Haverhill, Essex Co., MA; Boston, MA; and Bradford, Essex Co., MA.
**Buried:** Holy Cross Cemetery, Malden, MA (North Lake Avenue, Path 10, Lot 54 West)
**References:** Thomas Kirwan and Henry Splaine. *Memorial History of the 17th Regiment Massachusetts Volunteer Infantry.* Salem, MA, 1911. Pension File, National Archives.

*Henry Splaine*
*Massachusetts MOLLUS Collection, USAMHI.*

## Eben Francis Stone

Captain, Co. A, 48 MA Infantry, Sept. 16, 1862. Colonel, 48 MA Infantry, Dec. 8, 1862. Honorably mustered out, Sept. 3, 1863.

**Born:** Aug. 3, 1822 Newburyport, MA
**Died:** Jan. 22, 1895 Newburyport, MA
**Education:** Graduated Harvard University, Cambridge, MA, 1843. Graduated Harvard University Law School, Cambridge, MA, 1846.
**Occupation:** Lawyer
**Offices/Honors:** Massachusetts Senate, 1857-58, 1861. Massachusetts General Court, 1867, 1877-78, 1880. US House of Representatives, 1881-87.
**Miscellaneous:** Resided Newburyport, Essex Co., MA
**Buried:** Oak Hill Cemetery, Newburyport, MA (Elm Avenue, Lot 247)
**References:** John J. Currier. *"Ould Newbury": Historical and Biographical Sketches.* Boston, MA, 1896. *Exercises Commemorating the Life and Character of Hon. Eben Francis Stone.* Boston, MA, 1895. Albert Plummer. *History of the 48th Regiment Massachusetts Volunteer Militia During the Civil War.* Boston, MA, 1907.

*Right:*
*Henry Splaine*
*Memorial History of the 17th Regiment Massachusetts Infantry.*

## Thomas Redding Tannatt

1 Lieutenant, 4 US Artillery, May 14, 1861. GSW shoulder, Malvern Hill, VA, July 1, 1862. Colonel, 16 MA Infantry, July 14, 1862. Colonel, 1 MA Heavy Artillery, Dec. 28, 1862. Commanded 1 Brigade, Defenses South of the Potomac, 22 Army Corps, April 15-Aug. 11, 1863 and Sept. 16, 1863-March 10, 1864. Commanded Defenses South of the Potomac, 22 Army Corps, April 26-May 23, 1863. Captain, 4 US Artillery, Aug. 11, 1863. Commanded 2 Brigade, Defenses South of the Potomac, 22 Army Corps, March-May 1864. Commanded 2 Brigade, 3 Division, 2 Army Corps, Army of the Potomac, May 29-June 16, 1864. GSW head, Petersburg, VA, June 16, 1864. Resigned from volunteer service, July 15, 1864. Resigned from regular service, July 18, 1864.

*Eben Francis Stone*
*USAMHI. Whipple, 96 Washington Street, Boston, MA.*

**Born:** Sept. 27, 1833 Verplanck Point, NY

**Died:** Dec. 20, 1913 Spokane, WA

**Education:** Graduated US Military Academy, West Point, NY 1858.

**Occupation:** Civil engineer engaged in railway and mining enterprises.

**Miscellaneous:** Resided Manchester, Essex Co., MA; Black Hawk, Gilpin Co., CO; McMinnville, Warren Co., TN; Walla Walla, WA; Portland, OR; and Spokane, WA.

**Buried:** Fairmount Memorial Park, Spokane, WA (Lawn 12, Section D, Lot 12)

**References:** Obituary Circular, Whole No. 243, Oregon MOLLUS. Pension File, National Archives. Alfred S. Roe and Charles Nutt. *History of the 1st Regiment of Heavy Artillery Massachusetts Volunteers.* Worcester, MA, 1917. George W. Cullum. *Biographical Register of the Officers and Graduates of the US Military Academy.* Boston and New York, 1891.

*Left:*
*Thomas Redding Tannatt*
*Massachusetts MOLLUS Collection, USAMHI.*

## Henry Martyn Tremlett

1 Sergeant, 4 Battalion, MA Militia, April 25, 1861. Captain, Co. A, 20 MA Infantry, July 10, 1861. Major, 39 MA Infantry, Aug. 28, 1862. Lieutenant Colonel, 39 MA Infantry, July 13, 1864. *Colonel,* 39 MA Infantry, Jan. 5, 1865. GSW right leg (amputated), White Oak Road, VA, March 31, 1865. Bvt. Colonel, USV, March 31, 1865, for distinguished gallantry in front of Petersburg, and at the battle of White Oak Road, VA.

**Born:** July 15, 1833 Dorchester, MA
**Died:** June 6, 1865 DOW Boston, MA
**Education:** Attended Chauncey Hall School, Boston, MA.
**Occupation:** Merchant
**Miscellaneous:** Resided Boston, MA.
**Buried:** Forest Hills Cemetery, Jamaica Plain, MA (Asphodel Path, Lot 1346)
**References:** Alfred S. Roe. *The 39th Regiment Massachusetts Volunteers.* Worcester, MA, 1914. Military Service File, National Archives. Obituary, *Boston Post*, June 7, 1865.

*Henry Martyn Tremlett*
*Massachusetts MOLLUS Collection, USAMHI. Black & Case, Photographic Artists, Boston & Newport, RI.*

*Thomas Redding Tannatt (postwar)*
*Massachusetts MOLLUS Collection, USAMHI.*

*Henry Martyn Tremlett*
*Massachusetts MOLLUS Collection, USAMHI.*

*Right:*
*Henry Martyn Tremlett*
*Massachusetts MOLLUS Collection, USAMHI.*

*Opposite, below right:*
*Henry Martyn Tremlett*
*Massachusetts MOLLUS Collection, USAMHI*

## James Tucker

*James Tucker*
*Massachusetts MOLLUS Collection, USAMHI.*

1 Sergeant, Co. D, 3 Battalion MA Rifles, April 19, 1861. Honorably mustered out, Aug. 3, 1861. 1 Lieutenant, Co. C, 25 MA Infantry, Oct. 12, 1861. Captain, Co. C, 25 MA Infantry, Oct. 29, 1862. GSW right arm, Petersburg, VA, June 18, 1864. Lieutenant Colonel, 25 MA Infantry, Jan. 1, 1865. *Colonel,* 25 MA Infantry, Jan. 10, 1865. Commanded 3 Brigade, 1 Division, 23 Army Corps, June 17-July 13, 1865. Honorably mustered out, July 13, 1865. Bvt. Colonel, USV, March 13, 1865, for gallant and meritorious conduct throughout the whole war, especially at Cold Harbor, June 3, 1864.

**Born:** June 9, 1836 Boston, MA
**Died:** Nov. 26, 1910 Chelsea, MA
**Occupation:** Master plumber.
**Miscellaneous:** Resided Somerville, Middlesex Co., MA; and San Francisco, CA.
**Buried:** Cedar Grove Cemetery, Dorchester, MA (Section 10, Rear Tulip Path, Lot 310)
**References:** Charles W. Hall, editor. *Regiments and Armories of Massachusetts.* Boston, MA, 1899-1901. Pension File, National Archives. J. Waldo Denny. *Wearing the Blue in the 25th Massachusetts Volunteer Infantry.* Worcester, MA, 1879.

## Mason Whiting Tyler

*James Tucker*
*Massachusetts MOLLUS Collection, USAMHI.*

1 Lieutenant, Co. F, 37 MA Infantry, Aug. 13, 1862. Captain, Co. F, 37 MA Infantry, Jan. 17, 1863. Shell wound neck and chin, Winchester, VA, Sept. 19, 1864. Major, 37 MA Infantry, March 4, 1865. GSW right knee, Petersburg, VA, March 25, 1865. *Lieutenant Colonel,* 37 MA Infantry, May 19, 1865. *Colonel,* 37 MA Infantry, June 26, 1865. Honorably mustered out, June 21, 1865.

**Born:** June 17, 1840 Amherst, MA
**Died:** July 2, 1907 New York City, NY
**Education:** Attended Williston Seminary, Easthampton, MA. Graduated Amherst (MA) College, 1862. Attended Columbia College Law School, New York City, NY.
**Occupation:** Lawyer, in partnership with Bvt. Brig. Gen. Henry E. Tremain from 1869 to 1893.
**Miscellaneous:** Resided Amherst, Hampshire Co., MA; New York City, NY; and Plainfield, Union Co., NJ.
**Buried:** Hillside Cemetery, Plainfield, NJ (Section A, Division 5, Lot 30)
**References:** Mason W. Tyler. *Recollections of the Civil War.* New York and London, 1912. Obituary Circular, Whole

*Mason Whiting Tyler*
*Recollections of the Civil War.*

*Mason Whiting Tyler*
*Recollections of the Civil War.*

No. 923, New York MOLLUS. James L. Bowen. *History of the 37th Regiment Massachusetts Volunteers.* Holyoke, MA, 1884. Robert S. Fletcher and Malcolm O. Young, editors. *Amherst College Biographical Record.* Centennial Edition. Amherst, MA, 1927.

## Edwin Upton

Colonel, 25 MA Infantry, Sept. 9, 1861. Resigned Oct. 28, 1862, due to declining health caused by malarial poisoning.

**Born:** Dec. 9, 1815 Fitchburg, MA
**Died:** May 10, 1890 Fitchburg, MA
**Occupation:** Lumberman, farmer and builder
**Offices/Honors:** For 25 years actively connected with the Massachusetts Volunteer Militia, rising to the rank of colonel of the 9th Regiment. Storekeeper, Boston Custom House, 1863-69. Master of Fitchburg House of Correction, 1869-75.
**Miscellaneous:** Resided Fitchburg, Worcester Co., MA; and Boston, MA
**Buried:** Forest Hill Cemetery, Fitchburg, MA
**References:** John A. Vinton. *The Upton Memorial: A Genealogical Record of the Descendants of John Upton of North Reading, MA.* Bath, ME, 1874. Pension File and Military Service File, National Archives. J. Waldo Denny. *Wearing the Blue in the 25th Massachusetts Volunteer Infantry.* Worcester, MA, 1879. Henry A. Willis. *Fitchburg in the War of the Rebellion.* Fitchburg, MA, 1866.

*Opposite:*
*Edwin Upton*
*Massachusetts MOLLUS Collection, USAMHI.*

*Right:*
*Edwin Upton*
*Massachusetts MOLLUS Collection, USAMHI.*

## Henry Walker

1 Lieutenant, Adjutant, 4 MA Infantry, April 22, 1861. Honorably mustered out, July 22, 1861. Colonel, 4 MA Infantry, Dec. 6, 1862. Honorably mustered out, Sept. 3, 1863.

**Born:** Dec. 25, 1832 Boston, MA
**Died:** Dec. 20, 1914 Newton, MA
**Education:** Graduated Harvard University, Cambridge, MA, 1855
**Occupation:** Lawyer
**Offices/Honors:** Boston License Commissioner, 1877-78. Boston Police Commissioner, 1879-82.
**Miscellaneous:** Resided Quincy, Norfolk Co., MA; Boston, MA; and Newton, Middlesex Co., MA. The first Harvard graduate to enlist for the Civil War, according to inscription on his tombstone.
**Buried:** Mount Wollaston Cemetery, Quincy, MA (Old Section, Lot 494)
**References:** Obituary, *Boston Evening Transcript*, Dec. 21, 1914. Oliver A. Roberts. *History of the Ancient and Honorable Artillery Company of Massachusetts, 1637-1888.* Vol. 4. Boston, MA, 1901. George W. Nason. *Minute Men of '61.* Boston, MA, 1910.

*Left:*
*Henry Walker*
*Massachusetts MOLLUS Collection, USAMHI. J.W. Black, 173 Washington Street, Boston, MA.*

Henry Walker (1855)
Harvard College Portraits, Class of 1855, 1851-1905.

Henry Walker
Roger D. Hunt Collection, USAMHI. Silsbee, Case & Co., Photographers, Boston, MA.

## David William Wardrop

Colonel, 3 MA Infantry, April 23, 1861. Honorably mustered out, July 22, 1861. Colonel, 99 NY Infantry, Aug. 21, 1861. Commanded Reserve Brigade, 7 Army Corps, Department of Virginia, April 24, 1863-May 13, 1863. Commanded Provisional Brigade, 7 Army Corps, Department of Virginia, June 1863. Commanded Sub-District of the Albemarle, District of North Carolina, April 21, 1864-Dec. 10, 1864. Honorably discharged, Dec. 10, 1864, on account of the reduced strength of his command.

**Born:** May 18, 1824 Philadelphia, PA
**Died:** July 10, 1898 Dorchester, MA
**Occupation:** Merchant connected with the shipping and whaling interests of New Bedford, MA, before war. Inspector in the Boston Custom House after war.
**Miscellaneous:** Resided New Bedford, Bristol Co., MA; and Dorchester, Suffolk Co., MA.
**Buried:** Cedar Grove Cemetery, Dorchester, MA (Section 5, Dahlia Path, Lot 1021)
**References:** Pension File and Military Service File, National Archives. Philip Corell. *History of the Naval Brigade, 99th New York Volunteers, Union Coast Guard.* New York City, NY, 1905. Obituary, *Boston Evening Transcript*, July 11, 1898. John G. Gammons. *The 3rd Massachusetts Regiment Volunteer Militia in the War of the Rebellion.* Providence, RI, 1906.

## Fletcher Webster

Colonel, 12 MA Infantry, June 26, 1861. GSW arm and chest, 2nd Bull Run, VA, Aug. 30, 1862.

**Born:** July 23, 1813 Portsmouth, NH
**Died:** Aug. 30, 1862 KIA Manassas, VA
**Education:** Graduated Harvard University, Cambridge, MA, 1833.
**Occupation:** Lawyer.
**Offices/Honors:** US Undersecretary of State, 1840-43. US Secretary of Legation to China, 1843-45. US Surveyor of the Port of Boston, 1845-61.
**Miscellaneous:** Resided Marshfield, Plymouth Co., MA. Son of the noted statesman Daniel Webster.
**Buried:** Winslow Cemetery, Marshfield, MA

*David William Wardrop*
*Massachusetts MOLLUS Collection, USAMHI. J.W. Black, 173 Washington Street, Boston, MA.*

*David William Wardrop*
*USAMHI.*

**References:** Thomas W. Higginson. *Harvard Memorial Biographies.* Cambridge, MA, 1866. Benjamin F. Cook. *History of the 12th Massachusetts Volunteers.* Boston, MA, 1882.

## Joseph Henry Wheelock

Colonel, 7 MA Infantry, Nov. 20, 1861. Resigned Jan. 30, 1862, his health being "too feeble to endure the hardships of camp life in this latitude and at this season of the year."

**Born:** Jan. 13, 1829 Sturbridge, MA
**Died:** May 8, 1862 Washington, DC

**Education:** Attended Quaboag Seminary, Warren, MA. Graduated US Military Academy, West Point, NY, 1850.

**Occupation:** Regular Army (1 Lieutenant, 4 US Artillery, resigned March 31, 1857).

**Miscellaneous:** Resided Warren, Worcester Co., MA; and Boston, MA.

**Buried:** Soldiers Home National Cemetery, Washington, DC (Section B, Grave 569)

**References:** Military Service File, National Archives. USMA Cadet Application Papers, National Archives. *Vital Records of Sturbridge, MA, to the Year 1850.* Boston, MA, 1906. Nelson V. Hutchinson. *History of the 7th Massachusetts Volunteer Infantry in the War of the Rebellion.* Taunton, MA, 1890.

*Fletcher Webster*
*Massachusetts MOLLUS Collection, USAMHI.*

*Above right:*
*Fletcher Webster*
*Massachusetts MOLLUS Collection, USAMHI.*

*Right:*
*Fletcher Webster*
*Massachusetts MOLLUS Collection, USAMHI.*

## John Chadwick Whiton

Lieutenant Colonel, 43 MA Infantry, Oct. 13, 1862. Honorably mustered out, July 30, 1863. Lieutenant Colonel, 58 MA Infantry, March 8, 1864. GSW right side, Cold Harbor, VA, June 3, 1864. *Colonel,* 58 MA Infantry, Aug. 31, 1864. Bvt. Colonel, USV, April 2, 1865, for gallant and meritorious conduct before Petersburg, VA. Honorably mustered out, July 14, 1865.

**Born:** Aug. 21, 1828 Hingham, MA
**Died:** Jan. 2, 1905 Boston, MA
**Occupation:** Clerk and bookkeeper for wholesale grocery firm before war. Employed after war as Boston municipal official, first in the auditor's department and later in the corrections department.
**Offices/Honors:** Master of the Suffolk Co. House of Corrections, 1889-1905.
**Miscellaneous:** Resided Hingham, Plymouth Co., MA; and Boston, MA.
**Buried:** Hingham Center Cemetery, Hingham, MA
**References:** Pension File, National Archives. *American Series of Popular Biographies.* Massachusetts Edition. Boston, MA, 1901. Edward H. Rogers. *Reminiscences of Military Service in the 43rd Regiment Massachusetts Infantry.* Boston, MA, 1883. Frederick E. Cushman. *History of the 58th Regiment Massachusetts Volunteers.* Washington, DC, 1865.

*John Chadwick Whiton*
*Massachusetts MOLLUS Collection, USAMHI.*

*John Chadwick Whiton (postwar)*
*Massachusetts MOLLUS Collection, USAMHI.*

*John Chadwick Whiton*
*Massachusetts MOLLUS Collection, USAMHI.*

*John Chadwick Whiton*
*Massachusetts MOLLUS Collection, USAMHI.*

*John Chadwick Whiton*
*Massachusetts MOLLUS Collection, USAMHI.*

## Henry Wilson

Colonel, 22 MA Infantry, Sept. 2, 1861. Resigned Oct. 29, 1861, in order to resume his duties as US Senator.

**Born:** Feb. 16, 1812 Farmington, NH
**Died:** Nov. 22, 1875 Washington, DC
**Education:** Attended Strafford (NH) Academy; Wolfeboro (NH) Academy; and Concord (NH) Academy
**Occupation:** Farmer, school teacher and shoe manufacturer
**Offices/Honors:** Massachusetts Legislature, 1840-41, 1844-46, 1850-52. US Senate, 1855-73. Vice President of the United States, 1873-75.
**Miscellaneous:** Resided Natick, Middlesex Co., MA; Boston, MA; and Washington, DC
**Buried:** Dell Park Cemetery, Natick, MA
**References:** *Dictionary of American Biography.* Elias Nason and Thomas Russell. *The Life and Public Services of Henry Wilson.* N.p., 1876. John L. Parker. *History of the 22nd Massachusetts Infantry.* Boston, MA, 1887.

*Henry Wilson*
*Massachusetts MOLLUS Collection, USAMHI. Brady's National Photographic Portrait Gallery, Washington, DC.*

*Henry Wilson*
*Massachusetts MOLLUS Collection, USAMHI.*

*Henry Wilson*
*Massachusetts MOLLUS Collection, USAMHI.*

*Henry Wilson*
*Massachusetts MOLLUS Collection, USAMHI.*

## Levi Parker Wright

Major, 1 MA Heavy Artillery, July 5, 1861. Lieutenant Colonel, 1 MA Heavy Artillery, June 10, 1862. Detached as Superintendent of Military Railroads running from Chattanooga, TN, to July 1, 1864. *Colonel,* 1 MA Heavy Artillery, Jan. 26, 1865. Detached as Superintendent of Military Railroads running from Memphis, TN, in 1865. Honorably mustered out, May 16, 1865.

**Born:** Sept. 17, 1824 Dunstable, MA
**Died:** Jan. 3, 1913 Bevier, KY
**Education:** Attended Hancock (NH) Academy
**Occupation:** Railroad superintendent before war. Public works contractor after war.
**Offices/Honors:** Chicago Police Commissioner, 1873. Register of Wills, Washington, DC. Collector of the Port of Nome, Alaska.

*Right:*
*Levi Parker Wright*
*Massachusetts MOLLUS Collection, USAMHI. R. W. Addis, McClees' Gallery, 308 Penna. Avenue, Washington, DC.*

*Levi Parker Wright*
*Massachusetts MOLLUS Collection, USAMHI. J.W. Black, 173 Washington Street, Boston, MA*

**Miscellaneous:** Resided Lawrence, Essex Co., MA; Chicago, IL, 1867-76; Washington, DC, 1876-1905; and Bevier, Muhlenberg Co., KY, 1905-13

**Buried:** Arlington National Cemetery, Arlington, VA (Section 3, Lot 1757)

**References:** Alfred S. Roe and Charles Nutt. *History of the 1st Regiment of Heavy Artillery Massachusetts Volunteers.* Worcester, MA, 1917. Pension File, National Archives.

*Levi Parker Wright*
*Massachusetts MOLLUS Collection, USAMHI.*

## Powell Tremlett Wyman

Colonel, 16 MA Infantry, July 13, 1861. GSW right arm and heart, Glendale, VA, June 30, 1862.

**Born:** Jan. 29, 1828 Boston, MA

**Died:** June 30, 1862 KIA Glendale, VA

**Education:** Graduated US Military Academy, West Point, NY, 1850.

**Occupation:** Regular Army (1 Lieutenant, Adjutant, 1 US Artillery, resigned July 13, 1860).

**Miscellaneous:** Resided Boston, MA. His alleged adulterous affair with the wife of Brig. Gen. John M. Brannan is the subject of several letters between Major Gen. Benjamin F. Butler and Governor John A. Andrew in *Official Records*, Series 3, Vol. 1, pp. 855-858.

**Buried:** Mount Auburn Cemetery, Cambridge, MA (Sweetbrier Path, Lot 3262)

**References:** *New England Historical and Genealogical Register.* Vol. 16 (Oct. 1862). Obituary, *Boston Post*, July 4, 1862. Pension File, National Archives.

*Right:*
*Powell Tremlett Wyman*
*Massachusetts MOLLUS Collection, USAMHI. L.H. Hale, Photographer, 293 Washington Street, Boston, MA.*

*Chapter IV*

# NEW HAMPSHIRE

| **1st Cavalry** | | |
|---|---|---|
| John L. Thompson | March 17, 1864 | Mustered out July 15, 1865 **Bvt. Brig. Gen.** |

**2nd Cavalry** (See 8th Infantry)

| **1st Heavy Artillery** | | |
|---|---|---|
| Charles H. Long | Sept. 29, 1864 | Mustered out June 15, 1865 |

| **1st Infantry** | | |
|---|---|---|
| Mason W. Tappan | April 29, 1861 | Mustered out Aug. 9, 1861 |

| **2nd Infantry** | | |
|---|---|---|
| Gilman Marston | June 4, 1861 | Promoted **Brig. Gen., USV** Nov. 29, 1862 |
| Edward L. Bailey | April 18, 1863 | Mustered out June 21, 1864 |
| Joab N. Patterson | Jan. 10, 1865 | Mustered out Dec. 19, 1865 **Bvt. Brig. Gen.** |

| **3rd Infantry** | | |
|---|---|---|
| Enoch Q. Fellows | Aug. 10, 1861 | Discharged June 26, 1862 |
| John H. Jackson | June 27, 1862 | Discharged Feb. 24, 1864 |
| John Bedel | April 6, 1864 | Mustered out July 20, 1865 **Bvt. Brig. Gen.** |

| **4th Infantry** | | |
|---|---|---|
| Thomas J. Whipple | Aug. 20, 1861 | Resigned March 18, 1862 |
| Louis Bell | May 16, 1862 | DOW Jan. 16, 1865 |
| William Badger | Feb. 21, 1865 | Not mustered |

| **5th Infantry** | | |
|---|---|---|
| Edward E. Cross | Aug. 27, 1861 | KIA July 2, 1863 |
| Charles E. Hapgood | July 3, 1863 | Mustered out Oct. 17, 1864 |
| Richard E. Cross | Feb. 21, 1865 | Commission revoked |
| Welcome A. Crafts | April 29, 1865 | Mustered out June 28, 1865 |

| **6th Infantry** | | |
|---|---|---|
| Nelson Converse | Oct. 26, 1861 | Resigned March 8, 1862 |
| Simon G. Griffin | April 22, 1862 | Promoted **Brig. Gen., USV** May 12, 1864 |
| Phineas P. Bixby | Feb. 21, 1865 | Mustered out July 17, 1865 |

| **7th Infantry** | | |
|---|---|---|
| Haldimand S. Putnam | Oct. 15, 1861 | KIA July 18, 1863 |
| Joseph C. Abbott | July 22, 1863 | Mustered out July 20, 1865 **Bvt. Brig. Gen.** |

| **8th Infantry** (designated 2nd Cavalry, Dec. 16, 1863 - July 25, 1864) | | |
|---|---|---|
| Hawkes Fearing, Jr. | Sept. 24, 1861 | Mustered out Jan. 18, 1865 |
| James H. Landers | Oct. 28, 1865 | Mustered out Dec. 21, 1865 |

| **9th Infantry** | | |
|---|---|---|
| Enoch Q. Fellows | June 14, 1862 | Discharged Nov. 21, 1862 |
| Herbert B. Titus | Nov. 22, 1862 | Mustered out June 10, 1865 **Bvt. Brig. Gen.** |

| **10th Infantry** | | |
|---|---|---|
| Michael T. Donohoe | Aug. 6, 1862 | Mustered out June 21, 1865 **Bvt. Brig. Gen.** |

| **11th Infantry** | | |
|---|---|---|
| Walter Harriman | Aug. 26, 1862 | Mustered out June 4, 1865 **Bvt. Brig. Gen.** |

| **12th Infantry** | | |
|---|---|---|
| Joseph H. Potter | Sept. 17, 1862 | Promoted **Brig. Gen., USV** May 1, 1865 |
| Thomas E. Barker | May 26, 1865 | Mustered out June 21, 1865 |

| **13th Infantry** | | |
|---|---|---|
| Aaron F. Stevens | Aug. 26, 1862 | Mustered out June 21, 1865 **Bvt. Brig. Gen.** |

| **14th Infantry** | | |
|---|---|---|
| Robert Wilson | Sept. 19, 1862 | Discharged Sept. 6, 1864 |
| Alexander Gardiner | Sept. 12, 1864 | DOW Oct. 7, 1864 **Bvt. Brig. Gen.** |
| Carroll D. Wright | Dec. 6, 1864 | Discharged March 6, 1865 |
| Theodore A. Ripley | March 24, 1865 | Mustered out May 15, 1865 **Bvt. Brig. Gen.** |

| **15th Infantry** | | |
|---|---|---|
| John W. Kingman | Oct. 7, 1862 | Mustered out Aug. 13, 1863 |

| **16th Infantry** | | |
|---|---|---|
| James Pike | Nov. 1, 1862 | Mustered out Aug. 20, 1863 |

| **17th Infantry** | | |
|---|---|---|
| Henry O. Kent | Oct. 23, 1862 | Mustered out April 16, 1863 |

| **18th Infantry** | | |
|---|---|---|
| Charles H. Bell | Aug. 22, 1864 | Resigned Oct. 24, 1864 |
| Thomas L. Livermore | Jan. 17, 1865 | Mustered out June 23, 1865 |
| Joseph M. Clough | July 29, 1865 | Mustered out July 29, 1865 **Bvt. Brig. Gen.** |

## William Badger

Captain, Co. D, 4 NH Infantry, Sept. 18, 1861. Dismissed June 4, 1864, for mistakenly ordering the retreat of pickets on the Bermuda Hundred line, May 21, 1864. Disability resulting from dismissal removed, Jan. 21, 1865. *Colonel,* 4 NH Infantry, Feb. 21, 1865. Captain, Co. B, 9 US Veteran Volunteers, June 9, 1865. Honorably mustered out, April 20, 1866.

**Born:** Aug. 1, 1826 Gilmanton, NH
**Died:** May 11, 1897 Jamaica Plain, MA
**Education:** Graduated Dartmouth College, Hanover, NH, 1848.
**Occupation:** Textile manufacturer before war. Regular Army (Captain, 6 US Infantry, retired Jan. 15, 1889).
**Miscellaneous:** Resided Gilmanton, Belknap Co., NH; and Boston, MA. Son of NH Governor William Badger.
**Buried:** Smith Meeting House Cemetery, Gilmanton, NH
**References:** John C. Badger. *Giles Badger and his Descendants.* Manchester, NH, 1909. John G. Hutchinson. *Roster 4th Regiment New Hampshire Volunteers.* Manchester, NH, 1896. William H. Hodgkins, editor. *Military Record of the Sons of Dartmouth.* Boston, MA, 1907. Pension File and Military Service File, National Archives.

*William Badger*
*Courtesy of Henry Deeks. Thomas H. Martin, Photographer, 82 Chatham Street, New York, NY.*

*William Badger (postwar)*
*Massachusetts MOLLUS Collection, USAMHI.*

*Right:*
*William Badger*
*Stephen Allen Collection, USAMHI.*

## Edward Lyon Bailey

Captain, Co. I, 2 NH Infantry, May 9, 1861. GSW slight, Williamsburg, VA, May 5, 1862. GSW slight, Glendale, VA, June 30, 1862. Major, 2 NH Infantry, July 26, 1862. Lieutenant Colonel, 2 NH Infantry, Oct. 23, 1862. Colonel, 2 NH Infantry, April 18, 1863. GSW slight, Gettysburg, PA, July 2, 1863. Honorably mustered out, June 21, 1864.

**Born:** Dec. 10, 1841 Manchester, NH
**Died:** March 12, 1930 Manchester, NH
**Occupation:** Chief Clerk, Manchester (NH) Post Office, before war. Regular Army (Captain, 4 US Infantry, dismissed Oct. 15, 1893, for conduct unbecoming an officer and a gentleman in borrowing money from a fellow officer and not repaying it, although repeatedly promising to do so; in entering a private house, in uniform, without permission, in the absence of the owner, beckoning to the owner's wife with his hand; refusing to leave the house when requested to do so by her; and in going to a public saloon in Boise City, ID, and chasing a prostitute about the saloon, and in going to a corner of the saloon, holding a conversation with her while in the uniform of a commissioned officer).
**Miscellaneous:** Resided Manchester, NH; Boise, ID, 1893-97; and Bedford, Hillsborough Co., NH, 1897-1930.
**Buried:** Piscataquog Cemetery, Manchester, NH
**References:** Pension File and Military Service File, National Archives. Obituary, *Manchester Union*, March 13, 1930. Martin A. Haynes. *History of the 2nd Regiment New Hampshire Volunteer Infantry.* Lakeport, NH, 1896. Otis F. R. Waite. *New Hampshire in the Great Rebellion.* Claremont, NH, 1870.

*Edward Lyon Bailey*
*Roger D. Hunt Collection, USAMHI.*

## Thomas Erskine Barker

Corporal, Co. B, 2 NH Infantry, June 1, 1861. Captured 1st Bull Run, VA, July 21, 1861. Confined Richmond, VA; New Orleans, LA; and Salisbury, NC. Paroled June 2, 1862 and discharged July 2, 1862. Captain, Co. B, 12 NH Infantry, Sept. 8, 1862. GSW left leg, Chancellorsville, VA, May 3, 1863. Lieutenant Colonel, 12 NH Infantry, Sept. 30, 1864. *Colonel,* 12 NH Infantry, May 26, 1865. Honorably mustered out, June 21, 1865.

**Born:** March 13, 1839 Canterbury, NH
**Died:** Dec. 17, 1896 Malden, MA

*Right:*
*Thomas Erskine Barker*
*Massachusetts MOLLUS Collection, USAMHI.*

**Occupation:** Wholesale grocer and commission merchant.

**Offices/Honors:** Treasurer, Massachusetts Soldiers' Home, Chelsea, MA, 1892-96. Massachusetts Legislature.

**Miscellaneous:** Resided Gilmanton, Belknap Co., NH; and Malden, Middlesex Co., MA.

**Buried:** Forest Dale Cemetery, Malden, MA (Section 24, Lot 25-A)

**References:** Asa W. Bartlett. *History of the 12th Regiment New Hampshire Volunteers.* Concord, NH, 1897. Obituary, *Boston Evening Transcript*, Dec. 18, 1896. Pension File, National Archives. Martin A. Haynes. *History of the 2nd Regiment New Hampshire Volunteer Infantry.* Lakeport, NH, 1896.

*Thomas Erskine Barker*
*Massachusetts MOLLUS Collection, USAMHI.*

*Thomas Erskine Barker*
*USAMHI.*

*Right:*
*Thomas Erskine Barker (postwar)*
*Massachusetts MOLLUS Collection, USAMHI.*

## Charles Henry Bell

*Colonel,* 18 NH Infantry, Aug. 22, 1864. Resigned Oct. 24, 1864, having concluded that "I ought no longer to quit my urgent private business for the contingency of the completion of the regiment."

**Born:** Nov. 18, 1823 Chester, NH
**Died:** Nov. 11, 1893 Exeter, NH
**Education:** Graduated Dartmouth College, Hanover, NH, 1844
**Occupation:** Lawyer and author
**Offices/Honors:** New Hampshire House of Representatives, 1858-60 and 1872-73. New Hampshire Senate, 1863-64. US Senate, 1879. Governor of New Hampshire, 1881-83.
**Miscellaneous:** Resided Exeter, Rockingham Co., NH. For 19 years President of the New Hampshire Historical Society. Author of numerous works on New Hampshire history.
**Buried:** Exeter Cemetery, Exeter, NH
**References:** *National Cyclopedia of American Biography.* Charles H. Bell. *The Bench and Bar of New Hampshire.* Boston and New York, 1894. Thomas L. Livermore. *History of the 18th New Hampshire Volunteers.* Boston, MA, 1904.

*Charles Henry Bell (postwar)*
*Frederick H. Meserve. Historical Portraits. Courtesy of New York State Library.*

## Louis Bell

Captain, Co. A, 1 NH Infantry, April 30, 1861. Honorably mustered out, Aug. 9, 1861. Lieutenant Colonel, 4 NH Infantry, Sept. 3, 1861. Acting AIG, Staff of Brig. Gen. Thomas W. Sherman, Nov.-Dec. 1861. Colonel, 4 NH Infantry, March 18, 1862. Commanded Post of St. Augustine, FL, Department of the South, April-July 1862. Commanded 1 Brigade, 3 Division, 10 Army Corps, May 16-18, 1864. Commanded 3 Brigade, 3 Division, 18 Army Corps, June 9-19, 1864. Commanded 3 Brigade, 2 Division, 10 Army Corps, June 20-Aug. 13, 1864 and Sept. 23-Dec. 3, 1864. Commanded 3 Brigade, 2 Division, 24 Army Corps, Dec. 3, 1864-Jan. 15, 1865. GSW left breast, Fort Fisher, NC, Jan. 15, 1865.

**Born:** March 8, 1837 Chester, NH
**Died:** Jan. 16, 1865 DOW Fort Fisher, NC
**Education:** Attended Brown University, Providence, RI.
**Occupation:** Lawyer
**Miscellaneous:** Resided Farmington, Strafford Co., NH. Son of NH Governor Samuel Bell. Biographer John B. Bouton claimed that Bell posthumously received brevet brigadier general commission, but there is no record of this at the National Archives.

*Louis Bell*
*Roger D. Hunt Collection, USAMHI.*

*Louis Bell*
*Massachusetts MOLLUS Collection, USAMHI.*

*Louis Bell*
*Massachusetts MOLLUS Collection, USAMHI.*

**Buried:** Village Cemetery, Chester, NH

**References:** John B. Bouton. *A Memoir of General Louis Bell.* New York City, NY, 1865. Henry S. Burrage. *Brown University in the Civil War.* Providence, RI, 1868. John G. Hutchinson. *Roster 4th Regiment New Hampshire Volunteers.* Manchester, NH, 1896. Military Service File, National Archives.

## Phineas P. Bixby

1 Lieutenant, Adjutant, 6 NH Infantry, Nov. 30, 1861. Captured 2nd Bull Run, VA, Aug. 29, 1862. Confined Libby Prison, Richmond, VA. Exchanged Sept. 21, 1862. Major, 6 NH Infantry, Oct. 15, 1862. GSW left shoulder, Petersburg, VA, July 14, 1864. Lieutenant Colonel, 6 NH Infantry, July 28, 1864. Colonel, 6 NH Infantry, Feb. 21, 1865. Bvt. Colonel, USV, April 2, 1865, for gallant and highly meritorious conduct in the assault before Petersburg, VA. Honorably mustered out, July 17, 1865.

**Born:** May 9, 1829 Piermont, NH

**Died:** Jan. 16, 1877 Concord, NH

**Occupation:** Printer and grocer before war. Surveyor in Boston Custom House, grocer, and chief clerk in the New Hampshire Treasurer's office after war.

*Phineas P. Bixby*
*Roger D. Hunt Collection, USAMHI.*

**Miscellaneous:** Resided Concord, Merrimack Co., NH; and Boston, MA.
**Buried:** Blossom Hill Cemetery, Concord, NH (North Addition, Lot 16)
**References:** Willard G. Bixby. *Bixby Genealogy: Descendants of Joseph Bixby.* New York City, NY, 1914. Pension File, National Archives. Obituary, *Concord Daily Monitor*, Jan. 16, 1877. Lyman Jackman. *History of the 6th New Hampshire Regiment in the War for the Union.* Concord, NH, 1891. Otis F. R. Waite. *New Hampshire in the Great Rebellion.* Claremont, NH, 1870.

*Phineas P. Bixby (postwar)*
*Massachusetts MOLLUS Collection, USAMHI.*

## Nelson Converse

Colonel, 6 NH Infantry, Oct. 26, 1861. Discharged for disability, March 8, 1862, due to chronic diarrhea.

**Born:** Oct. 18, 1810 Marlborough, NH
**Died:** April 27, 1894 Marlborough, NH
**Occupation:** Farmer, quarryman, and boarding house operator
**Offices/Honors:** Major General, New Hampshire State Militia, 1860-61. New Hampshire Legislature.
**Miscellaneous:** Resided Marlborough, Cheshire Co., NH
**Buried:** Graniteville Cemetery, Marlborough, NH
**References:** Charles A. Converse, compiler. *Some of the Ancestors and Descendants of Samuel Converse, Jr.* Boston, MA, 1905. Pension File, National Archives. Charles A. Bemis. *History of the Town of Marlborough, NH.* Boston, MA, 1881. Otis F. R. Waite. *New Hampshire in the Great Rebellion.* Claremont, NH, 1870. Lyman Jackman. *History of the 6th New Hampshire Regiment in the War for the Union.* Concord, NH, 1891.

## Welcome Alonzo Crafts

1 Sergeant, Co. F, 2 NH Infantry, June 4, 1861. 1 Lieutenant, Co. B, 5 NH Infantry, Oct. 12, 1861. Captured Malvern Hill, VA, July 1, 1862. Confined Libby Prison, Richmond, VA. Exchanged Aug. 27, 1862. Captain, Co. B, 5 NH Infantry, Sept. 11, 1862. GSW left leg, Fredericksburg, VA, Dec. 13, 1862. Commanded Point Lookout (MD) Prison Camp, April 1864. Major, 5 NH Infantry, Sept. 6, 1864. Lieutenant Colonel, 5 NH Infantry, Oct. 28, 1864. Bvt. Colonel, USV, March 13, 1865, for gallant and meritorious conduct during the war. *Colonel,* 5 NH Infantry, April 29, 1865. Honorably mustered out, June 28, 1865.

*Welcome Alonzo Crafts*
*Courtesy of Henry Deeks. Case & Getchell, Photographic Artists 2-9 1/2 Washington Street, Boston, MA.*

**Born:** Jan. 23, 1835 Milan, NH
**Died:** Jan. 12, 1891 Brownsville, TX
**Occupation:** Law student before war. Regular Army (Captain, 26 US Infantry, honorably mustered out Jan. 1, 1871)
**Miscellaneous:** Resided Milan, Coos Co., NH; and Brownsville, Cameron Co., TX
**Buried:** City Cemetery, Brownsville, TX (Block 45, Lot 24)
**References:** Pension File, National Archives. James M. and William F. Crafts, compilers. *The Crafts Family.* Northampton, MA, 1893. William Child. *A History of the 5th Regiment New Hampshire Volunteers.* Bristol, NH, 1893.

Edward Everett Cross
Massachusetts MOLLUS Collection, USAMHI.

## Edward Everett Cross

Colonel, 5 NH Infantry, Aug. 27, 1861. GSW left thigh, Fair Oaks, VA, June 1, 1862. Shell wounds breast, mouth and forehead, Fredericksburg, VA, Dec. 13, 1862. Commanded 1 Brigade, 1 Division, 2 Army Corps, Army of the Potomac, May 22, 1863-July 2, 1863. GSW abdomen, Gettysburg, PA, July 2, 1863.

**Born:** April 22, 1832 Lancaster, NH
**Died:** July 3, 1863 DOW Gettysburg, PA
**Occupation:** Newspaper editor and correspondent early in life. Later traveled extensively in the West, led a mining expedition into Arizona, and accepted an army position in Sonora, Mexico.
**Miscellaneous:** Resided Lancaster, Coos Co., NH; and Cincinnati, OH. Brother of Bvt. Brig. Gen. Nelson Cross and Colonel Richard E. Cross.
**Buried:** Wilder Cemetery, Lancaster, NH
**References:** William Child. *A History of the 5th Regiment New Hampshire Volunteers.* Bristol, NH, 1893. A. N. Somers. *History of Lancaster, NH.* Concord, NH, 1899. Otis F. R. Waite. *New Hampshire in the Great Rebellion.* Claremont, NH, 1870.

## Richard Everett Cross

Artificer, Co. A, Corps of Engineers, Feb. 20, 1860. 1 Lieutenant, Co. H, 5 NH Infantry, Oct. 12, 1861. Captain, Co. K, 5 NH Infantry, Feb. 17, 1862. GSW left leg and right hand, Fair Oaks, VA, June 1, 1862. Major, 5 NH Infantry, Dec. 14, 1862. Shell

*Right:*
*Edward Everett Cross*
*Massachusetts MOLLUS Collection, USAMHI. Brady's National Photographic Portrait Gallery.*

wound chest, Chancellorsville, VA, May 3, 1863. Lieutenant Colonel, 5 NH Infantry, July 3, 1863. Cashiered Aug. 4, 1864, for "disobedience of orders and breach of arrest." Disability resulting from dismissal removed, Jan. 16, 1865. *Colonel,* 5 NH Infantry, Feb. 21, 1865. Appointment as colonel revoked, April 29, 1865.

**Born:** 1835? Lancaster, NH
**Died:** Sept. 16, 1894 Washington, DC
**Occupation:** Printer and Regular Army enlisted man before war. Oil business, railroad contractor and physician after war. Watchman, US Treasury Department, when he died.
**Miscellaneous:** Resided Lancaster, Coos Co., NH; Glencoe, Ontario; Franklin, Venango Co., PA; Norwich, Chenango Co., NY; Montreal, Quebec; Concord, Merrimack Co., NH; and Washington, DC. Brother of Bvt. Brig. Gen. Nelson Cross and Colonel Edward E. Cross.
**Buried:** Wilder Cemetery, Lancaster, NH
**References:** Pension File and Military Service File, National Archives. A. N. Somers. *History of Lancaster, NH.* Concord, NH, 1899. William Child. *A History of the 5th Regiment New Hampshire Volunteers.* Bristol, NH, 1893. Obituary, *Washington Evening Star*, Sept. 17, 1894.

*Richard Everett Cross*
*Massachusetts MOLLUS Collection, USAMHI.*

## Hawkes Fearing, Jr.

Lieutenant Colonel, 4 MA Infantry, April 22, 1861. Honorably mustered out, July 22, 1861. Colonel, 8 NH Infantry, Sept. 25, 1861. Shell wound leg, Fort Bisland, LA, April 13, 1863. Commanded 2 Brigade, 3 Division, 19 Army Corps, May 1863 and July 10-Aug. 15, 1863. Commanded 3 Division, 19 Army Corps, June 14-July 6, 1863. Colonel, 2 NH Cavalry, Dec. 16, 1863. Honorably mustered out, Jan. 17, 1865.

**Born:** May 20, 1826 Hingham, MA
**Died:** Feb. 9, 1908 Hingham, MA
**Occupation:** Merchant dealing in clothing and furnishing goods before war. Municipal official in Hingham, MA, after war. Librarian of Hingham Public Library, 1873-1908.
**Offices/Honors:** Massachusetts Legislature, 1871-72. Hingham (MA) Postmaster, 1872-79.
**Miscellaneous:** Resided Manchester, Hillsborough Co., NH; and Hingham, Plymouth Co., MA
**Buried:** Hingham Center Cemetery, Hingham, MA

*Right:*
*Richard Everett Cross*
*Massachusetts MOLLUS Collection, USAMHI.*

Hawkes Fearing, Jr.
*Massachusetts MOLLUS Collection, USAMHI. J. Morgan, Corner Main & Warren Streets, Opposite the Phoenix, Concord, NH.*

Hawkes Fearing, Jr.
*Massachusetts MOLLUS Collection, USAMHI.*

**References:** John M. Stanyan. *History of the 8th Regiment of New Hampshire Volunteers.* Concord, NH, 1892. Pension File, National Archives. Obituary, *Boston Evening Transcript*, Feb. 10, 1908. Otis F. R. Waite. *New Hampshire in the Great Rebellion.* Claremont, NH, 1870.

*Hawkes Fearing, Jr.*
*From a private collection.*

## Enoch Quimby Fellows

1 Lieutenant, Adjutant, 1 NH Infantry, April 30, 1861. Colonel, 3 NH Infantry, Aug. 10, 1861. Commanded Post of Hilton Head, SC, Department of the South, Jan. 27-April 5, 1862. Commanded Post of Edisto Island, SC, Department of the South, April 5-23, 1862. Colonel, 9 NH Infantry, June 14, 1862. Discharged for disability, Nov. 21, 1862, due to neuralgia and deafness.

**Born:** June 20, 1825 Sandwich, NH
**Died:** May 6, 1897 Tilton, NH
**Education:** Attended US Military Academy, West Point, NY (Class of 1848)
**Occupation:** Farmer, tanner and saw mill operator before war. After the war connected with Carroll County Savings Bank and served as assistant assessor and deputy collector of internal revenue.

**Offices/Honors:** Doorkeeper, New Hampshire State Senate, 1851-54. Inspector, Boston Custom House, 1854-57. Brigadier General, New Hampshire Militia, 1858. New Hampshire Legislature, 1868-69, 1877.
**Miscellaneous:** Resided Center Sandwich, Carroll Co., NH; St. Paul, MN; and Tilton, Belknap Co., NH
**Buried:** Grove Cemetery, Center Sandwich, NH
**References:** Daniel Eldredge. *The Third New Hampshire and All About It.* Boston, MA, 1893. Pension File, National Archives. Georgia D. Merrill. *History of Carroll County, NH.* Boston, MA, 1889. Otis F. R. Waite. *New Hampshire in the Great Rebellion.* Claremont, NH, 1870.

*Enoch Quimby Fellows*
*The Third New Hampshire and All About It. Kimball, Concord, NH.*

*Enoch Quimby Fellows*
*Massachusetts MOLLUS Collection, USAMHI.*

## Charles Edward Hapgood

Captain, Co. I, 5 NH Infantry, Oct. 12, 1861. Lieutenant Colonel, 5 NH Infantry, Dec. 14, 1862. Colonel, 5 NH Infantry, July 3, 1863. GSW right arm, Petersburg, VA, June 16, 1864. Honorably mustered out, Oct. 14, 1864.

**Born:** Dec. 11, 1830 Shrewsbury, MA
**Died:** Sept. 24, 1909 Chelsea, MA

*Charles Edward Hapgood*
*Massachusetts MOLLUS Collection, USAMHI. Brady's National Photographic Portrait Gallery, Washington, DC.*

**Occupation:** Learned the trade of gun making, but soon went into mercantile business, which he continued until he entered service. Wool commission merchant after war.
**Offices/Honors:** Superintendent, Massachusetts Soldiers' Home, Chelsea, MA, 1906-09.
**Miscellaneous:** Resided Amherst, Hillsborough Co., NH; Boston, MA; and Brookline, Norfolk Co., MA
**Buried:** Mountain View Cemetery, Shrewsbury, MA (Section 12, Lot 366)
**References:** Warren Hapgood. *The Hapgood Family: Descendants of Shadrach, 1656-1898.* Boston, MA, 1898. Obituary, *Boston Evening Transcript*, Sept. 24, 1909. Pension File, National Archives. William Child. *A History of the 5th Regiment New Hampshire Volunteers.* Bristol, NH, 1893. Otis F. R. Waite. *New Hampshire in the Great Rebellion.* Claremont, NH, 1870.

*Charles Edward Hapgood*
*Massachusetts MOLLUS Collection, USAMHI.*

## John Henry Jackson

Lieutenant Colonel, 3 NH Infantry, Aug. 6, 1861. Colonel, 3 NH Infantry, June 27, 1862. Shell wound left breast, Fort Wagner, SC, July 18, 1863. Discharged for disability, Feb. 24, 1864, due to chronic bronchitis.

**Born:** Oct. 20, 1814 Portsmouth, NH
**Died:** April 10, 1890 Boston, MA
**Other Wars:** Mexican War (Captain, 9 US Infantry)
**Occupation:** Inspector, Boston Custom House, 1853-61 and 1867-90.
**Miscellaneous:** Resided Portsmouth, NH; and Boston, MA.
**Buried:** Proprietors' Cemetery (now part of South Cemetery), Portsmouth, NH
**References:** Daniel Eldredge. *The Third New Hampshire and All About It.* Boston, MA, 1893. Joseph Foster. *The Soldiers' Memorial, Portsmouth, NH, 1893-1923.* Portsmouth, NH, 1923. Otis F. R. Waite. *New Hampshire in the Great Rebellion.* Claremont, NH, 1870.

*John Henry Jackson*
*The Third New Hampshire and All About It.*

## Henry Oakes Kent

Colonel, 17 NH Infantry, Oct. 23, 1862. Honorably mustered out, April 16, 1863.

**Born:** Feb. 7, 1834 Lancaster, NH
**Died:** March 21, 1909 Lancaster, NH
**Education:** Graduated Norwich (VT) University, 1854
**Occupation:** Newspaper editor, paper manufacturer, banker and politician

**Offices/Honors:** New Hampshire House of Representatives, 1862, 1868-69, 1882-83. New Hampshire Senate, 1884. Naval Officer, Port of Boston, 1886-90.
**Miscellaneous:** Resided Lancaster, Coos Co., NH. First cousin of Bvt. Brig. Gen. Loren Kent.
**Buried:** Summer Street Cemetery, Lancaster, NH
**References:** William A. Ellis, editor. *History of Norwich University, 1819-1911.* Montpelier, VT, 1911. John B. Clarke, editor. *Sketches of Successful New Hampshire Men.* Manchester, NH, 1882. Charles N. Kent. *History of the 17th Regiment New Hampshire Volunteer Infantry.* Concord, NH, 1898.

*Henry Oakes Kent*
*Courtesy of the author.*

## John William Kingman

Colonel, 15 NH Infantry, Oct. 7, 1862. Honorably mustered out, Aug. 13, 1863.

**Born:** Jan. 1, 1821 Barrington, NH
**Died:** Dec. 17, 1903 Cedar Falls, IA
**Education:** Attended Phillips Exeter Academy, Exeter, NH. Graduated Harvard University, Cambridge, MA, 1843.
**Occupation:** Lawyer and judge. Late in life engaged with his son in the operation of a paper mill and an oat meal mill.

*John William Kingman*
*History of the 15th Regiment New Hampshire Volunteers.*

*Left:*
*John William Kingman (postwar on horseback)*
*History of the 15th Regiment New Hampshire Volunteers.*

**Offices/Honors:** Associate Justice, Wyoming Territory Supreme Court, 1869-73.

**Miscellaneous:** Resided Dover, Strafford Co., NH, to 1869; Cheyenne, WY, 1869-83; and Cedar Falls, Black Hawk Co., IA, 1883-1903

**Buried:** Pine Hill Cemetery, Dover, NH (Section 4, Avenue H, Lot 169)

**References:** Charles McGregor. *History of the 15th Regiment New Hampshire Volunteers.* Concord, NH, 1900. Obituary, *Cedar Falls Semi-Weekly Gazette*, Dec. 22, 1903. Obituary, *Foster's Weekly Democrat and Dover Enquirer*, Dec. 25, 1903. Otis F. R. Waite. *New Hampshire in the Great Rebellion.* Claremont, NH, 1870.

## James H. Landers

2 Lieutenant, Co. I, 8 NH Infantry, Dec. 20, 1861. 1 Lieutenant, Co. I, 8 NH Infantry, Oct. 28, 1862. Captain, Co. I, 8 NH Infantry, May 6, 1863. Captain, Co. A, 8 NH Veteran Infantry, Jan. 2, 1865. Assistant Commissary of Musters, Staff of Major Gen. Henry W. Slocum, July 21-Oct. 1865. *Colonel,* 8 NH Veteran Infantry, Oct. 28, 1865. Honorably mustered out, Dec. 21, 1865.

**Born:** Aug. 2, 1827 Lee, MA

**Died:** Aug. 18, 1870 Vidalia, LA

**Occupation:** Musical instrument manufacturer before war. Judge of Concordia Parish, LA, after war.

**Offices/Honors:** Member of the Louisiana State Constitutional Convention, 1867.

**Miscellaneous:** Resided Concord, Merrimack Co., NH; and Vidalia, Concordia Parish, LA.

**Buried:** On cenotaph in Blossom Hill Cemetery, Concord, NH, his place of burial is given as Natchez (MS) National Cemetery, but records there do not indicate that he is buried there.

**References:** John M. Stanyan. *History of the 8th Regiment of New Hampshire Volunteers.* Concord, NH, 1892. Obituary, *Concord Republican Statesman*, Sept. 2, 1870.

*Above right:*
*James H. Landers*
*Massachusetts MOLLUS Collection, USAMHI.*

*Right:*
*James H. Landers*
*A History of the 8th Regiment New Hampshire Volunteers.*

## Thomas Leonard Livermore

Private, Co. F, 1 NH Infantry, May 3, 1861. Honorably mustered out, Aug. 9, 1861. 1 Sergeant, Co. K, 5 NH Infantry, Oct. 12, 1861. 2 Lieutenant, Co. K, 5 NH Infantry, June 10, 1862. Shell wound leg, Malvern Hill, VA, July 1, 1862. 1 Lieutenant, Co. K, 5 NH Infantry, Dec. 14, 1862. Captain, Co. E, 5 NH Infantry, March 3, 1863. Captain, Chief of Ambulances, 2 Army Corps, Army of the Potomac, July 1-Dec. 13, 1863. Acting ADC and Acting AQM, Staff of Brig. Gen. Edward W. Hinks, April 20-June 29, 1864. Acting ADC and Acting AIG, Staff of Major Gen. William F. Smith, June 29-July 19, 1864. Acting AIG, Staff of Major Gen. Edward O. C. Ord, July 22-Sept. 3, 1864. Acting AIG, Staff of Major Gen. Winfield S. Hancock, Sept. 3-Nov. 26, 1864. Major, 5 NH Infantry, Oct. 28, 1864. Acting AIG, Staff of Major Gen. Andrew A. Humphreys, Nov. 26, 1864-April 8, 1865. Colonel, 18 NH Infantry, Jan. 17, 1865. Bvt. Colonel, USV, April 7, 1865, for highly valuable and meritorious services. Honorably mustered out, June 23, 1865.

**Born:** Feb. 7, 1844 Galena, IL
**Died:** Jan. 9, 1918 Boston, MA
**Education:** Attended Lombard University, Galesburg, IL.
**Occupation:** Lawyer and mining company executive. Vice President of the Calumet & Hecla Copper Mining Co. for more than 20 years.
**Offices/Honors:** Boston Park Commissioner, 1889-93.
**Miscellaneous:** Resided Milford, Hillsborough Co., NH; Manchester, Hillsborough Co., NH; and Boston, MA.
**Buried:** West Street Cemetery, Milford, NH
**References:** Obituary, *Boston Evening Transcript*, Jan. 10, 1918. Thomas L. Livermore. *Days and Events, 1860-1866.* Boston and New York, 1920. George A. Ramsdell. *History of Milford, NH.* Concord, NH, 1901. William Child. *A History of the 5th Regiment New Hampshire Volunteers.* Bristol, NH, 1893. Thomas L. Livermore. *History of the 18th New Hampshire Volunteers.* Boston, MA, 1904. Obituary Circular, Whole No. 550, Massachusetts MOLLUS.

*Thomas Leonard Livermore*
*Roger D. Hunt Collection, USAMHI. A. Sonrel, 46 School Street Boston, MA.*

*Right:*
*Thomas Leonard Livermore*
*Massachusetts MOLLUS Collection, USAMHI.*

*Thomas Leonard Livermore*
*Massachusetts MOLLUS Collection, USAMHI.*

*Thomas Leonard Livermore*
*Massachusetts MOLLUS Collection, USAMHI.*

*Thomas Leonard Livermore*
*Massachusetts MOLLUS Collection, USAMHI.*

*Thomas Leonard Livermore (postwar)*
*Massachusetts MOLLUS Collection, USAMHI.*

*Thomas Leonard Livermore (postwar)*
*Massachusetts MOLLUS Collection, USAMHI.*

## Charles Hatch Long

Captain, Co. G, 5 NH Infantry, Oct. 12, 1861. GSW left arm, Antietam, MD, Sept. 17, 1862. Lieutenant Colonel, 17 NH Infantry, Oct. 23, 1862. Captain, Co. A, 1 NH Heavy Artillery, April 17, 1863. Commanded Fort Constitution, Portsmouth, NH, July 1863-April 1864. Colonel, 1 NH Heavy Artillery, Sept. 29, 1864. Commanded 1 Brigade, Hardin's Division, Department of Washington, Nov. 10, 1864-June 15, 1865. Honorably mustered out, June 15, 1865.

**Born:** March 14, 1834 Claremont, NH
**Died:** May 30, 1908 Claremont, NH
**Education:** Graduated Norwich (VT) University, 1855.
**Occupation:** Farmer before war. Railroad station agent after war.
**Miscellaneous:** Resided Claremont, Sullivan Co., NH.
**Buried:** West Claremont Burying Ground, Claremont, NH
**References:** *Biographical Review Merrimack and Sullivan Counties, NH.* Boston, MA, 1897. William A. Ellis, editor. *History of Norwich University, 1819-1911.* Montpelier, VT, 1911. Pension File, National Archives. Charles N. Kent. *History of the 17th Regiment New Hampshire Volunteer Infantry.* Concord, NH, 1898.

*Charles Hatch Long*
*Massachusetts MOLLUS Collection, USAMHI.*

*Charles Hatch Long*
*Roger D. Hunt Collection, USAMHI. H.O. Bly, 25 Main Street, Hanover, NH.*

## Thomas Prescott Pierce

Colonel, 2 NH Infantry, April 30, 1861. Resigned June 4, 1861.

**Born:** Aug. 30, 1820 Chelsea, MA
**Died:** Oct. 14, 1887 Nashua, NH
**Other Wars:** Mexican War (1 Lieutenant, 9 US Infantry)
**Occupation:** Carriage and ornamental painter before war. Manufacturer of card board and glazed paper after war.
**Offices/Honors:** Postmaster of Manchester, NH, 1853-61. New Hampshire Senate, 1874. Sheriff of Hillsborough Co., NH, 1875-76.
**Miscellaneous:** Resided Manchester, Hillsborough Co., NH, until 1866; and Nashua, Hillsborough Co., NH, after 1866.
**Buried:** Woodlawn Cemetery, Nashua, NH
**References:** John B. Clarke, editor. *Sketches of Successful New Hampshire Men.* Manchester, NH, 1882. Edward E. Parker, editor. *History of the City of Nashua, NH.* Nashua, NH, 1897. Obituary, *Concord Evening Monitor*, Oct. 15, 1887.

*Thomas Prescott Pierce (postwar)*
*Sketches of Successful New Hampshire Men.*

## James Pike

Colonel, 16 NH Infantry, Nov. 1, 1862. Honorably mustered out, Aug. 20, 1863.

**Born:** Nov. 10, 1818 Salisbury, Essex Co., MA
**Died:** July 26, 1895 Newfields, NH
**Education:** Attended Wesleyan University, Middletown, CT
**Occupation:** Methodist clergyman
**Offices/Honors:** US House of Representatives, 1855-59.
**Miscellaneous:** Resided Newfields, Rockingham Co., NH, after serving many cities in Massachusetts and New Hampshire during his ministerial career. Brother-in-law of Bvt. Brig. Gen. Thornton F. Brodhead.
**Buried:** Locust Grove Cemetery, Newfields, NH
**References:** Luther T. Townsend. *History of the 16th Regiment New Hampshire Volunteers.* Washington, DC, 1897. James H. Fitts. *History of Newfields, NH.* Concord, NH, 1912. *Biographical Directory of the American Congress.*

*James Pike*
*Roger D. Hunt Collection, USAMHI. Davis Brothers, 17 Pleasant Street, Portsmouth, NH.*

## Haldimand Sumner Putnam

2 Lieutenant, Topographical Engineers, April 1, 1861. Acting ADC, Staff of Brig. Gen. Irvin McDowell, May 27-Oct. 17, 1861. 1 Lieutenant, Topographical Engineers, Aug. 3, 1861. Colonel, 7 NH Infantry, Dec. 14, 1861. Commanded Post of St. Augustine, FL, Department of the South, Sept. 3, 1862-March 28, 1863 and April 16-May 10, 1863. Captain, Corps of

Engineers, March 3, 1863. Commanded Post of Fernandina, FL, Department of the South, May 10-June 7, 1863. Commanded 1 Brigade, US Forces Folly Island, SC, Department of the South, June 17-July 14, 1863. Commanded 2 Brigade, US Forces Morris Island, SC, Department of the South, July 14-18, 1863. GSW head, Fort Wagner, SC, July 18, 1863.

**Born:** Oct. 6, 1836 Cornish, NH
**Died:** July 18, 1863 KIA Fort Wagner, SC
**Education:** Graduated US Military Academy, West Point, NY, 1857
**Occupation:** Regular Army (Captain, Corps of Engineers)
**Miscellaneous:** Resided Cornish, Sullivan Co., NH. "As brave a soldier, as courteous a gentleman, as true a man as ever walked beneath the Stars and Stripes." *Official Records,* Vol. 28, Part 1, p. 348.
**Buried:** Fort Wagner, Morris Island, SC (Body never recovered). Cenotaph in Trinity Cemetery, Cornish, NH.
**References:** Henry F. W. Little. *The 7th Regiment New Hampshire Volunteers in the War of the Rebellion.* Concord, NH, 1896. George W. Cullum. *Biographical Register of the Officers and Graduates of the US Military Academy.* Boston and New York, 1891. Otis F. R. Waite. *New Hampshire in the Great Rebellion.* Claremont, NH, 1870. William H. Child. *History of the Town of Cornish, NH.* Concord, NH, 1910.

*Haldimand Sumner Putnam*
*Massachusetts MOLLUS Collection, USAMHI.*

*Right:*
*Haldimand Sumner Putnam*
*Courtesy of Henry Deeks. D.O. Furnald, Manchester, NH.*

*Haldimand Sumner Putnam*
*Frederick H. Meserve. Historical Portraits. Courtesy of New York State Library.*

*Haldimand Sumner Putnam (1857)*
*US Military Academy Library, West Point, NY.*

*Right:*
*Haldimand Sumner Putnam*
*The 7th Regiment New Hampshire Volunteers.*

## Mason Weare Tappan

Colonel, 1 NH Infantry, April 29, 1861. Honorably mustered out, Aug. 9, 1861.

**Born:** Oct. 20, 1817 Newport, NH
**Died:** Oct. 25, 1886 Bradford, NH
**Education:** Attended Kimball Union Academy, Meriden, NH
**Occupation:** Lawyer
**Offices/Honors:** New Hampshire Legislature, 1853-55. US House of Representatives, 1855-61. New Hampshire Attorney General, 1876-86.
**Miscellaneous:** Resided Bradford, Merrimack Co., NH
**Buried:** Pleasant Hill Cemetery, Bradford, NH
**References:** Charles H. Bell. *The Bench and Bar of New Hampshire.* Boston and New York, 1894. Stephen G. Abbott. *The 1st Regiment New Hampshire Volunteers in the Great Rebellion.* Keene, NH, 1890. Mildred H. Gunscheon. *Two Hundred Plus: Bradford, NH, in Retrospect.* Canaan, NH, 1976.

*Mason Weare Tappan*
*Roger D. Hunt Collection, USAMHI. Carr & Morrill, 114 Main Street, Concord, NH.*

*Mason Weare Tappan*
*Roger D. Hunt Collection, USAMHI. Carr's, 114 Main Street, Concord, NH.*

*Mason Weare Tappan*
*Frederick H. Meserve. Historical Portraits. Courtesy of New York State Library.*

*Mason Weare Tappan (postwar)*
*Massachusetts MOLLUS Collection, USAMHI.*

## Thomas Jefferson Whipple

Lieutenant Colonel, 1 NH Infantry, April 29, 1861. Honorably mustered out, Aug. 9, 1861. Colonel, 4 NH Infantry, Aug. 20, 1861. Resigned March 18, 1862, following several instances of "gross intoxication" during which he "deported himself in a manner prejudicial to his position as an officer and a gentleman."

**Born:** Jan. 30, 1816 Wentworth, NH
**Died:** Dec. 21, 1889 Laconia, NH
**Education:** Attended Norwich (VT) University.
**Other Wars:** Mexican War (1 Lieutenant, Adjutant, 9 US Infantry).
**Occupation:** Lawyer
**Miscellaneous:** Resided Laconia, Belknap Co., NH.
**Buried:** Union Cemetery, Laconia, NH
**References:** Stephen G. Abbott. *The 1st Regiment New Hampshire Volunteers in the Great Rebellion.* Keene, NH, 1890. John G. Hutchinson. *Roster 4th Regiment New Hampshire Volunteers.* Manchester, NH, 1896. Charles H. Bell. *The Bench and Bar of New Hampshire.* Boston and New York, 1894. Military Service File, National Archives. Otis F. R. Waite. *New Hampshire in the Great Rebellion.* Claremont, NH, 1870.

## Robert Wilson

Colonel, 14 NH Infantry, Sept. 19, 1862. Commanded District of Carrollton, LA, Department of the Gulf, April 22, 1864-June 12, 1864. Discharged for disability, Sept. 6, 1864, due to the effects of diphtheria, diarrhea and rheumatism.

**Born:** Sept. 24, 1811 Peterborough, NH
**Died:** April 8, 1870 Keene, NH
**Education:** Attended Phillips Exeter Academy, Exeter, NH. Attended Harvard University, Cambridge, MA. Graduated Amherst (MA) College, 1832.
**Occupation:** Lawyer

Thomas Jefferson Whipple
Roger D. Hunt Collection, USAMHI. Kimball & Son, State Block, Corner of Main & School Streets, Concord, NH.

*Robert Wilson*
*Courtesy of Dave Zullo. Brady's National Photographic Portrait Gallery, Broadway & Tenth Street, New York.*

**Offices/Honors:** New Hampshire Legislature, 1868-69
**Miscellaneous:** Resided Keene, Cheshire Co., NH
**Buried:** Woodland Cemetery, Keene, NH
**References:** Francis H. Buffum. *A Memorial of the Great Rebellion: Being a History of the 14th Regiment New Hampshire Volunteers.* Boston, MA, 1882. Otis F. R. Waite. *New Hampshire in the Great Rebellion.* Claremont, NH, 1870.

## Carroll Davidson Wright

2 Lieutenant, Co. C, 14 NH Infantry, Sept. 22, 1862. Acting ADC, Staff of Brig. Gen. John H. Martindale, June 29, 1863-Nov. 7, 1863. 1 Lieutenant, Adjutant, 14 NH Infantry, Dec. 8, 1863. Acting AAG, Staff of Brig. Gen. Henry W. Birge, June 29, 1864-Dec. 28, 1864. Colonel, 14 NH Infantry, Dec. 28, 1864. Discharged for disability, March 18, 1865, due to debility resulting from typho-malarial fever.

**Born:** July 25, 1840 Dunbarton, NH
**Died:** Feb. 20, 1909 Worcester, MA
**Education:** Attended academies in Washington, NH; Alstead, NH; and Chester, VT.
**Occupation:** Lawyer, social economist and statistician. While chief of the Massachusetts Bureau of Labor, he pioneered the compilation of labor statistics.

**Offices/Honors:** Massachusetts State Senate, 1871-72. US Commissioner of Labor, 1885-1905. President of Clark College, Worcester, MA, 1902-09.

**Miscellaneous:** Resided Keene, Cheshire Co., NH; Cambridge, Middlesex Co., MA; Lynn, Essex Co., MA; Boston, MA; Washington, DC; and Worcester, MA.

**Buried:** Laurel Hill Cemetery, Reading, MA

**References:** *Dictionary of American Biography. National Cyclopedia of American Biography.* Francis H. Buffum. *A Memorial of the Great Rebellion: Being a History of the 14th Regiment New Hampshire Volunteers.* Boston, MA, 1882. Pension File, National Archives.

*Carroll Davidson Wright*
*Courtesy of Dave Zullo. B. P. Paige, Photographer, "Plumb Gallery," Washington, DC.*

*Carroll Davidson Wright*
*Roger D. Hunt Collection, USAMHI. G.L. Hurd, 19 Westminster Street, Providence, RI.*

*Right:*
*Carroll Davidson Wright*
*Massachusetts MOLLUS Collection, USAMHI.*

*Chapter V*

# RHODE ISLAND

**1st Cavalry**

| | | |
|---|---|---|
| Robert B. Lawton | Dec. 14, 1861 | Resigned July 1, 1862 |
| Alfred N. Duffie | July 4, 1862 | Promoted **Brig. Gen., USV** June 23, 1863 |

**3rd Cavalry**

| | | |
|---|---|---|
| Willard Sayles | July 1, 1863 | Mustered out Nov. 29, 1865 |

**3rd Heavy Artillery**

| | | |
|---|---|---|
| Asher R. Eddy | Aug. 19, 1861 | Resigned Sept. 17, 1861 |
| Nathaniel W. Brown | Sept. 17, 1861 | Died Oct. 30, 1862 |
| Edwin Metcalf | Nov. 11, 1862 | Resigned Feb. 5, 1864 |
| Charles R. Brayton | March 22, 1864 | Mustered out Oct. 5, 1864 **Bvt. Brig. Gen.** |
| William Ames | Oct. 10, 1864 | Mustered out Aug. 27, 1865 **Bvt. Brig. Gen.** |

**5th Heavy Artillery**

| | | |
|---|---|---|
| Henry T. Sisson | Nov. 5, 1862 | Discharged Oct. 5, 1864 |
| George W. Tew | Oct. 14, 1864 | Mustered out June 26, 1865 **Bvt. Brig. Gen.** |

**14th Heavy Artillery (Colored)**

| | | |
|---|---|---|
| Jacob Hale Sypher | July 5, 1864 | Mustered out Oct. 2, 1865 **Bvt. Brig. Gen.** |

**1st Light Artillery**

| | | |
|---|---|---|
| Charles H. Tompkins | Sept. 13, 1861 | Discharged April 21, 1865 **Bvt. Brig. Gen.** |

**1st Detached Militia**

| | | |
|---|---|---|
| Ambrose E. Burnside | May 2, 1861 | Mustered out Aug. 2, 1861 Later **Major Gen., USV** |

**2nd Infantry**

| | | |
|---|---|---|
| John S. Slocum | June 5, 1861 | KIA July 21, 1861 |
| Frank Wheaton | July 21, 1861 | Promoted **Brig. Gen., USV** Nov. 29, 1862 |
| Nelson Viall | Dec. 13, 1862 | Resigned Jan. 25, 1863 **Bvt. Brig. Gen.** |
| Horatio Rogers, Jr. | Jan. 31, 1863 | Resigned Jan. 15, 1864 **Bvt. Brig. Gen.** |
| Samuel B. M. Read | June 1, 1864 | Mustered out June 17, 1864 |
| George E. Church | Dec. 31, 1864 | Not mustered |
| Elisha H. Rhodes | July 18, 1865 | Mustered out July 28, 1865 |

**4th Infantry**

| | | |
|---|---|---|
| Justus I. McCarty | Aug. 15, 1861 | Commission revoked |
| Isaac P. Rodman | Oct. 30, 1861 | Promoted **Brig. Gen., USV** May 16, 1862 |
| William H. P. Steere | June 12, 1862 | Mustered out Oct. 15, 1864 **Bvt. Brig. Gen.** |

**7th Infantry**

| | | |
|---|---|---|
| Zenas R. Bliss | Aug. 14, 1862 | Mustered out June 28, 1865 |

**9th Infantry**

| | | |
|---|---|---|
| Charles T. Robbins | May 25, 1862 | To Major Gen., RI National Guard, June 1862 |
| John T. Pitman | July 3, 1862 | Mustered out Sept. 2, 1862 |

**10th Infantry**

| | | |
|---|---|---|
| Zenas R. Bliss | May 26, 1862 | To 7th RI Infantry, Aug. 6, 1862 |
| James Shaw, Jr. | Aug. 11, 1862 | Mustered out Sept. 1, 1862 **Bvt. Brig. Gen.** |

**11th Infantry**

| | | |
|---|---|---|
| Edwin Metcalf | Sept. 15, 1862 | To 3rd RI Heavy Artillery, Nov. 11, 1862 |
| Horatio Rogers, Jr. | Dec. 27, 1862 | To 2nd RI Infantry, Jan. 31, 1863 **Bvt. Brig. Gen.** |
| George E. Church | Feb. 11, 1863 | Mustered out July 13, 1863 |

**12th Infantry**

| | | |
|---|---|---|
| George H. Browne | Sept. 18, 1862 | Mustered out July 29, 1863 |

## Zenas Randall Bliss

1 Lieutenant, 8 US Infantry, Oct. 17, 1860. Captured San Lucas Spring, TX, May 9, 1861. Captain, 8 US Infantry, May 14, 1861. Confined at San Antonio, TX, and Richmond, VA. Paroled April 5, 1862. Colonel, 10 RI Infantry, May 26, 1862. Colonel, 7 RI Infantry, Aug. 21, 1862. Commanded 1 Brigade, 2 Division, 9 Army Corps, Aug. 30, 1863-Sept. 30, 1863; May 5-6, 1864; July 4-11, 1864; and July 25, 1864-Aug. 21, 1864. Commanded 2 Division, 9 Army Corps, March 16, 1864-April 2, 1864. Honorably mustered out of volunteer service, June 28, 1865.

**Born:** April 17, 1835 Johnston, RI
**Died:** Jan. 2, 1900 Washington, DC
**Education:** Graduated US Military Academy, West Point, NY, 1854
**Occupation:** Regular Army (Major General, retired May 22, 1897)
**Offices/Honors:** Medal of Honor, Fredericksburg, VA, Dec. 13, 1862. "This officer, to encourage his regiment which had never before been in action and which had been or-

*Zenas Randall Bliss*
*Roger D. Hunt Collection, USAMHI. Henry Ulke, 278 Pennsylvania Avenue, Washington, DC.*

*Zenas Randall Bliss*
*Courtesy of Michael J. McAfee.*

Zenas Randall Bliss (left), with Major Jacob Babbitt
Massachusetts MOLLUS Collection, USAMHI.

Zenas Randall Bliss (postwar)
Massachusetts MOLLUS Collection, USAMHI.

dered to lie down to protect itself from the enemy's fire, rose to his feet, advanced in front of the line, and himself fired several shots at the enemy at short range, being fully exposed to their fire at the time."

**Miscellaneous:** Resided Providence, RI; and Washington, DC

**Buried:** Arlington National Cemetery, Arlington, VA (Section 1, Lot 8-B)

**References:** William P. Hopkins. *The 7th Regiment Rhode Island Volunteers in the Civil War.* Providence, RI, 1903. Aaron T. Bliss. *Genealogy of the Bliss Family in America.* Midland, MI, 1982. William A. Spicer. *History of the 9th and 10th Regiments Rhode Island Volunteers.* Providence, RI, 1892.

## Nathaniel Williams Brown

Nathaniel Williams Brown
Massachusetts MOLLUS Collection, USAMHI.

Captain, Co. D, 1 RI Detached Militia, May 2, 1861. Honorably mustered out, Aug. 2, 1861. Colonel, 3 RI Heavy Artillery, Sept. 17, 1861. Commanded Post of Hilton Head, SC, Department of the South, June 1862. Commanded US Forces, Hilton Head, SC, Department of the South, Sept. 3-Oct. 5, 1862. Chief of Artillery, Staff of Major General Ormsby M. Mitchel, Department of the South, Oct. 11, 1862-Oct. 30, 1862.

**Born:** Feb. 22, 1811 Dighton, MA
**Died:** Oct. 30, 1862 Hilton Head, SC, of yellow fever
**Occupation:** Manufacturer of woolen goods
**Offices/Honors:** For several years, Lieutenant Colonel, 1st Light Infantry of Providence, RI
**Miscellaneous:** Resided Dighton, Bristol Co., MA; and Providence, RI
**Buried:** North Burial Ground, Providence, RI (Section 14, Lot 566)
**References:** John Russell Bartlett. *Memoirs of Rhode Island Officers*. Providence, RI, 1867. Obituary, *Providence Journal*, Nov. 6, 1862. Frederic Denison. *Shot and Shell: The 3rd Rhode Island Heavy Artillery Regiment in the Rebellion*. Providence, RI, 1879.

*Nathaniel Williams Brown*
*Massachusetts MOLLUS Collection, USAMHI.*

## George Huntington Browne

Colonel, 12 RI Infantry, Sept. 18, 1862. Honorably mustered out, July 29, 1863.

**Born:** Jan. 6, 1818 Glocester, RI
**Died:** Sept. 26, 1885 Providence, RI
**Education:** Graduated Brown University, Providence, RI, 1840
**Occupation:** Lawyer
**Offices/Honors:** US District Attorney for Rhode Island, 1853-61. US House of Representatives, 1861-63. Rhode Island Senate, 1872-73. Declined Chief Judgeship of the Rhode Island Supreme Court, 1874.
**Miscellaneous:** Resided Chepachet, Providence Co., RI; and Providence, RI
**Buried:** Swan Point Cemetery, Providence, RI (Group 194, Lot 4)
**References:** Obituary, *Providence Journal*, Sept. 27, 1885. *History of the 12th Regiment Rhode Island Volunteers in the Civil War*. Providence, RI, 1904. John Russell Bartlett. *Memoirs of Rhode Island Officers*. Providence, RI, 1867.

## George Earl Church

Captain, Co. C, 7 RI Infantry, Sept. 4, 1862. Lieutenant Colonel, 7 RI Infantry, Jan. 7, 1863. Colonel, 11 RI Infantry, Feb. 11, 1863. Commanded 2 Brigade, 1 Division, 4 Army Corps, Department of Virginia, June 17, 1863-July 13, 1863. Honorably mustered out, July 13, 1863. Appointed Colonel, 2 RI In-

*Right:*
*George Huntington Browne*
*Massachusetts MOLLUS Collection, USAMHI. Manchester Brothers, Photographers, 73 Westminster Street, Providence, RI.*

fantry, Dec. 31, 1864, but never joined regiment because the reduced strength of the regiment would not permit the mustering of a colonel.

**Born:** Dec. 7, 1835 New Bedford, MA
**Died:** Jan. 5, 1910 London, England
**Occupation:** Civil engineer, primarily engaged in railroad construction in South America. Became a leading authority on the history, geography and resources of tropical South America through participation in many exploring expeditions and various enterprises aimed at opening the continent to economic development.
**Offices/Honors:** Vice President of the Royal Geographical Society of England for four years.
**Miscellaneous:** Resided Providence, RI; and London, England
**Buried:** Brompton Cemetery, London, England
**References:** John A. Church. *Descendants of Richard Church of Plymouth, MA.* Rutland, VT, 1913. Obituary Circular, Whole No. 1019, New York MOLLUS. Obituary, *London Times*, Jan. 6, 1910. William P. Hopkins. *The 7th Regiment Rhode Island Volunteers in the Civil War.* Providence, RI, 1903.

*George Earl Church*
*The 7th Regiment Rhode Island Volunteers in the Civil War.*

## Asher Robbins Eddy

Captain, AQM, USA, Feb. 12, 1861. *Colonel*, 3 RI Infantry (later 3 RI Heavy Artillery), Aug. 19, 1861. Resigned Sept. 17, 1861, in order to resume Regular Army position. Chief Quartermaster, Springfield, IL, Sept. 27, 1861-Jan. 25, 1862. Depot Quartermaster, Memphis, TN, Oct. 1862-Aug. 24, 1864. Disbursing Officer, US Military Railroads, Nashville, TN, Sept. 27-Dec. 31, 1864. Chief Quartermaster, District of West Tennessee, April 24-Oct. 16, 1865. Chief Quartermaster, Department of the Tennessee, Nov. 6, 1865-April 6, 1866. Bvt. Colonel, USA, March 13, 1865, for faithful and meritorious services during the war.

**Born:** Nov. 1, 1823 Newport, RI
**Died:** Jan. 27, 1879 Island of Malta
**Education:** Graduated US Military Academy, West Point, NY, 1844
**Occupation:** Regular Army (Lieutenant Colonel, Deputy Quartermaster General, June 6, 1872)
**Miscellaneous:** Resided San Francisco, CA
**Buried:** San Francisco National Cemetery, San Francisco, CA (Section OS, Plot 6, Grave 6)
**References:** *Annual Reunion,* Association of the Graduates of the USMA, 1879. George W. Cullum. *Biographical Register of the Officers and Graduates of the USMA.* Boston and New York, 1891. Edwin W. Stone. *Rhode Island in the Rebellion.* Providence, RI, 1864. Ruth A. Breck, editor. *The Eddy Family in America. Supplement 1968.* Middleboro, MA, 1971. Pension File, National Archives.

## Robert Brown Lawton

Colonel, 1 RI Cavalry, Dec. 14, 1861. Claiming debility due to diarrhea and hemorrhage, he left his regiment and hid away in Bridgewater, MA, while Rhode Island Governor William Sprague, citing his "inattention and carelessness," petitioned the War Department for his dismissal. Discharged July 1, 1862, by order of the Secretary of War.

**Born:** Feb. 8, 1806 Newport, RI
**Died:** May 11, 1876 Newport, RI
**Other Wars:** Seminole War (1 Lieutenant, 2 US Dragoons, resigned Oct. 8, 1841). Mexican War (Captain of the Port of Vera Cruz).
**Occupation:** Followed the trade of a machinist after spending several years as a sailor. As evidence of his mechanical ingenuity, he received a patent for a form of hose coupling.

**Miscellaneous:** Resided Pawtucket, RI; and Newport, RI
**Buried:** Common Burial Ground, Newport, RI
**References:** Obituary, *Providence Journal*, May 12-13, 15, 1876. Obituary, *Newport Daily News*, May 12, 1876. Elva Lawton. *The Descendants of George Lawton of Portsmouth, RI.* Seattle, WA, 1977. Military Service File, National Archives. Frederic Denison. *Sabres and Spurs: The 1st Regiment Rhode Island Cavalry in the Civil War.* Central Falls, RI, 1876.

## Justus Ingersoll McCarty

*Colonel*, 4 RI Infantry, Aug. 15, 1861. Commission revoked, Oct. 30, 1861.

**Born:** 1816? NY
**Died:** June 8, 1881 Washington, DC
**Other Wars:** Mexican War (Major, 10 US Infantry)
**Occupation:** Lawyer
**Miscellaneous:** Resided New York City, NY; and Washington, DC
**Buried:** Oak Hill Cemetery, Washington, DC (Lot 260 East, unmarked)
**References:** Obituary, *Washington Evening Star*, June 9, 1881. Pension File, National Archives. George H. Allen. *Forty-Six Months with the 4th Rhode Island Volunteers.* Providence, RI, 1887.

*Robert Brown Lawton*
*Massachusetts MOLLUS Collection, USAMHI. Brady's National Photographic Portrait Gallery, 352 Pennsylvania Avenue, Washington, DC.*

*Left:*
*Justus Ingersoll McCarty (postwar)*
*Massachusetts MOLLUS Collection, USAMHI.*

## Edwin Metcalf

Major, 3 RI Heavy Artillery, Aug. 27, 1861. Colonel, 11 RI Infantry, Sept. 15, 1862. Colonel, 3 RI Heavy Artillery, Nov. 11, 1862. Commanded Artillery Brigade, Department of the South, April 1863. Chief of Artillery and Ordnance, 10 Army Corps, May 5-July 6, 1863. Commanded US Forces, Hilton Head, SC, Department of the South, July 6, 1863-Aug. 6, 1863.

Commanded Fort Pulaski, near Savannah, GA, Nov. 22, 1863-Feb. 5, 1864. Resigned Feb. 5, 1864, with charges of habitual intoxication pending, to "relieve the regiment from the unpleasant consequences of my recent conduct."

**Born:** Aug. 23, 1823 Providence, RI
**Died:** Jan. 18, 1894 Providence, RI
**Education:** Graduated Brown University, Providence, RI, 1842. Attended Harvard University Law School, Cambridge, MA.
**Occupation:** Lawyer
**Offices/Honors:** Rhode Island House of Representatives, 1861-62. Speaker of Rhode Island House of Representatives, 1873-74. Rhode Island Senate, 1874-75. Rhode Island Attorney General, 1886.
**Miscellaneous:** Resided Providence, RI
**Buried:** Swan Point Cemetery, Providence, RI (Group FCS, Lot 354)
**References:** *Biographical Cyclopedia of Representative Men of Rhode Island.* Providence, RI, 1881. John Russell Bartlett. *Memoirs of Rhode Island Officers.* Providence, RI, 1867. Obituary, *Providence Journal*, Jan. 19, 1894. Military Service File, National Archives.

*Edwin Metcalf*
*Courtesy of the Rhode Island Historical Society.*

*Edwin Metcalf (postwar)*
*National Archives.*

*Right:*
*Edwin Metcalf (postwar)*
*Courtesy of the Rhode Island Historical Society.*

## John Talbot Pitman

Captain, Co. G, 1 RI Detached Militia, May 11, 1861. Honorably mustered out, Aug. 2, 1861. Major, 9 RI Infantry, May 26, 1862. Lieutenant Colonel, 9 RI Infantry, June 9, 1862. Colonel, 9 RI Infantry, July 3, 1862. Honorably mustered out, Sept. 2, 1862. Lieutenant Colonel, 11 RI Infantry, Sept. 16, 1862. "I see him now, mounted on his horse, ... wearing a moth-eaten blouse and an exceedingly dilapidated straw hat, with a very black 'T.D.' clay pipe stuck in his mouth, the bowl downwards." Nickerson. Honorably mustered out, July 13, 1863.

**Born:** Nov. 26, 1813 Salem, MA
**Died:** Oct. 30, 1892 Frankford, Philadelphia Co., PA
**Education:** Attended Harvard University Law School, Cambridge, MA
**Occupation:** Lawyer and US pension agent
**Miscellaneous:** Resided Providence, RI
**Buried:** Swan Point Cemetery, Providence, RI (Group 96, Lot 2)
**References:** Obituary, *Providence Journal*, Nov. 1, 1892. Obituary, *Philadelphia Public Ledger*, Nov. 1, 1892. Ansel D. Nickerson. *A Raw Recruit's War Experiences.* Providence, RI, 1888. William A. Spicer. *History of the 9th and 10th Regiments Rhode Island Volunteers.* Providence, RI, 1892. John C. Thompson. *History of the 11th Regiment Rhode Island Volunteers in the War of the Rebellion.* Providence, RI, 1881.

## Samuel Brinton Mumford Read

1 Lieutenant, Co. E, 2 RI Infantry, June 6, 1861. Captain, Co. I, 2 RI Infantry, July 22, 1861. Acting AAG, 2 Brigade, 3 Division, 6 Army Corps, Dec. 1862-April 1863. Lieutenant Colonel, 2 RI Infantry, March 13, 1863. Acting AIG, 3 Division, 6 Army Corps, July 31, 1863-March 1864. GSW thigh, Wilderness, VA, May 5, 1864. Shell wound head and neck, Spotsylvania, VA, May 12, 1864. *Colonel,* 2 RI Infantry, June 1, 1864. Honorably mustered out, June 17, 1864.

**Born:** Dec. 22, 1834 Newport, RI
**Died:** June 5, 1895 Cambridge, MA
**Occupation:** Jeweller before war. Provisions merchant and express messenger after war.

*Right:*
*John Talbot Pitman*
*Massachusetts MOLLUS Collection, USAMHI. Brady's National Photographic Portrait Gallery, Broadway & Tenth Street, New York.*

**Miscellaneous:** Resided Sandusky, OH; Lincoln, NE; Providence, RI; Boston, MA; and Cambridge, MA.
**Buried:** Cambridge Cemetery, Cambridge, MA (Wisteria Path, Lot 2312)
**References:** Pension File, National Archives. Obituary, *Boston Evening Transcript*, June 6, 1895. Augustus Woodbury. *The 2nd Rhode Island Regiment.* Providence, RI, 1875. Robert Hunt Rhodes, editor. *All for the Union.* Lincoln, RI, 1985.

Samuel Brinton Mumford Read
Massachusetts MOLLUS Collection, USAMHI.

## Elisha Hunt Rhodes

Corporal, Co. D, 2 RI Infantry, June 5, 1861. Sergeant Major, 2 RI Infantry, March 1, 1862. 2 Lieutenant, Co. D, 2 RI Infantry, July 24, 1862. 1 Lieutenant, Co. D, 2 RI Infantry, March 2, 1863. 1 Lieutenant, Adjutant, 2 RI Infantry, Nov. 6, 1863. Captain, Co. B, 2 RI Infantry, June 26, 1864. Lieutenant Colonel, 2 RI Infantry, Feb. 6, 1865. Bvt. Colonel, USV, April 2, 1865, for gallant and meritorious services before Petersburg, VA. *Colonel,* 2 RI Infantry, July 18, 1865. Honorably mustered out, July 28, 1865.

**Born:** March 21, 1842 Pawtuxet, RI
**Died:** Jan. 14, 1917 Providence, RI
**Occupation:** Manufacturer of textile mill supplies
**Offices/Honors:** Senior Vice-Commander-in-Chief, GAR, 1877. US Collector of Internal Revenue, District of Rhode Island, 1875-85. Brig. Gen., Rhode Island State Militia, 1879-93.
**Miscellaneous:** Resided Pawtuxet, RI; and Providence, RI
**Buried:** Swan Point Cemetery, Providence, RI (Group 416, Lot 94)
**References:** Robert Hunt Rhodes, editor. *All for the Union.* Lincoln, RI, 1985. John Russell Bartlett. *Memoirs of Rhode Island Officers.* Providence, RI, 1867. Augustus Woodbury. *The 2nd Rhode Island Regiment.* Providence, RI, 1875. Obituary, *Providence Journal*, Jan. 15, 1917.

Samuel Brinton Mumford Read
Massachusetts MOLLUS Collection, USAMHI.

## Charles Thomas Robbins

*Colonel*, 9 RI Infantry, May 25, 1862. Accompanied regiment to Washington, DC, but then yielded colonelcy to Lieutenant Colonel John Talbot Pitman, and returned to position as Brig. Gen., RI National Guard.

**Born:** July 31, 1822 Providence, RI
**Died:** Nov. 4, 1868 Providence, RI
**Occupation:** Bank cashier and politician

*Elisha Hunt Rhodes*
*Massachusetts MOLLUS Collection, USAMHI. Carpenter & Lord, Photographers, successors to Frank Rowell, 25 Westminster Street, Providence, RI.*

*Elisha Hunt Rhodes*
*Massachusetts MOLLUS Collection, USAMHI.*

*Right:*
*Elisha Hunt Rhodes (postwar)*
*Massachusetts MOLLUS Collection, USAMHI.*

**Offices/Honors:** Brigadier General, and later Major General, RI National Guard. President, Providence Common Council, 1855-56.
**Miscellaneous:** Resided Providence, RI
**Buried:** Swan Point Cemetery, Providence, RI (Group 18, Lot 3)
**References:** *Transactions of the Rhode Island Society for the Encouragement of Domestic Industry in the Year 1868.* Providence, RI, 1869. Obituary, *Providence Daily Journal*, Nov. 5, 1868. William A. Spicer. *History of the 9th and 10th Regiments Rhode Island Volunteers.* Providence, RI, 1892.

*Willard Sayles (postwar)*
*Representative Men and Old Families of Rhode Island.*

## Willard Sayles

Major, 1 RI Cavalry, Sept. 27, 1861. Lieutenant Colonel, 1 RI Cavalry, Feb. 21, 1862. Resigned July 7, 1862, due to the "appointment of a colonel (Alfred N. Duffie) to our regiment who is a foreigner and an entire stranger to officers and men." Colonel, 3 RI Cavalry, July 1, 1863. Commanded Post of Napoleonville, LA, District of La Fourche, Department of the Gulf, Oct. 1864-May 1865. Honorably mustered out, Nov. 29, 1865.

**Born:** Aug. 30, 1822 Mendon, MA
**Died:** April 18, 1903 Providence, RI
**Education:** Graduated Brown University, Providence, RI, 1844
**Occupation:** Lawyer
**Offices/Honors:** Providence City Solicitor, 1855. Rhode Island Attorney General, 1867-82.
**Miscellaneous:** Resided Providence, RI; and New Orleans, LA
**Buried:** Swan Point Cemetery, Providence, RI (Group 155, Lot 5)
**References:** *Representative Men and Old Families of Rhode Island.* Chicago, IL, 1908. Obituary, *Providence Journal*, April 19, 1903. Judith A. Hurst. *Sayles Country.* Baltimore, MD, 1986. Frederic Denison. *Sabres and Spurs: The 1st Regiment Rhode Island Cavalry in the Civil War.* Central Falls, RI, 1876.

*Henry Tillinghast Sisson*
*Massachusetts MOLLUS Collection, USAMHI.*

## Henry Tillinghast Sisson

1 Lieutenant, Paymaster, 1 RI Detached Militia, May 2, 1861. Honorably mustered out, Aug. 2, 1861. Major, 3 RI Heavy Artillery, April 11, 1862. Resigned Aug. 6, 1862, to recruit another regiment. Colonel, 5 RI Heavy Artillery, Nov. 5, 1862. Discharged for disability, Oct. 5, 1864, due to malarial disease with chronic diarrhea.

*Henry Tillinghast Sisson*
*Massachusetts MOLLUS Collection, USAMHI.*

*John Stanton Slocum*
*Massachusetts MOLLUS Collection, USAMHI.*

**Born:** Aug. 20, 1831 Fall River, MA
**Died:** Oct. 19, 1910 East Providence, RI
**Education:** Attended Gorham (ME) Academy and University Grammar School, Providence, RI
**Occupation:** Farmer, merchant and manufacturer before war. Cotton mills superintendent and graphite manufacturer after war.
**Offices/Honors:** Lieutenant Governor of Rhode Island, 1875-77. Statue at his gravesite was jointly financed by the states of Massachusetts and Rhode Island in recognition for his role in raising the siege of Washington, NC, April 13, 1863.
**Miscellaneous:** Resided Little Compton, Newport Co., RI, to 1901; East Providence, RI, 1901-10.
**Buried:** Union Cemetery, Little Compton, RI
**References:** Richard M. Bayles, editor. *History of Newport County, RI.* New York City, NY, 1888. Pension File, National Archives. John Russell Bartlett. *Memoirs of Rhode Island Officers.* Providence, RI, 1867. John K. Burlingame. *History of the 5th Regiment of Rhode Island Heavy Artillery.* Providence, RI, 1892.

## John Stanton Slocum

Major, 1 RI Detached Militia, May 2, 1861. Colonel, 2 RI Infantry, June 5, 1861. GSW head, Bull Run VA, July 21, 1861.

**Born:** Nov. 1, 1824 Richmond, RI
**Died:** July 21, 1861 KIA Bull Run, VA
**Education:** Attended Trinity College, Hartford, CT
**Other Wars:** Mexican War (Captain, 9 US Infantry)
**Occupation:** Engaged with his father-in-law, Charles T. James, in the improvement, manufacture, and sale of the James cannon and projectiles
**Miscellaneous:** Resided Providence, RI
**Buried:** Swan Point Cemetery, Providence, RI (Group 236, Lot 3)
**References:** *Memorial of Colonel John Stanton Slocum.* Providence, RI, 1886. John R. Bartlett. *Memoirs of Rhode Island Officers.* Providence, RI, 1867. Augustus Woodbury. *A Narrative of the Campaign of the 1st Rhode Island Regiment.* Providence, RI, 1862. Augustus Woodbury. *The 2nd Rhode Island Regiment.* Providence, RI, 1875.

*Chapter VI*

# VERMONT

**1st Cavalry**

| | | |
|---|---|---|
| Lemuel B. Platt | Sept. 4, 1861 | Resigned Feb. 27, 1862 |
| Jonas P. Holliday | Feb. 14, 1862 | Died April 5, 1862 |
| Charles H. Tompkins | April 24, 1862 | Resigned Sept. 9, 1862 **Bvt. Brig. Gen.** |
| Edward B. Sawyer | Sept. 16, 1862 | Resigned April 28, 1864 |
| Addison W. Preston | April 29, 1864 | KIA June 3, 1864 |
| William Wells | June 4, 1864 | Promoted **Brig. Gen., USV** May 19, 1865 |
| Josiah Hall | May 23, 1865 | Mustered out June 21, 1865 |

**1st Heavy Artillery**

| | | |
|---|---|---|
| James M. Warner | Aug. 15, 1862 | Promoted **Brig. Gen., USV** May 8, 1865 |
| Charles Hunsdon | May 23, 1865 | Mustered out June 24, 1865 |

**1st Infantry**

| | | |
|---|---|---|
| John W. Phelps | April 26, 1861 | Promoted **Brig. Gen., USV** May 17, 1861 |

**2nd Infantry**

| | | |
|---|---|---|
| Henry Whiting | June 6, 1861 | Resigned Feb. 9, 1863 |
| James H. Walbridge | Feb. 9, 1863 | Resigned April 1, 1864 |
| Newton Stone | April 2, 1864 | KIA May 5, 1864 |
| John S. Tyler | May 6, 1864 | DOW May 23, 1864 |
| Amasa S. Tracy | June 7, 1865 | Mustered out July 15, 1865 |

**3rd Infantry**

| | | |
|---|---|---|
| William F. Smith | April 27, 1861 | Promoted **Brig. Gen., USV** Aug. 13, 1861 |
| Breed N. Hyde | Aug. 13, 1861 | Resigned Jan. 15, 1863 |
| Thomas O. Seaver | Jan. 15, 1863 | Mustered out July 27, 1864 |
| Horace W. Floyd | June 4, 1865 | Mustered out July 11, 1865 |

**4th Infantry**

| | | |
|---|---|---|
| Edwin H. Stoughton | Aug. 1, 1861 | Promoted **Brig. Gen., USV** Nov. 5, 1862 |
| Charles B. Stoughton | Nov. 5, 1862 | Resigned Feb. 2, 1864 **Bvt. Brig. Gen.** |
| George P. Foster | Feb. 3, 1864 | Mustered out July 13, 1865 **Bvt. Brig. Gen.** |

**5th Infantry**

| | | |
|---|---|---|
| Henry A. Smalley | July 30, 1861 | Resigned Sept. 10, 1862 **Bvt. Brig. Gen.** |
| Lewis A. Grant | Sept. 16, 1862 | Promoted **Brig. Gen., USV** April 27, 1864 |
| John R. Lewis | May 6, 1864 | To VRC Sept. 4, 1864 **Bvt. Brig. Gen.** |
| Ronald A. Kennedy | June 9, 1865 | Mustered out June 29, 1865 |

**6th Infantry**

| | | |
|---|---|---|
| Nathan Lord, Jr. | Sept. 16, 1861 | Resigned Dec. 18, 1862 |
| Oscar S. Tuttle | Dec. 18, 1862 | Resigned March 18, 1863 |
| Elisha L. Barney | March 18, 1863 | DOW May 10, 1864 |
| Sumner H. Lincoln | June 4, 1865 | Mustered out June 26, 1865 |

**7th Infantry**

| | | |
|---|---|---|
| George T. Roberts | Dec. 5, 1861 | DOW Aug. 7, 1862 |
| William C. Holbrook | Aug. 27, 1862 | Resigned June 2, 1865 |
| David B. Peck | June 29, 1865 | Mustered out Aug. 26, 1865 |
| Henry M. Porter | Sept. 1, 1865 | Mustered out March 14, 1866 |

**8th Infantry**

| | | |
|---|---|---|
| Stephen Thomas | Nov. 12, 1861 | Promoted **Brig. Gen., USV** Feb. 1, 1865 |
| John B. Mead | March 4, 1865 | Mustered out June 28, 1865 |

**9th Infantry**

| | | |
|---|---|---|
| George J. Stannard | May 21, 1862 | Promoted **Brig. Gen., USV** March 11, 1863 |
| Dudley K. Andross | March 20, 1863 | Resigned May 22, 1863 |
| Edward H. Ripley | May 22, 1863 | Mustered out June 13, 1865 **Bvt. Brig. Gen.** |

**10th Infantry**

| | | |
|---|---|---|
| Albert B. Jewett | Aug. 26, 1862 | Resigned April 25, 1864 |
| William W. Henry | April 26, 1864 | Resigned Dec. 17, 1864 **Bvt. Brig. Gen.** |
| George B. Damon | June 15, 1865 | Mustered out June 28, 1865 |

**11th Infantry** (see 1st Heavy Artillery)

**12th Infantry**

| | | |
|---|---|---|
| Asa P. Blunt | Sept. 19, 1862 | Mustered out July 14, 1863<br>**Bvt. Brig. Gen.** |

**13th Infantry**

| | | |
|---|---|---|
| Francis V. Randall | Sept. 24, 1862 | Mustered out July 21, 1863 |

**14th Infantry**

| | | |
|---|---|---|
| William T. Nichols | Sept. 25, 1862 | Mustered out July 30, 1863 |

**15th Infantry**

| | | |
|---|---|---|
| Redfield Proctor | Sept. 26, 1862 | Mustered out Aug. 5, 1863 |

**16th Infantry**

| | | |
|---|---|---|
| Wheelock G. Veazey | Sept. 27, 1862 | Mustered out Aug. 10, 1863 |

**17th Infantry**

| | | |
|---|---|---|
| Francis V. Randall | Feb. 10, 1864 | Mustered out July 14, 1865 |

## Dudley Kimball Andross

Captain, Co. D, 1 VT Infantry, May 1, 1861. Honorably mustered out, Aug. 15, 1861. Lieutenant Colonel, 9 VT Infantry, May 26, 1862. Captured Harper's Ferry, WV, Sept. 15, 1862. Sent to Chicago, IL, as paroled prisoner. Exchanged Jan. 10, 1863. Colonel, 9 VT Infantry, March 20, 1863. Discharged for disability, May 22, 1863, due to chronic bronchitis and acute tonsilitis. "... tall, straight, soldierly, rough in his way, but kind in deed, he was a favorite with the men." Vermont MOLLUS.

**Born:** Sept. 12, 1823 Bradford, VT
**Died:** Nov. 28, 1906 Bradford, VT
**Occupation:** Early in life a lumberman, he also engaged in railroad building and the fur business. Farmer and grist mill operator in later years.
**Miscellaneous:** Resided Bradford, Orange Co., VT.
**Buried:** Sawyer Cemetery, Bradford, VT
**References:** Silas McKeen. *History of Bradford, VT.* Montpelier, VT, 1875. Pension File, National Archives. George G. Benedict. *Vermont in the Civil War.* Burlington, VT, 1886. Obituary Circular, Whole No. 147, Vermont MOLLUS.

*Dudley Kimball Andross*
*USAMHI. S.M. Fassett, Artist, 122 & 124 Clark Street, Chicago, IL.*

## Elisha L. Barney

Captain, Co. K, 6 VT Infantry, Oct. 15, 1861. GSW head, Crampton's Gap, MD, Sept. 14, 1862. Major, 6 VT Infantry, Oct. 15, 1862. Lieutenant Colonel, 6 VT Infantry, Dec. 18, 1862. Colonel, 6 VT Infantry, March 18, 1863. GSW head, Wilderness, VA, May 5, 1864.

**Born:** April 13, 1832 Swanton, VT
**Died:** May 10, 1864 DOW Fredericksburg, VA
**Occupation:** Merchant in partnership with Colonel Albert B. Jewett.
**Miscellaneous:** Resided Swanton, Franklin Co., VT; and Dubuque, IA, 1851-59.
**Buried:** Church Street Cemetery, Swanton, VT
**References:** George G. Benedict. *Vermont in the Civil War.* Burlington, VT, 1886. Eugene D. Preston. *Genealogy of the Barney Family in America.* N.p., 1990. Obituary, *Rutland Weekly Herald*, May 26, 1864.

*Right:*
*Elisha L. Barney*
*Massachusetts MOLLUS Collection, USAMHI. Brady's National Portrait Gallery. Published by E. & H. T. Anthony, 501 Broadway, New York.*

## George B. Damon

Captain, Co. G, 10 VT Infantry, Aug. 12, 1862. Judge Advocate, 3 Division, 3 Army Corps, Nov. 1863-March 24, 1864. Judge Advocate, 3 Division, 6 Army Corps, March 24-Dec. 18, 1864. Major, 10 VT Infantry, Dec. 19, 1864. Lieutenant Colonel, 10 VT Infantry, Jan. 2, 1865. Bvt. Colonel, USV, April 2, 1865, for gallant and meritorious services before Petersburg, VA. *Colonel,* 10 VT Infantry, June 15, 1865. Honorably mustered out, June 28, 1865.

**Born:** March 31, 1835 Hatley, Quebec, Canada
**Died:** April 20, 1885 Des Moines, IA
**Education:** Attended academies of Glover and Barton, VT.
**Occupation:** Lawyer before war. Lawyer and school book agent after war.
**Miscellaneous:** Resided Bradford, Orange Co., VT; Cincinnati, OH; St. Louis, MO; Boston, MA; and Des Moines, IA.
**Buried:** Woodland Cemetery, Des Moines, IA (Public Ground, Row 1, Grave 29, unmarked)
**References:** Edwin M. Haynes. *A History of the 10th Regiment Vermont Volunteers.* Rutland, VT, 1894. Obituary, *Des Moines Iowa State Register*, April 21, 1885. Pension File, National Archives. George G. Benedict. *Vermont in the Civil War.* Burlington, VT, 1886.

*George B. Damon*
*Roger D. Hunt Collection, USAMHI. Styles' Vermont Gallery of Art (on the first floor), 150 Church Street, Burlington, VT.*

## Horace Whitmore Floyd

2 Lieutenant, Co. A, 3 VT Infantry, May 21, 1861. 1 Lieutenant, Co. F, 3 VT Infantry, Aug. 13, 1861. 1 Lieutenant, Co. A, 3 VT Infantry, Dec. 1, 1861. Captain, Co. C, 3 VT Infantry, Sept. 22, 1862. GSW hand, Spotsylvania, VA, May 12, 1864. Major, 3 VT Infantry, Aug. 4, 1864. Lieutenant Colonel, 3 VT Infantry, Oct. 18, 1864. Bvt. Colonel, USV, Oct. 19, 1864, for gallantry and good conduct throughout the present campaign before Richmond, VA, and in the Shenandoah Valley. *Colonel,* 3 VT Infantry, June 4, 1865. Honorably mustered out, July 11, 1865.

**Born:** Nov. 9, 1833 Lebanon, NH
**Died:** Oct. 4, 1870 Springfield, VT
**Occupation:** Tailor
**Miscellaneous:** Resided Springfield, Windsor Co., VT. Brother of Colonel Elbridge G. Floyd.
**Buried:** Summer Hill Cemetery, Springfield, VT
**References:** C. Horace Hubbard and Justus Dartt. *History of the Town of Springfield, VT.* Boston, MA, 1895. Pension File, National Archives. George G. Benedict. *Vermont in the Civil War.* Burlington, VT, 1886.

*Horace Whitmore Floyd*
*USAMHI. H. Cushing, Photographer, Windsor, VT.*

## Josiah Hall

Captain, Co. F, 1 VT Cavalry, Oct. 17, 1861. Major, 1 VT Cavalry, Oct. 4, 1862. Captured near Morrisville, VA, Oct. 12, 1863. Confined at Richmond, VA; Charleston, SC; and Macon, GA. Paroled Aug. 3, 1864. Lieutenant Colonel, 1 VT Cavalry, Nov. 19, 1864. Colonel, 1 VT Cavalry, May 23, 1865. Honorably mustered out, June 21, 1865.

**Born:** Feb. 5, 1835 Westminster, VT
**Died:** March 15, 1912 Duncard District, Fresno Co., CA
**Education:** Attended Norwich (VT) University, receiving B.S. degree in 1904.
**Occupation:** Clerk and bookkeeper before war. Farmer and surveyor after war.
**Miscellaneous:** Resided Brattleboro, Windham Co., VT, to 1866; Greenfield, Franklin Co., MA, 1866-75; Hanford, Tulare Co., CA, 1875-82; Montague City, Franklin Co., MA, 1883-87; and Fresno, Fresno Co., CA, 1888-1912.
**Buried:** Mountain View Cemetery, Fresno, CA (East Addition, Block G, Lot 19)
**References:** William A. Ellis, editor. *History of Norwich University, 1819-1911.* Montpelier, VT, 1911. Pension File, National Archives. Obituary, *Boston Evening Transcript*, March 16, 1912.

*Josiah Hall*
*USAMHI. C.L. Howe, Photographer, Union Block, Brattleboro, VT.*

## William Cune Holbrook

1 Lieutenant, Co. F, 4 VT Infantry, Sept. 7, 1861. Major, 7 VT Infantry, Jan. 22, 1862. Colonel, 7 VT Infantry, Aug. 27, 1862. Commanded District of Pensacola (FL), Department of the Gulf, April 21, 1863-May 21, 1863 and June 18, 1863-Nov. 7, 1863. Commanded 1 Brigade (Post of Barrancas), District of West Florida, Department of the Gulf, Nov. 9, 1863-July 1864. Resigned June 2, 1865, "in view of the entire cessation of hostilities."

**Born:** July 14, 1842 Brattleboro, VT
**Died:** March 27, 1904 New York City, NY
**Education:** Attended Harvard University Law School, Cambridge, MA
**Occupation:** Mercantile clerk before war. Lawyer and judge after war.
**Offices/Honors:** Justice of the Court of Special Sessions, New York City, NY, 1895-1904
**Miscellaneous:** Resided Brattleboro, Windham Co., VT; and New York City, NY. Son of Vermont Governor Frederick Holbrook.
**Buried:** Prospect Hill Cemetery, Brattleboro, VT

*William Cune Holbrook*
*Annals of Brattleboro, 1681-1895.*

*William Cune Holbrook (postwar)*
*Proceedings at the First and Second Reunions of the 7th Regiment Vermont Volunteers.*

*William Cune Holbrook (postwar)*
*National Archives.*

**References:** Obituary Circular, Whole No. 818, New York MOLLUS. Jacob G. Ullery, compiler. *Men of Vermont.* Brattleboro, VT, 1894. Mary R. Cabot, editor. *Annals of Brattleboro, 1681-1895.* Brattleboro, VT, 1922. William C. Holbrook. *A Narrative of the 7th Regiment of Vermont Volunteers.* New York City, NY, 1882.

## Jonas P. Holliday

Captain, 2 US Dragoons, May 9, 1861. Captain, 2 US Cavalry, Aug. 3, 1861. Colonel, 1 VT Cavalry, Feb. 26, 1862.

**Born:** Jan. 24, 1829 NY
**Died:** April 5, 1862 near Strasburg, VA (committed suicide by pistol shot in the forehead)
**Education:** Graduated US Military Academy, West Point, NY, 1850
**Occupation:** Regular Army (Captain, 2 US Cavalry).

*Right:*
*Jonas P. Holliday*
*National Archives.*

**Miscellaneous:** Resided Burns, Allegany Co., NY.
**Buried:** Burns Cemetery, Burns, NY
**References:** Obituary, *New York World*, April 11, 1862. Obituary, *Hornellsville Tribune*, April 10, 1862. USMA Application Papers and Military Service File, National Archives. George G. Benedict. *Vermont in the Civil War.* Burlington, VT, 1886. George W. Cullum. *Biographical Register of the Officers and Graduates of the US Military Academy.* Boston and New York, 1891.

## Charles Hunsdon

Captain, Co. B, 1 VT Heavy Artillery, Aug. 13, 1862. Major, 1 VT Heavy Artillery, Nov. 2, 1863. Lieutenant Colonel, 1 VT Heavy Artillery, Sept. 2, 1864. Commanded 2 Brigade, 2 Division, 6 Army Corps, Dec. 26, 1864-Jan. 16, 1865. Colonel, 1 VT Heavy Artillery, May 23, 1865. Honorably mustered out, June 24, 1865.

*Charles Hunsdon*
*Roger D. Hunt Collection, USAMHI.*

**Born:** March 22, 1830 Shoreham, VT
**Died:** Sept. 20, 1899 South Nyack, NY
**Education:** Attended Pennsylvania Military Institute, Harrisburg, PA. Attended Norwich (VT) University.
**Occupation:** Farmer and merchant before war. Fire insurance agent and Methodist clergyman after war.
**Offices/Honors:** Vermont House of Representatives, 1861-62 and 1865.
**Miscellaneous:** Resided Shoreham, Addison Co., VT, to 1869; Albany, NY, 1869-78; Odessa, Schuyler Co., NY, 1878-80; Gerry, Chautauqua Co., NY, 1880-82; Elba, Genesee Co., NY; Bellbrook, Greene Co., OH; and Springfield, Clark Co., OH
**Buried:** Ferncliff Cemetery, Springfield, OH (Section M, Lot 4)
**References:** Pension File, National Archives. William A. Ellis, editor. *History of Norwich University, 1819-1911.* Montpelier, VT, 1911. George G. Benedict. *Vermont in the Civil War.* Burlington, VT, 1886.

## Breed Noyes Hyde

Lieutenant Colonel, 3 VT Infantry, June 6, 1861. Colonel, 3 VT Infantry, Aug. 13, 1861. Resigned Jan. 15, 1863 to avoid court martial on charges of cowardice at Fredericksburg, VA, Dec. 13, 1862.

**Born:** May (or Aug.) 14, 1831 Hyde Park, VT
**Died:** Oct. 5, 1918 Pottsville, PA
**Education:** Attended US Military Academy, West Point, NY (Class of 1854)
**Occupation:** Merchant before war. Mining engineer and librarian after war.
**Miscellaneous:** Resided Hyde Park, Lamoille Co., VT; St. Louis, MO; and Pottsville, Schuylkill Co., PA.
**Buried:** Charles Baber Cemetery, Pottsville, PA (Section X, Lot 7)
**References:** Reuben H. Walworth. *Hyde Genealogy.* Albany, NY, 1864. Obituary, *Pottsville Republican*, Oct. 5, 1918. Henry L. Abbot. *Half Century of a West Point Class, 1850-1854.* Boston, MA, 1904. George G. Benedict. *Vermont in the Civil War.* Burlington, VT, 1886. Military Service File, National Archives.

## Albert Burton Jewett

1 Lieutenant, Co. A, 1 VT Infantry, May 9, 1861. Honorably mustered out, Aug. 15, 1861. Colonel, 10 VT Infantry, Aug. 26, 1862. Commanded Jewett's Independent Brigade, Department of Washington, Feb. 2, 1863-June 26, 1863. Discharged for disability, April 25, 1864, due to chronic inflammation of the kidneys.

**Born:** March 20, 1829 Swanton, VT
**Died:** March 6, 1887 Jacksonville, FL

*Breed Noyes Hyde*
*Massachusetts MOLLUS Collection, USAMHI.*

Albert Burton Jewett
*Roger D. Hunt Collection, USAMHI. Bogardus, Photographer, 363 Broadway, New York City, NY.*

**Occupation:** In mercantile business with Colonel Elisha L. Barney before war. Railroad superintendent after war, being connected with the St. Johnsbury and Montpelier Railroad.

**Miscellaneous:** Resided Swanton, Franklin Co., VT; and St. Johnsbury, Caledonia Co., VT.

**Buried:** Church Street Cemetery, Swanton, VT

**References:** Pension File, National Archives. Frederic C. Jewett. *History and Genealogy of the Jewetts of America.* Rowley, MA, 1908. Obituary, *Burlington Daily Free Press*, March 8, 1887. Edwin M. Haynes. *A History of the 10th Regiment Vermont Volunteers.* Rutland, VT, 1894.

## Ronald A. Kennedy

Sergeant, Co. I, 3 VT Infantry, June 1, 1861. 2 Lieutenant, Co. D, 3 VT Infantry, Sept. 22, 1862. 1 Lieutenant, Co. I, 3 VT Infantry, Oct. 13, 1862. Shell wound left side, Salem Heights, VA, May 4, 1863. Captain, Co. K, 3 VT Infantry, Jan. 8, 1864. Lieutenant Colonel, 5 VT Infantry, Feb. 20, 1865. *Colonel,* 5 VT Infantry, June 9, 1865. Honorably mustered out, June 29, 1865.

Albert Burton Jewett
*Massachusetts MOLLUS Collection, USAMHI. Brady's National Photographic Portrait Gallery.*

**Born:** Sept. 25, 1837 VT

**Died:** June 13, 1902 New Albany, IN

**Occupation:** Farmer and flour and feed merchant.

**Offices/Honors:** Nebraska Legislature. Superintendent, New Albany (IN) National Cemetery, 1897-1902.

**Miscellaneous:** Resided Concord, Essex Co., VT; Waterford, VT; Marshalltown, Marshall Co., IA, 1865-66; Pawnee City, Pawnee Co., NE, 1866-86; Omaha, Boone Co., AR; and New Albany, Floyd Co., IN.

**Buried:** New Albany National Cemetery, New Albany, IN (Section A, Grave 2939)

**References:** Obituary, *New Albany Daily Ledger*, June 14, 1902. Pension File, National Archives. Alfred T. Andreas. *History of Nebraska.* Chicago, IL, 1882.

## Sumner H. Lincoln

Private, Co. B, 1 VT Infantry, May 2, 1861. Honorably mustered out, Aug. 15, 1861. Corporal, Co. B, 6 VT Infantry, Sept. 17, 1861. 1 Lieutenant, Adjutant, 6 VT Infantry, Feb. 3, 1863. Acting Commissary of Subsistence, 2 Brigade, 2 Division, 6 Army Corps, Oct. 1863-Jan. 1864. GSW left knee, Wilderness, VA, May 5, 1864. GSW left side of head, Winchester, VA, Sept. 19, 1864. Major, 6 VT Infantry, Oct. 21, 1864. Acting AIG, 2

Ronald A. Kennedy
Courtesy Vermont Historical Society.

Ronald A. Kennedy
Courtesy of Ed Italo.

Brigade, 2 Division, 6 Army Corps, Sept.-Nov. 1864. Lieutenant Colonel, 6 VT Infantry, Jan. 7, 1865. *Colonel,* 6 VT Infantry, June 4, 1865. Honorably mustered out, June 26, 1865.

**Born:** Dec. 21, 1840 Gardner, MA
**Died:** April 17, 1928 Washington, DC
**Education:** Attended Winchendon (MA) Academy. Attended Norwich (VT) University.
**Other Wars:** Spanish American War (Colonel, 10 US Infantry)
**Occupation:** Chain maker before war. Regular Army (Brigadier General, retired June 9, 1902).
**Miscellaneous:** Resided Hartford, Windsor Co., VT; Fern Bank, OH; and Washington, DC.
**Buried:** Arlington National Cemetery, Arlington, VA (Section 2, Lot 908)
**References:** Obituary Circular, Whole No. 1314, Ohio MOLLUS. Obituary, *Washington Post*, April 17, 1928. *Who Was Who in America, 1897-1942.* ACP File and Military Service File, National Archives. George G. Benedict. *Vermont in the Civil War.* Burlington, VT, 1886.

*Sumner H. Lincoln*
*Courtesy of Nicholas Picerno.*

## Nathan Lord, Jr.

Captain, Co. G, 7 IN Infantry, April 21, 1861. Honorably mustered out, Aug. 2, 1861. Colonel, 6 VT Infantry, Sept. 16, 1861. Discharged for disability, Dec. 18, 1862, due to "chronic dysentery."

**Born:** July 17, 1831 Hanover, NH
**Died:** Oct. 16, 1885 near Cincinnati, OH
**Education:** Graduated Dartmouth College, Hanover, NH, 1851.
**Occupation:** Lawyer and railroad agent before war. Lawyer after war.
**Miscellaneous:** Resided Montpelier, Washington Co., VT; Cincinnati, OH; Lawrenceburg, Dearborn Co., IN; and Louisville, KY.
**Buried:** Cave Hill Cemetery, Louisville, KY (Section P, Lot N)
**References:** George T. Chapman. *Sketches of the Alumni of Dartmouth College.* Cambridge, MA, 1867. William H. Hodgkins, editor. *Military Record of the Sons of Dartmouth.* Boston, MA, 1907. George G. Benedict. *Vermont in the Civil War.* Burlington, VT, 1886. Obituary, *Louisville Courier Journal*, Oct. 17, 1885. Military Service File, National Archives.

*Sumner H. Lincoln (postwar)*
*National Archives.*

*Nathan Lord, Jr.*
*Roger D. Hunt Collection, USAMHI. Brady's National Photographic Portrait Gallery, 352 Pennsylvania Avenue, Washington, DC.*

## John Boardman Mead

2 Lieutenant, Co. G, 8 VT Infantry, Jan. 7, 1862. Captured Bayou Des Allemands, LA, Sept. 4, 1862. Confined at Opelousas, LA, and Vicksburg, MS. Paroled Nov. 13, 1862. 1 Lieutenant, Co. G, 8 VT Infantry, April 2, 1863. Captain, Co. G, 8 VT Infantry, May 5, 1863. Major, 8 VT Infantry, July 26, 1864. GSW right side, Cedar Creek, VA, Oct. 19, 1864. Lieutenant Colonel, 8 VT Infantry, Nov. 24, 1864. Colonel, 8 VT Infantry, March 4, 1865. Honorably mustered out, June 28, 1865.

**Born:** March 15, 1831 Stratham, NH
**Died:** Dec. 16, 1887 Randolph, VT
**Occupation:** Farmer and stock raiser.
**Offices/Honors:** Vermont Legislature, 1867-68, 1878. Vermont Superintendent of Agriculture, 1878-80. Commissioner to New Orleans Exposition, 1884-86.
**Miscellaneous:** Resided Randolph, Orange Co., VT.
**Buried:** Randolph Center Cemetery, Randolph Center, VT
**References:** Nickerson and Cox, compilers. *Illustrated Historical Souvenir of Randolph, VT.* N.p., 1895. Pension File, National Archives. George N. Carpenter. *History of the 8th Regiment Vermont Volunteers.* Boston, MA, 1886.

*Nathan Lord, Jr.*
*National Archives.*

*John Boardman Mead*
*National Archives.*

*Right:*
*John Boardman Mead (postwar)*
*History of the 8th Regiment Vermont Volunteers.*

## William Thomas Nichols

Private, Co. K, 1 VT Infantry, May 9, 1861. Honorably mustered out, Aug. 15, 1861. Colonel, 14 VT Infantry, Sept. 25, 1862. Honorably mustered out, July 30, 1863.

**Born:** March 24, 1829 Clarendon, VT
**Died:** April 10, 1882 Maywood, Cook Co., IL
**Occupation:** Lawyer and manufacturer
**Offices/Honors:** Vermont Legislature, 1861-62
**Miscellaneous:** Resided Rutland, Rutland Co., VT; Chicago, IL; and Maywood, Cook Co., IL
**Buried:** Evergreen Cemetery, Rutland, VT (Section 22, Lot 12)
**References:** Pension File, National Archives. Nathan R. Nichols. *Nichols Genealogy.* N.p., 1923. George G. Benedict. *A Short History of the 14th Vermont Regiment.* Bennington, VT, 1887. George G. Benedict. *Vermont in the Civil War.* Burlington, VT, 1886.

*William Thomas Nichols*
*National Archives.*

*Right:*
*William Thomas Nichols*
*Courtesy of Michael J. McAfee.*

## David Brainerd Peck

Captain, Co. H, 1 VT Infantry, May 2, 1861. Honorably mustered out, Aug. 15, 1861. Captain, Co. A, 7 VT Infantry, Jan. 14, 1862. Lieutenant Colonel, 7 VT Infantry, Aug. 27, 1862. *Colonel,* 7 VT Infantry, June 29, 1865. Honorably mustered out, Aug. 26, 1865.

**Born:** March 15, 1833 Pompey, NY
**Died:** Dec. 28, 1912 Washington, DC
**Occupation:** Merchant. Later clerk in the Secret Service division of the US Treasury Department.
**Miscellaneous:** Resided Burlington, Chittenden Co., VT; Pensacola, Escambia Co., FL; Washington, DC, 1866-73; Cleveland, OH, 1873-1903; and Washington, DC, 1903-12.
**Buried:** Mentor Municipal Cemetery, Mentor, OH (Section 8, Lot 19)
**References:** Pension File, National Archives. Obituary, *Washington Evening Star*, Dec. 30, 1912. Ira B. Peck. *A Genealogical History of the Descendants of Joseph Peck.* Boston, MA, 1868. William C. Holbrook. *A Narrative of the 7th Regiment of Vermont Volunteers.* New York City, NY, 1882.

*David Brainerd Peck*
*Courtesy Vermont Historical Society.*

*David Brainerd Peck (postwar)*
*National Archives.*

*David Brainerd Peck*
*Ed Italo Collection, USAMHI. C. Miller, Burlington, VT.*

## Lemuel B. Platt

Colonel, 1 VT Cavalry, Sept. 4, 1861. Resigned Feb. 27, 1862.

**Born:** Feb. 1, 1811 Milton, VT
**Died:** Feb. 12, 1880 Winooski, VT
**Occupation:** Farmer before war. Engaged in lumber and manufacturing enterprises after war.
**Offices/Honors:** Vermont Senate, 1849-50.
**Miscellaneous:** Resided Colchester, Chittenden Co., VT; Burlington, Chittenden Co., VT; and Winooski, Chittenden Co., VT
**Buried:** Green Mount Cemetery, Burlington, VT
**References:** Obituary, *Burlington Free Press*, Feb. 13, 1880. George G. Benedict. *Vermont in the Civil War.* Burlington, VT, 1886. Military Service File, National Archives.

*Henry Martyn Porter*
*USAMHI.*

## Henry Martyn Porter

Private, Co. B, 7 NY State Militia, April 26, 1861. Honorably mustered out, June 3, 1861. Captain, Co. C, 7 VT Infantry, Jan. 15, 1862. Major, 7 VT Infantry, Aug. 28, 1862. Provost Marshal, Ascension Parish, LA, March-Aug. 1863. Provost Marshal, Brashear City, LA, Sept. 1863. Provost Marshal, New Orleans, LA, Oct. 1863-Oct. 1864. Lieutenant Colonel, 7 VT Infantry, June 29, 1865. *Colonel,* 7 VT Infantry, Sept. 1, 1865. Honorably mustered out, March 14, 1866.

**Born:** April 25, 1835 Middlebury, VT
**Died:** Feb. 6, 1907 Poughkeepsie, NY
**Education:** Graduated Middlebury (VT) College, 1857.
**Occupation:** School teacher and hardware merchant before war. Banker (connected with the American Bank Note Co.) and insurance agent after war.
**Miscellaneous:** Resided Middlebury, Addison Co., VT; New York City, NY; and Middletown, Orange Co., NY. Married adopted daughter of Major General John C. Fremont.
**Buried:** West Cemetery, Middlebury, VT
**References:** Obituary Circular, Whole No. 916, New York MOLLUS. *General Catalogue of Middlebury College.* Middlebury, VT, 1950. Henry Whittemore. *History of George Washington Post 103, G. A. R.* Detroit, MI, 1885. Pension File and Military Service File, National Archives. William C. Holbrook. *A Narrative of the 7th Regiment of Vermont Volunteers.* New York City, NY, 1882. Obituary, *Poughkeepsie Daily Eagle*, Feb. 8, 1907.

*Right:*
*Henry Martyn Porter*
*Jack McCormack Collection, USAMHI.*

*Henry Martyn Porter (left) in a moment of leisure.*
*USAMHI.*

## Addison Webster Preston

Addison Webster Preston
National Archives.

Captain, Co. D, 1 VT Cavalry, Oct. 15, 1861. Lieutenant Colonel, 1 VT Cavalry, Sept. 16, 1862. GSW right arm, Ashby's Gap, VA, Sept. 22, 1862. Commanded 2 Brigade, 3 Division, Cavalry Corps, Army of the Potomac, Feb. 27, 1864-April 17, 1864. *Colonel,* 1 VT Cavalry, April 29, 1864. GSW chest, Haw's Shop, VA, June 3, 1864.

**Born:** Dec. 8, 1830 Burke, VT
**Died:** June 3, 1864 KIA Haw's Shop, VA
**Education:** Attended Brown University, Providence, RI (Class of 1855).
**Occupation:** Engaged in farming after spending several adventurous years in Australia and California upon leaving college.
**Miscellaneous:** Resided Danville, Caledonia Co., VT. Brig. Gen. George A. Custer described him as "the best fighting colonel in the Cavalry Corps."
**Buried:** Green Cemetery, Danville, VT
**References:** *Historical Catalogue of Brown University, 1764-1904.* Providence, RI, 1905. *Zeta Psi Semi-Centennial Biographical Catalogue.* New York City, NY, 1899. George G. Benedict. *Vermont in the Civil War.* Burlington, VT, 1886.

## Redfield Proctor

1 Lieutenant, RQM, 3 VT Infantry, June 19, 1861. Quartermaster, Staff of Brig. Gen. William F. Smith, July-Sept. 1861. Major, 5 VT Infantry, Sept. 25, 1861. Resigned July 11, 1862, due to ill health. Colonel, 15 VT Infantry, Sept. 26, 1862. Honorably mustered out, Aug. 5, 1863.

**Born:** June 1, 1831 Proctorsville, Windsor Co., VT
**Died:** March 4, 1908 Washington, DC
**Education:** Graduated Dartmouth College, Hanover, NH, 1851. Graduated Albany (NY) Law School, 1859.
**Occupation:** Lawyer and marble company executive. In 1880 became President of the Vermont Marble Company.
**Offices/Honors:** Vermont House of Representatives, 1867-68 and 1888. Vermont Senate, 1874-75. Lieutenant Governor of Vermont, 1876-78. Governor of Vermont, 1878-80. US Secretary of War, 1889-91. US Senate, 1891-1908.
**Miscellaneous:** Resided Proctor, Rutland Co., VT; Boston, MA; Rutland, Rutland Co., VT; and Washington, DC

*Right:*
*Addison Webster Preston*
*Massachusetts MOLLUS Collection, USAMHI.*

**Buried:** City Cemetery, Proctor, VT

**References:** Obituary Circular, Whole No. 161, Vermont MOLLUS. *Dictionary of American Biography.* Jacob G. Ullery, compiler. *Men of Vermont.* Brattleboro, VT, 1894. George G. Benedict. *Vermont in the Civil War.* Burlington, VT, 1886. William L. Proctor. *A Genealogy of Descendants of Robert Proctor.* Ogdensburg, NY, 1898.

*Redfield Proctor (postwar)*
*Massachusetts MOLLUS Collection, USAMHI.*

## Francis Voltaire Randall

Captain, Co. F, 2 VT Infantry, May 20, 1861. Colonel, 13 VT Infantry, Sept. 24, 1862. Commanded 3 Brigade, 3 Division, 1 Army Corps, Army of the Potomac, July 3-11, 1863. Honorably mustered out, July 21, 1863. Colonel, 17 VT Infantry, Feb. 10, 1864. Honorably mustered out, July 14, 1865.

**Born:** Feb. 13, 1824 Braintree, VT

**Died:** March 1, 1885 Northfield, VT

**Occupation:** Lawyer and farmer.

**Miscellaneous:** Resided Northfield, Washington Co., VT; Montpelier, Washington Co., VT; and Brookfield, Orange Co., VT.

**Buried:** Elmwood Cemetery, Northfield, VT

*Francis Voltaire Randall*
*Massachusetts MOLLUS Collection, USAMHI. Brady's National Photographic Portrait Gallery, Broadway & Tenth Street, New York.*

**References:** Ralph O. Sturtevant. *Pictorial History 13th Regiment Vermont Volunteers.* N.p., 1910. Pension File, National Archives. George G. Benedict. *Vermont in the Civil War.* Burlington, VT, 1886.

## George Tisdale Roberts

1 Lieutenant, Co. K, 1 VT Infantry, May 2, 1861. Honorably mustered out, Aug. 15, 1861. Colonel, 7 VT Infantry, Dec. 5, 1861. GSW neck and thigh, Baton Rouge, LA, Aug. 5, 1862.

**Born:** Oct. 3, 1824 Clarendon, VT

**Died:** Aug. 7, 1862 DOW Baton Rouge, LA

**Occupation:** Superintended the construction of railroads in the West, and later managed marble quarries in West Rutland, VT.

**Miscellaneous:** Resided Rutland, Rutland Co., VT.

**Buried:** Evergreen Cemetery, Rutland, VT (Section 12, Lot 2)

**References:** Almon D. Hodges, Jr., compiler. *Genealogical Record of the Hodges Family of New England.* Boston,

*Left:*
*Francis Voltaire Randall*
*Pictorial History 13th Regiment Vermont Volunteers.*

MA, 1896. William C. Holbrook. *A Narrative of the 7th Regiment of Vermont Volunteers.* New York City, NY, 1882. George G. Benedict. *Vermont in the Civil War.* Burlington, VT, 1886.

*George Tisdale Roberts*
*A Narrative of the 7th Regiment of Vermont Volunteers.*

*George Tisdale Roberts*
*National Archives.*

## Edward Bertrand Sawyer

Captain, Co. I, 1 VT Cavalry, Oct. 21, 1861. Major, 1 VT Cavalry, April 25, 1862. Colonel, 1 VT Cavalry, Sept. 16, 1862. Commanded 1 Brigade, 3 Division, Cavalry Corps, Army of the Potomac, July 25, 1863-Aug. 21, 1863. Commanded 2 Brigade, 3 Division, Cavalry Corps, Army of the Potomac, Sept. 14, 1863-Oct. 9, 1863 and Dec. 15-20, 1863. Resigned April 28, 1864, due to "family and personal business requiring his attention."

**Born:** April 16, 1828 Hyde Park, VT
**Died:** March 17, 1918 Hyde Park, VT
**Occupation:** Lawyer and county clerk before war. After the war edited the Lamoille News-Dealer for three years and conducted a hotel for seven years before resuming his law practice.
**Miscellaneous:** Resided Hyde Park, Lamoille Co., VT. First in VT to undertake the artificial breeding of trout. Active in the Republican party, he was secretary of the Vermont delegation to the convention that nominated Lincoln.
**Buried:** Village Cemetery, Hyde Park, VT
**References:** Obituary, *Burlington Daily Free Press*, March 19, 1918. Pension File and Military Service File, National Archives. George G. Benedict. *Vermont in the Civil War.* Burlington, VT, 1886.

*Edward Bertrand Sawyer*
*Roger D. Hunt Collection, USAMHI. Hugo Bartels, Photographer, 262 Pennsylvania Avenue, Washington, DC.*

## Thomas Orville Seaver

Captain, Co. F, 3 VT Infantry, May 24, 1861. Major, 3 VT Infantry, Aug. 13, 1861. Lieutenant Colonel, 3 VT Infantry, Sept. 27, 1862. Colonel, 3 VT Infantry, Jan. 15, 1863. Commanded 2 Brigade, 2 Division, 6 Army Corps, Dec. 1863-Jan. 1864. Honorably mustered out, July 27, 1864.

**Born:** Dec. 23, 1833 Cavendish, VT
**Died:** July 11, 1912 Woodstock, VT
**Education:** Attended Tufts College, Medford, MA. Graduated Union College, Schenectady, NY, 1859.
**Occupation:** Lawyer and probate judge
**Offices/Honors:** Vermont Railroad Commissioner, 1884. Medal of Honor, Spotsylvania, VA, May 10, 1864. "At the head of three regiments and under a most galling fire, attacked and occupied the enemy's works."
**Miscellaneous:** Resided Cavendish, Windsor Co., VT; and Woodstock, Windsor Co., VT
**Buried:** River Street Cemetery, Woodstock, VT
**References:** Pension File, National Archives. George G. Benedict. *Vermont in the Civil War.* Burlington, VT, 1886.

*Edward Bertrand Sawyer*
*National Archives.*

*Right:*
*Thomas Orville Seaver*
*Courtesy of Henry Deeks. Cushing, Woodstock, VT.*

*Bottom right:*
*Thomas Orville Seaver*
*Courtesy of Thomas Harris. Cushing, Woodstock, VT.*

Andrew Van Vranken Raymond. *Union University.* New York City, NY, 1907.

## Newton Stone

1 Lieutenant, Co. A, 2 VT Infantry, May 16, 1861. Captain, Co. I, 2 VT Infantry, Jan. 22, 1862. Major, 2 VT Infantry, Jan. 8, 1863. Lieutenant Colonel, 2 VT Infantry, Feb. 9, 1863. Acting AIG, 2 Division, 6 Army Corps, Jan. 1863-March 1864. Colonel, 2 VT Infantry, April 2, 1864. GSW head, Wilderness, VA, May 5, 1864.

**Born:** Dec. 9, 1838 Readsboro, VT
**Died:** May 5, 1864 KIA Wilderness, VA
**Occupation:** Law student (admitted to the bar June 1861).
**Miscellaneous:** Resided Bennington, Bennington Co., VT. Brig. Gen. Lewis A. Grant eulogized him as "a good officer, gallant by nature, prompt in his duties, and urbane in his manner."

*Newton Stone*
*USAMHI. Schoonmaker, 282 River Street, Troy, NY.*

**Buried:** Old First Cemetery, Bennington, VT

**References:** George G. Benedict. *Vermont in the Civil War.* Burlington, VT, 1886. Obituary, *Rutland Weekly Herald,* May 19, 1864. *Official Records,* Vol. 36, Part 1, p. 700.

## Amasa Sawyer Tracy

1 Lieutenant, Co. K, 2 VT Infantry, May 28, 1861. Captain, Co. H, 2 VT Infantry, Jan. 24, 1862. GSW left leg, Chancellorsville, VA, May 3, 1863. Major, 2 VT Infantry, April 2, 1864. Lieutenant Colonel, 2 VT Infantry, June 17, 1864. Shell wound left hip, Cedar Creek, VA, Oct. 19, 1864. Commanded 2 Brigade, 2 Division, 6 Army Corps, Oct. 19, 1864 and April 2, 1865. Bvt. Colonel, USV, April 2, 1865, for gallant and meritorious services in the assault before Petersburg, VA. *Colonel,* 2 VT Infantry, June 7, 1865. Honorably mustered out, July 15, 1865.

**Born:** March 16, 1829 Dover, ME

**Died:** Feb. 26, 1908 North Troy, VT

**Occupation:** Carpenter before war. Merchant and carriage maker after war.

**Offices/Honors:** Postmaster, Middlebury, VT, 1870-82. Appointed Deputy Collector of Customs, District of Vermont, 1889. Medal of Honor, Cedar Creek, VA, Oct. 19, 1864. "Took command and led the brigade in the assault on the enemy's works."

**Miscellaneous:** Resided Middlebury, Addison Co., VT; and North Troy, Orleans Co., VT.

**Buried:** West Cemetery, Middlebury, VT

**References:** Obituary Circular, Whole No. 160, Vermont MOLLUS. Pension File, National Archives. George G. Benedict. *Vermont in the Civil War.* Burlington, VT, 1886.

*Amasa Sawyer Tracy*
*Courtesy of Henry Deeks. O.A. Taft's Gallery, Opposite Post Office, Middlebury, VT.*

*Amasa Sawyer Tracy*
*Courtesy of Tom MacDonald. G.F. Child, 304 Pennsylvania Avenue, Washington, DC.*

## Oscar S. Tuttle

Captain, Co. E, 1 VT Infantry, May 9, 1861. Honorably mustered out, Aug. 15, 1861. Major, 6 VT Infantry, Sept. 25, 1861. Lieutenant Colonel, 6 VT Infantry, Sept. 19, 1862. Colonel, 6 VT Infantry, Dec. 18, 1862. Discharged for disability, March 18, 1863, due to persistent stomach illness.

**Born:** Aug. 23, 1832 Weathersfield, VT

**Died:** Dec. 15, 1881 Holyoke, MA

**Occupation:** Dry goods merchant

**Offices/Honors:** Assessor of Internal Revenue

**Miscellaneous:** Resided Cavendish, Windsor Co., VT; and Holyoke, Hampden Co., MA

*Oscar S. Tuttle*
*USAMHI. J. D. Powers, Springfield, VT.*

*Oscar S. Tuttle*
*Massachusetts MOLLUS Collection, USAMHI.*

**Buried:** Forestdale Cemetery, Holyoke, MA (Section L, Lilac Avenue)

**References:** Pension File, National Archives. Obituary, *Springfield Republican*, Dec. 16, 1881. George G. Benedict. *Vermont in the Civil War.* Burlington, VT, 1886.

## John Steele Tyler

1 Lieutenant, Co. C, 2 VT Infantry, May 17, 1861. Captain, Co. C, 2 VT Infantry, Jan. 23, 1862. Major, 2 VT Infantry, Feb. 9, 1863. Lieutenant Colonel, 2 VT Infantry, April 2, 1864. GSW thigh, Wilderness, VA, May 5, 1864. *Colonel,* 2 VT Infantry, May 6, 1864.

*Right:*
*John Steele Tyler*
*USAMHI. C.L. Howe, Photographer, Union Block, Brattleboro, VT.*

**Born:** April 29, 1843 Brattleboro, VT
**Died:** May 23, 1864 DOW New York City, NY
**Occupation:** Law student
**Miscellaneous:** Resided Brattleboro, Windham Co., VT.
**Buried:** Prospect Hill Cemetery, Brattleboro, VT
**References:** Dorothy Sutherland Melville. *Tyler-Browns of Brattleboro.* Jericho, NY, 1973. George G. Benedict. *Vermont in the Civil War.* Burlington, VT, 1886. Mary R. Cabot, editor. *Annals of Brattleboro, 1681-1895.* Brattleboro, VT, 1922.

*John Steele Tyler*
*Annals of Brattleboro, 1681-1895.*

## Wheelock Graves Veazey

Captain, Co. A, 3 VT Infantry, May 21, 1861. Major, 3 VT Infantry, Aug. 10, 1861. Lieutenant Colonel, 3 VT Infantry, Aug. 13, 1861. Colonel, 16 VT Infantry, Sept. 27, 1862. Honorably mustered out, Aug. 10, 1863.

**Born:** Dec. 5, 1835 Brentwood, NH
**Died:** March 22, 1898 Washington, DC
**Education:** Attended Phillips Exeter Academy, Exeter, NH. Graduated Dartmouth College, Hanover, NH, 1859. Graduated Albany (NY) Law School, 1860.
**Occupation:** Lawyer and judge

*Wheelock Graves Veazey (postwar)*
*Massachusetts MOLLUS Collection, USAMHI.*

*Wheelock Graves Veazey*
*Courtesy of Henry Deeks.*

**Offices/Honors:** Associate Justice, Vermont Supreme Court, 1879-89. Interstate Commerce Commissioner, 1889-97. Commander-in-Chief, GAR, 1890. Medal of Honor, Gettysburg, PA, July 3, 1863. "Rapidly assembled his regiment and charged the enemy's flank; changed front under heavy fire, and charged and destroyed a Confederate brigade, all this with new troops in their first battle."

**Miscellaneous:** Resided Springfield, Windsor Co., VT; Rutland, Rutland Co., VT; and Washington, DC

**Buried:** Arlington National Cemetery, Arlington, VA (Section 2, Lot 1026)

**References:** *National Cyclopedia of American Biography.* Pension File, National Archives. George G. Benedict. *Vermont in the Civil War.* Burlington, VT, 1886.

*Wheelock Graves Veazey*
*Courtesy of Ed Italo.*

## James Hicks Walbridge

Captain, Co. A, 2 VT Infantry, May 16, 1861. Major, 2 VT Infantry, May 21, 1862. Lieutenant Colonel, 2 VT Infantry, Jan. 8, 1863. Colonel, 2 VT Infantry, Feb. 9, 1863. Discharged for disability, April 1, 1864, suffering from pain and poor circulation in his legs.

**Born:** July 29, 1826 Hinsdillville, Bennington Co., VT

**Died:** Dec. 15, 1913 North Bennington, VT

**Occupation:** Early in life engaged in mackerel fishing and paper manufacturing. Returning to Vermont in 1857 after five years in California, he engaged in farming and the Internal Revenue service.

**Offices/Honors:** Assistant Assessor and Deputy Collector of Internal Revenue for 15 years after war

**Miscellaneous:** Resided North Bennington, Bennington Co., VT; and also San Francisco, CA, 1852-57, where he prospected for gold, established a printing firm, and was a member of the famous Vigilance Committee

**Buried:** Grandview Cemetery, North Bennington, VT

**References:** William G. Wallbridge, compiler. *Descendants of Henry Wallbridge.* Litchfield, CT, 1898. Obituary, *Bennington Evening Banner*, Dec. 15, 1913. Pension File, National Archives. George G. Benedict. *Vermont in the Civil War.* Burlington, VT, 1886.

*Right:*
*James Hicks Walbridge*
*USAMHI.*

## Henry Whiting

*Henry Whiting*
*USAMHI.*

Colonel, 2 VT Infantry, June 6, 1861. Commanded 2 Brigade, 2 Division, 6 Army Corps, Oct. 18, 1862-Feb. 1863. Resigned Feb. 9, 1863, due to dissatisfaction "at the neglect of what he considered to be his just claim for promotion."

**Born:** Feb. 7, 1818 Bath, NY
**Died:** June 23, 1887 Ypsilanti, MI
**Education:** Graduated US Military Academy, West Point, NY, 1840
**Occupation:** Regular Army (2 Lieutenant, 5 US Infantry, resigned 1846). Merchant.
**Miscellaneous:** Resided Bath, Steuben Co., NY; and St. Clair, St. Clair Co., MI.
**Buried:** Hillside Cemetery, St. Clair, MI
**References:** *History of St. Clair County, MI.* Chicago, IL, 1883. *American Biographical History of Eminent and Self-Made Men.* Michigan Volume. Cincinnati, OH, 1878. George G. Benedict. *Vermont in the Civil War.* Burlington, VT, 1886. Pension File, National Archives. Obituary, *Detroit Free Press*, June 24, 1887.

# Index


Abbot, Henry L., 10
Abbott, Joseph C., 155
Abert, William S., 63
Adams, Charles F., Jr., 63
Allen, Samuel Henderson, 41, 43
Ames, Adelbert, 42
Ames, William, 180
Amory, Thomas I. C., 64
Andrew, John A., 154
Andrews, George L., 63
Andross, Dudley Kimball, 194, 196
Arnold, John, 10, 12
Atwell, Seager Schuyler, 10, 12, 13
Atwood, George Marston, 42, 43, 44

Babbitt, Jacob, 182
Badger, William, 155, 156
Bailey, Edward Lyon, 155, 157
Banks, Gardner, 64, 67
Banks, Nathaniel P., 67
Barker, Thaddeus Lyscom, 65, 67, 68
Barker, Thomas Erskine, 155, 157, 158
Barlow, Francis C., 135
Barnes, James, 64
Barney, Elisha L., 194, 196, 202
Bartholomew, Walter Gustin, 65, 68
Bartlett, William F., 65, 66
Bates, James L., 64
Beach, Francis, 11, 13
Beal, George L., 41, 42
Bedel, John, 155
Bell, Charles Henry, 155, 159
Bell, Louis, 155, 159, 160
Bell, Samuel, 159
Berry, Hiram G., 41
Birge, Henry W., 11, 178
Birge, John Ward, 38
Bisbee, Horatio, Jr., 41, 44
Bissell, George Perkins, 11, 13, 14, 15
Bissell, Josiah W., 13
Bixby, Phineas P., 155, 160, 161
Blaisdell, William, 64
Blakeslee, Erastus, 10
Blinn, Charles D., 11, 15
Bliss, Zenas Randall, 180, 181, 182
Blunt, Asa P., 195
Bolan, Albion Keith, 42, 44, 45
Bostwick, Richard Stone, 11, 16
Bowler, George, 65, 69
Bowman, Henry, 65, 70
Boynton, Henry, 41
Brannan, John M., 154
Brayton, Charles R., 180
Briggs, Henry S., 64
Brodhead, Thornton F., 173
Brown, Nathaniel Williams, 180, 182, 183
Browne, George Huntington, 180, 183
Buckingham, William A., 38
Buckner, Simon B., 30
Burnham, George Sumner, 10, 11, 17, 18
Burnham, Hiram, 41
Burnside, Ambrose E., 180
Burpee, Thomas Francis, 11, 18
Burrell, Isaac Sanderson, 65, 70, 71, 72
Butler, Benjamin F., 54, 154
Byrnes, Richard, 65, 72

Cahill, Thomas William, 10, 19
Caldwell, John C., 42
Carruth, Sumner, 65
Cartwright, George W., 65, 73
Cass, Thomas, 64, 73, 74, 75
Chamberlain, Joshua L., 42
Chamberlain, Samuel E., 63
Chaplin, Daniel, 41
Chapman, George Dunham, 10, 19, 20
Chapman, William Henry, 65, 76
Chatfield, John Lyman, 10, 20
Chickering, Thomas E., 63
Church, George Earl, 180, 183, 184
Clark, George, Jr., 64, 76
Clark, William Smith, 64, 76, 77
Clarke, Thomas William, 65, 77, 78
Clough, Joseph M., 155
Codman, Charles Russell, 65, 78, 79, 80
Coffin, Frederic Jones, 64, 80, 119
Cogswell, William, 63
Colburn, Joseph, 66, 80, 81
Colburn, Ledyard, 10, 21
Connor, Selden, 42
Converse, Nelson, 155, 161
Cooke, Philip St. George, 13
Couch, Darius N., 64
Cowdin, Robert, 63
Crafts, Welcome Alonzo, 155, 161

Crosby, Hiram Benjamin, 11, 21, 22
Cross, Edward Everett, 155, 162
Cross, Nelson, 162, 163
Cross, Richard Everett, 155, 162, 163
Crowninshield, Caspar, 63
Custer, George A., 211

Daboll, Henry W., 10, 22, 23
Damon, George B., 194, 197
Davis, Nelson H., 64
Davis, Phineas Stearns, 65, 82
Deming, Henry Champion, 10, 23, 24
Devens, Charles, 64
Devens, William H., 113
Devereux, Arthur F., 64
Doane, Elisha, 65, 82, 83
Donohoe, Michael T., 155
Douty, Calvin Sanger, 41, 45, 46
Dow, Neal, 42
Drake, Albert Waldo, 10, 25
Dudley, Nathan A. M., 65
Duffie, Alfred N., 180, 190
Dunham, Thomas H., Jr., 64
Dunnell, Mark Hill, 41, 46, 47
Duryee, Redfield, 10, 25, 26
Dutton, Arthur H., 11
Dyer, Isaac, 42

Eddy, Asher Robbins, 180, 184
Edmands, J. Cushing, 65
Edwards, Clark S., 41
Edwards, Oliver, 65
Ellis, Theodore G., 11
Elwell, Andrew, 64, 84, 85
Ely, William G., 11
Emery, Sabine, 41, 47
Eustis, Henry L., 64

Farr, Alpha Burnham, 65, 85, 86
Fearing, Hawkes, Jr., 155, 163, 164
Fellows, Enoch Quimby, 155, 164, 165
Fellows, John Foster, 64, 86, 87
Ferris, Samuel Peters, 11, 26, 27
Ferry, Orris S., 10
Fessenden, Francis, 42
Finnicum, Mark, 39
Fish, William Stebbins, 10, 26, 27, 28, 29
Floyd, Elbridge G., 197
Floyd, Horace Whitmore, 194, 197
Fogler, William Henry, 42, 48
Follansbee, Albert S., 64, 88
Foster, George P., 194
Fowler, William, 113
Frankle, Jones, 63
Fremont, John C., 123, 209

Gardiner, Alexander, 155
Gelray, Joseph Wiley, 66, 89
Gilmore, Charles D., 42, 48
Goddard, John, 41, 49, 50
Gooding, Oliver P., 65
Gordon, George H., 63, 135
Gould, Jacob Parker, 66, 90
Gove, Jesse Augustus, 64, 91
Granger, George F., 41
Grant, Lewis A., 194, 215
Greeley, Edwin S., 10
Greene, William Batchelder, 63, 92, 135
Greenleaf, Halbert Stevens, 66, 93
Griffin, Simon G., 155
Griswold, Charles Edward, 64, 66, 93, 94, 95
Guiney, Patrick R., 64

Hall, Josiah, 194, 198
Hallowell, Edward N., 66, 96
Hallowell, Norwood Penrose, 66, 96, 97
Hancock, Winfield S., 169
Hapgood, Charles Edward, 155, 165, 166
Harland, Edward, 10
Harriman, Walter, 155
Hartwell, Alfred S., 66
Hawley, Joseph R., 10
Hayes, Joseph, 64
Heath, Francis E., 42
Henry, Guy V., 65
Henry, William W., 194
Hight, Thomas, 42, 51
Hill, Jonathan A., 42
Hinks, Edward W., 64, 169
Holbrook, Charles L., 65, 97, 98, 99
Holbrook, Frederick, 198
Holbrook, William Cune, 194, 198, 199
Holliday, Jonas P., 194, 199
Holmes, Charles Edward Latimer, 11, 28
Holmes, Oliver Wendell, 104
Honeycomb, George W., 122
Hooper, Charles Holden, 65, 99, 100
Hovey, Charles H., 107
Hovey, John G., 107
Howard, Oliver O., 41
Hubbard, James, 10
Hubbard, Nathaniel Hobbs, 42, 51
Hubbard, Thomas H., 42
Humphreys, Andrew A., 169
Hunsdon, Charles, 194, 200
Hyde, Breed Noyes, 194, 200, 201
Hyde, Thomas W., 41

Ingraham, Timothy, 65
Ives, Brayton, 10

Jackson, Amelia Lee, 104
Jackson, Anna Cabot, 104
Jackson, John Henry, 155, 166
Jackson, Joseph C., 13
Jackson, Nathaniel J., 41
James, Charles T., 193
Jameson, Charles D., 41
Jarves, Horatio D., 94, 95
Jenkins, Horatio, Jr., 63
Jerrard, Simon G., 42, 51
Jewett, Albert Burton, 194, 196, 200, 202
Johns, Thomas D., 64
Johnson, Elijah D., 42, 52
Jones, Edward F., 64, 65
Joslin, George Clesson, 64, 100, 101

Kellogg, Elisha Strong, 10, 29, 30
Kennedy, Ronald A., 194, 202, 203
Kent, Henry Oakes, 155, 166, 167
Kent, Loren, 167
Kimball, John W., 66
Kimball, William K., 42
King, William S., 63
Kingman, John William, 155, 167
Kingsbury, Henry Walter, 10, 30, 31
Kingsbury, Thomas Humphrey Cushing, 10, 30
Kingsley, Thomas Gibbs, 11, 32
Knowles, Abner, 41, 53
Kurtz, John, 64, 102

Lakeman, Moses B., 41, 53
Landers, James H., 155, 168
Lane, Everett, 98
Lawrence, Albert G., 30
Lawrence, Samuel Crocker, 64, 103, 104
Lawton, Robert Brown, 180, 184, 185

Lee, Francis L., 65, 104, 105
Lee, George Cabot, 104
Lee, Horace C., 65
Lee, William R., 64
Leonard, Samuel Haven, 64, 105, 106, 107
Lewis John R., 194
Lincoln, Rufus Pratt, 65, 107, 108
Lincoln, Sumner H., 194, 202, 204
Lincoln, William S., 65
Livermore, Thomas Leonard, 155, 169, 170, 171
Long, Charles Hatch, 155, 172
Lord Nathan, Jr., 194, 204, 205, 206
Lowell, Charles R., 63, 104, 135

Mackenzie, Ranald S., 10
Macy, George N., 64
Maggi, Alberto Camillo, 65, 108, 109
Manning, Jacob M., 98
Mansfield, Joseph K. F., 33
Mansfield, Samuel Mather, 11, 33, 34
Marsh, Lucius Bolles, 65, 110, 111
Marshall, Thomas Henry, 41, 54
Marston, Gilman, 155
Martindale, John H., 178
Mason, Edwin C., 41
Mattocks, Charles P., 42
McArthur, William M., 41
McCarty, Justus Ingersoll, 180, 185
McCluskey, John, 42, 54
McDowell, Irvin, 30, 173
McGilvery, Freeman, 41, 55
McKendry, Archibald, 63, 112
McLaughlen, Napoleon B., 63, 66
Mead, John Boardman, 194, 206
Messer, Carlos Page, 65, 112
Metcalf, Edwin, 180, 185, 186
Mitchel, Ormsby M., 182
Monteith, William, 65, 113
Morris, Dwight, 11, 34
Morse, Augustus, 64, 113
Morse, Charles Fessenden, 63, 114, 115
Munroe, Timothy, Jr., 64, 115

Nettleton, Edward Payson, 65, 116
Nichols, William Thomas, 195, 207
Nickerson, Frank S., 42
Noble, William H., 11
Nye, George H., 42

Ord, Edward O. C., 169
Ordway, Albert, 65
Osborn, Francis A., 65
Otis, John L., 10

Packard, Abner Butterfield, 63, 117
Packer, Warren Wightman, 10, 35
Palfrey, Francis W., 64
Parker, Francis Jewett, 65, 117, 118
Patterson, Joab N., 155
Peach, Benjamin Franklin, Jr., 64, 80, 119, 120
Peck, David Brainerd, 194, 208
Peck, Frank H., 21
Peirce, Ebenezer Weaver, 65, 120, 121, 132
Peirson, Charles L., 65
Peirson, George Henry, 64, 120, 122
Pettibone, Ira Welch, 10, 35
Phelps, John W., 194
Pickett, Josiah, 65
Pierce, Thomas Prescott, 155, 173
Pike, James, 155, 173
Pitman, John Talbot, 180, 187, 188
Plaisted, Harris M., 42
Platt, Lemuel B., 194, 209
Pope, Frederick G., 63, 122, 123, 133
Porter, Burr Baldwin, 63, 65, 123, 124
Porter, Henry Martyn, 194, 209, 210
Porter, P. H., 124
Porter, Thomas Whittier, 42, 56
Potter, Joseph H., 155
Prescott, George L., 65
Preston, Addison Webster, 194, 211
Proctor, Redfield, 195, 211, 212
Putnam, Haldimand Sumner, 155, 173, 174, 175

Quincy, Samuel M., 63

Rand, Arnold Augustus, 63, 124, 125, 126, 127, 128
Randall, Francis Voltaire, 195, 212, 213
Raymond, John William, 64, 129, 130
Read, Samuel Brinton Mumford, 180, 187, 188
Revere, Paul J., 64
Rhodes, Elisha Hunt, 180, 188, 189
Rice, Edmund, 64, 130, 131
Rice, Randall Hopkins, 10, 36
Rich, Rishworth, 41, 56
Richmond, Silas Peirce, 63, 132, 133
Ripley, Edward H., 194
Ripley, Theodore A., 155
Robbins, Charles Thomas, 180, 188
Roberts, Charles W., 41
Roberts, George Tisdale, 194, 212, 213
Roberts, Thomas A., 42, 57
Robinson, George D., 117
Robinson, Zina H., 41, 57
Rockwell, Alfred P., 10
Rodman, Isaac P., 180
Rogers, Horatio, Jr., 180
Roosevelt, Theodore, 104
Ross, Samuel, 11
Russell, Charles Lambert, 10, 36
Russell, David A., 64
Russell, Henry S., 63, 135
Rust, Henry, Jr., 42
Rust, John D., 41

Sargent, Horace B., 63
Sargent, Lorenzo Dow, 63, 123, 133
Sawtelle, Charles G., 118
Sawyer, Edward Bertrand, 194, 214
Saxton, Rufus, 124
Sayles, Willard, 180, 190
Scamman, Edward A., 41, 58
Schenck, Robert C., 26
Schley, William L., 47
Seaver, Thomas Orville, 194, 214, 215
Sewall, Frederic D., 42
Shatswell, Nathaniel, 63, 133, 134
Shaw, James, Jr., 180
Shaw, Robert Gould, 66, 92, 135, 136
Shepherd, Russell B., 41
Shepley, George F., 42
Sherman, Thomas W., 159
Shurtleff, William Steele, 65, 136, 137
Sisson, Henry Tillinghast, 180, 190, 191
Slocum, Henry W., 114, 168
Slocum, John Stanton, 180, 192, 193
Smalley, Henry A., 194
Smith, Charles H., 41
Smith, William F., 169, 194, 211
Spear, Ellis, 42
Splaine, Henry, 64, 138
Sprague, Augustus B. R., 63, 66
Sprague, William, 184
Stannard, George J., 194

Staples, Henry Genet, 41, 58
Starbird, Isaac W., 42
Stedman, Griffin A., Jr., 10
Steere, William H. P., 180
Stevens, Aaron F., 155
Stevenson, Thomas G., 65
Stone, Eben Francis, 65, 138, 139
Stone, Newton, 194, 215
Stoughton, Charles B., 194
Stoughton, Edwin H., 194
Strickland, Lee, 41, 59
Sypher, Jacob Hale, 180

Talbot, Thomas H., 41
Tannatt, Thomas Redding, 63, 64, 139, 140
Tapley, Rufus Preston, 42, 59
Tappan, Mason Weare, 155, 176, 177
Taylor, John McLean, 30
Taylor, Joseph P., 30
Terry, Alfred H., 10
Tew, George W., 180
Thomas, Stephen, 194
Thompson, John L., 155
Tilden, Charles W., 42
Tilton, William S., 64
Titus, Herbert B., 155
Tompkins, Charles H. (RI), 180
Tompkins, Charles H. (VT), 194
Tracy, Amasa Sawyer, 194, 216
Tremain, Henry E., 142
Tremlett, Henry Martyn, 65, 140, 141
Tucker, James, 65, 142
Turner, Henry A., 98
Tuttle, Oscar S., 194, 216, 217
Tyler, Daniel, 10
Tyler, John Steele, 194, 217, 218
Tyler, Mason Whiting, 65, 142, 143
Tyler, Robert O., 10

Underwood, Adin B., 65
Upham, Charles Leslie, 11, 37
Upton, Edwin, 65, 143, 144, 145

Varney, George, 41
Veazey, Wheelock Graves, 195, 218, 219
Viall, Nelson, 180
Virgin, William Wirt, 42, 59, 60

Walbridge, James Hicks, 194, 219
Walcott, Charles F., 66
Walker, Elijah, 41, 60
Walker, Henry, 63, 143, 145, 146
Ward, George H., 64
Ward, John Edward, 10, 37
Wardrop, David William, 63, 146, 147
Warner, James M., 194
Washburn, Francis, 63
Wass, Ansel D., 64, 66
Webster, Daniel, 146
Webster, Fletcher, 64, 146, 148
Welch, James William, 42, 60, 61
Weld, Stephen M., Jr., 66, 94, 95
Wells, George D., 65
Wells, William, 194
Wentworth, Mark F., 42
Wessells, Henry W., 38
Wessells, Leverette Ward, 10, 38
West, George W., 42
Wheaton, Frank, 180
Wheelock, Joseph Henry, 64, 147
Whipple, Thomas Jefferson, 155, 177, 178
White, Daniel, 42
Whiting, Henry, 194, 220
Whitlock, Charles, 113
Whitman, Royal Emerson, 42, 61
Whitney, James M., 98
Whiton, John Chadwick, 66, 98, 149, 150
Whittier, Francis H., 65
Wild, Edward A., 65
Wildes, Asa Waldo, 42, 62
Willcox, Orlando B., 21, 70
Williams, Robert, 63
Williams, Thomas, 19
Wilson, Henry, 64, 151, 152
Wilson, Robert, 155, 177, 178
Woodhouse, Levi, 10, 38, 39
Woodman, Ephraim Warren, 41, 42, 62
Wooster, William Burr, 11, 39
Wright, Carroll Davidson, 155, 178, 179
Wright, Dexter Russell, 11, 39, 40
Wright, Levi Parker, 63, 152, 153, 154
Wyman, Powell Tremlett, 64, 154